Santa Clara
County
Free Library

REFERENCE

5816

Santa Clara County Free Library
California

Alum Rock	Milpitas
Campbell	Morgan Hill
Cupertino	Saratoga
Gilroy	
Los Altos { Main	
Woodland	

Reference Center-Cupertino
For Bookmobile Service, request schedule
641092

Landmarks of the West

Kent Ruth   Landmarks of the **W**est

A Guide
to Historic Sites

University of Nebraska Press   Lincoln and London

Library of Congress Cataloging-in-Publication Data

Ruth, Kent.

Landmarks of the West.

Rev. ed. of: Great day in the West

by Kent Ruth. 1st ed. c1963.

Includes index.

1. Historic sites – West (U.S.) – Guide-books.

2. West (U.S.) – Description and travel – 1981-

– Guide-books. 3. West (U.S.) – History, Local.

I. Ruth, Kent. Great day in the West.   II. Title.

F595.3.R88 1986   917.8'0433   85-29014

ISBN 0-8032-3875-4 (alkaline paper)

ISBN 0-8032-8919-7 (paperback)

The paper used in this publication meets the minimum
requirements of American
National Standard for In-
formation Sciences – Permanence of Paper for Printed
Library Materials, ANSI
Z39.48 - 1984

To my father . . .

who, although he came west a bit too late
to qualify as a full-fledged pioneer,
displayed the same courage, resourcefulness,
and personal integrity that so strongly
characterize the pioneer spirit

Contents

Preface   ix
Map of the Western U.S.   2–3

Arizona
Tubac   4
Yuma   6
San Xavier del Bac   8
Tucson   10
Fort Bowie   12
Tombstone   14
Arkansas
Fort Smith   16
California
San Diego   18
Monterey   20
San Francisco   22
Los Angeles   24
Santa Barbara Mission   26
Fort Ross   28
New Helvetia   30
Coloma   32
Fort Tejón   34
Colorado
El Pueblo   36
Pike's Stockade   38
Bent's Fort   40
The South Platte Posts   42
Fort Garland   44
Denver   46
Leadville   48
Idaho
Fort Lemhi   50
Kullyspell House   52
Fort Hall   54
Fort Boise   56
Lapwai   58
Sacred Heart Mission   60
Silver City   62
Iowa
Council Bluffs   64
Fort Madison   66

Davenport   68
Mount Pisgah   70
Kansas
Fort Leavenworth   72
Shawnee Mission   74
Council Grove   76
Fort Scott   78
Fort Riley   80
Fort Larned   82
Fort Dodge   84
Fort Hays   86
Minnesota
Fort Snelling   88
Mendota   90
Missouri
St. Louis   92
St. Charles   94
Jefferson Barracks   96
Fort Osage   98
Franklin   100
Westport Landing   102
Independence   104
St. Joseph   106
Montana
Three Forks   108
Gates of the Mountains   110
Pompeys Pillar   112
St. Mary's Mission   114
Fort Benton   116
Butte   118
Bannack   120
Virginia City   122
Robbers' Roost   124
Last Chance Gulch   126
Custer Battlefield   128
Nebraska
Bellevue   130
Fort Atkinson   132
Scotts Bluff   134
Chimney Rock   136
Winter Quarters   138

Fort Kearny	140		**South Dakota**	
Homestead National Monument	142		Verendrye Hill	220
Fort Robinson	144		Fort Manuel	222
Nevada			Fort Pierre	224
Mormon Station	146		Fort Randall	226
Las Vegas Fort	148		Fort Sully	228
Lake's Crossing	150		Gordon Stockade	230
Comstock Lode	152		Deadwood	232
Fort Churchill	154		Wounded Knee Battlefield	234
New Mexico			**Texas**	
Tiguex	156		El Paso	236
Taos	158		San Antonio	238
El Morro	160		San José Mission	240
Santa Fe	162		San Felipe de Austin	242
Albuquerque	164		Fort Belknap	244
Fort Union	166		Fort Davis	246
Lincoln	168		Goodnight Ranch	248
Mesilla	170		**Utah**	
North Dakota			Miles Goodyear Farm	250
Pembina	172		Salt Lake City	252
Fort Mandan	174		Fort Utah	254
Fort Union	176		St. George	256
Fort Clark	178		Cove Fort	258
Fort Berthold	180		Promontory	260
Fort Abercrombie	182		Hole-in-the-Rock	262
Fort Rice	184		**Washington**	
Fort Abraham Lincoln	186		Baker Bay	264
Chateau de Mores	188		Spokane House	266
Oklahoma			Fort Okanogan	268
Fort Gibson	190		Fort Nez Percés	270
Fort Towson	192		Fort Vancouver	272
Park Hill	194		Fort Nisqually	274
Boggy Depot	196		Waiilatpu	276
Fort Washita	198		**Wyoming**	
Camp Supply	200		Green River Rendezvous	278
Fort Sill	202		Fort Laramie	280
Darlington Agency	204		South Pass	282
Oregon			Mormon Ferry	284
Fort Clatsop	206		Independence Rock	286
Astoria	208		Devil's Gate	288
Champoeg	210		Fort Bridger	290
Oregon City	212		Fort Supply	292
Methodist Mission	214		Fort Phil Kearny	294
The Dalles	216			
Cascades of the Columbia	218		Index	296

Preface

Landmarks of the West was born in 1963 as *Great Day in the West*—a profile of nearly 150 historically significant sites beyond the Mississippi at the time each was enjoying its "great day." The idea was to meet the need—of curious buff and, upon occasion, serious scholar as well—for basic information on the origin and early years of those important sites. With concise text and "then" and "now" illustrations on facing pages for each site, I tried to make it a source that was easy to use, dependably accurate, as detailed as space restrictions allowed, and—most important—interesting simply to read. The years have admittedly brought minor changes. In my view, however, none invalidates those original objectives; hence this updated edition.

How were those "significant sites" chosen over the many others for whom equally impressive credentials could be presented? Not by whim or prejudice. While cheerfully accepting full responsibility for the final selection, I would point out that I asked scores of historians and local authorities (with knowledge in the field far exceeding my own) to suggest sites they felt deserved inclusion. All of the sites finally profiled were included on one or more of their lists of recommendations.

Alas, the passage of twenty-plus years seems to have had a more devastating effect on the historians who helped shape that first edition than on the recorded history itself. Which is by way of recognizing that many of them are no longer on the scene. I am, however, nonetheless grateful for their assistance and do hereby acknowledge my indebtedness to them, as well as to those who helped with this new edition. Specifically, I would salute—and name—the one authority most responsible for the existence of both *Great Day* and *Landmarks*: Savoie Lottinville, long-time director of the University of Oklahoma Press.

Landmarks of the West

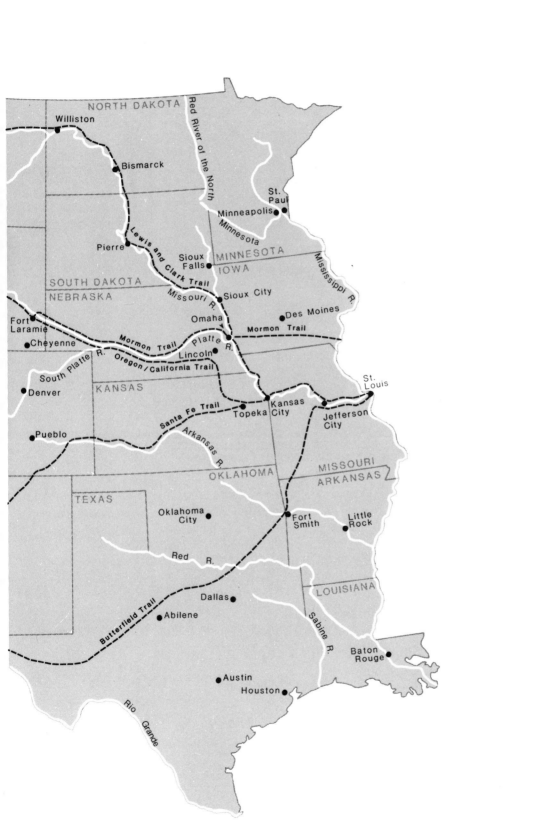

Tubac Arizona

Tubac did not impress John Russell Bartlett in July 1852: "As for this God-forsaken place, when I have said that it contains a few dilapidated buildings and one old church, with a miserable population, I have said about all." But this oldest white settlement in Arizona (off US 89 some forty-five miles south of Tucson) was merely passing through another of its frequent up-and-down cycles.

Tubac had been completely abandoned in December 1848. "I judged that its population must have been recent," Benjamin Butler Harris noted in July 1849, "for the wheat crop in the fields was ripe for the sickle. The bell and costly pictures, with other ornaments, were still in the church. Peaches and other fruits were ripening on the trees. . . . When our men rang the church bell, its hollow echoes seemed a bellowing mockery of all things human."

In 1854 the wheel of fortune turned again. Charles D. Poston, one of the state's most colorful pioneers, made Tubac headquarters for the Sonora Exploring and Mining Company and developed the Heintzelman mine, which subsequently produced $100,000 a year in silver. By 1858, the town was prosperous. Its population reached 800, five-sixths Mexican, and each family had its own orchard. "We had no law but love," Poston wrote of his community, "and no occupation but labor; no government, no taxes, no public debt, no politics. It was a community in a perfect state of nature. As syndic under New Mexico [Arizona did not become a separate territory until 1863], I opened a book of records, performed the marriage ceremony, baptized the children, and granted the divorce." (Tubac became something of a Gretna Green for runaway couples from Sonora, where the priest charged $25 for a marriage ceremony that Poston performed gratis, with a free treat for good measure.) Then in 1861, with U.S. troops withdrawn for Civil War service, marauding Apaches again brought virtual abandonment to Tubac.

(Fr. Eusebia Franciso Kino, a Jesuit, established a mission in this area in 1691. In 1752 it was renamed San José de Tumacacori. It is now a national monument located three miles south of Tubac.)

Tubac had become a Spanish frontier colony and supply center in 1752. Here, in 1776, Juan Bautista de Anza assembled his colonizing party for its epochal journey to San Francisco (*q.v.*). Indian hostility plagued the settlement intermittently until 1886, however, and it never regained its pre–Civil War prosperity or importance. A near-ghost for almost a century, its picturesque adobe ruins are now preserved as a state park.

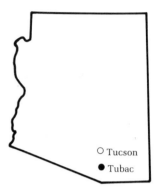

○ Tucson

● Tubac

Tubac (a Pima word meaning "burned place") in 1864. Founded more than a century earlier, it was abandoned repeatedly to marauding Indians. This view is from J. Ross Browne's Adventures in the Apache Country.

Courtesy California State Library

San José de Tumacacori. Construction of the present church, its impressive ruins stabilized by the National Park Service, began around 1800. It was in use by 1822 but was abandoned about 1848.

Courtesy Tucson News Service

4

Yuma   Arizona

Yuma and heat were synonymous. "It is said that a wicked soldier died here," J. Ross Browne related in the 1860's, "and was consigned to the fiery regions below for his manifold sins; but unable to stand the rigors of the climate, sent back for his blankets." Most of those subsequently sent to Yuma Territorial Prison (Arizona's notorious "Hell-Hole") would have understood. "Every thing dries; wagons dry; men dry; chickens dry; there is no juice left in any thing, living or dead, by the close of summer." Mules, Browne reported, "can only bray at midnight; and I have heard it hinted . . . that snakes find a difficulty in bending their bodies."

Even the Spaniards failed to conquer Yuma's heat. Colorado River navigator Hernando de Alarcón may have reached its granite bluff in 1540, but it took the discovery of gold in California almost three centuries later to bring permanent settlers. The mission Fr. Eusebio Francisco Kino established in 1697 lasted less than a year (he did, however, pioneer *El Camino del Diablo,* the desert route west on which hundreds of Argonauts of '49 died), and the mission Fr. Francisco Tomás Garcés founded across the river from Yuma in 1779 was destroyed by Apaches in 1781. When Lt. A. W. Whipple made his boundary survey in the fall of 1849 (a year after the region became American), he found it "populated only with Indians."

But L. J. F. Jaeger established a ferry that same year, and from then until 1877, when the Southern Pacific Railroad reached Yuma, ferrying was a profitable, highly competitive, and extremely important business enterprise (in the fall and spring of 1850–51, one ferry alone—operated by Dr. Able B. Lincoln, a Mexican War adventurer—carried an estimated sixty thousand California-bound gold seekers at two dollars a head). In 1850 the government established Fort Yuma on the west bank of the river. Yuma itself was platted in 1854. Near-by placer findings in 1858 brought additional growth, and on July 1, 1876, Yuma Territorial Prison was opened—to seven prisoners.

A symbol of harsh frontier justice for the next quarter-century, the prison stood naked to the desert heat atop a barren bluff overlooking the Colorado River. Adobe walls, eighteen feet high and eight feet thick at their base, surrounded the stone buildings, solid-rock dungeon cells, and sun-baked yard. Outside, a Gatling gun on a tower guarded the prison's single entrance. Beyond, would-be jailbreakers had yet to face a turbulent river, several hundred miles of desert, and Indians who were paid fifty dollars for each convict returned.

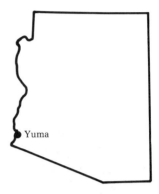

Fort Yuma, shown here in an 1854 water color by Henry C. Pratt, was established in 1850 on the California side of the Colorado River opposite Yuma.

Courtesy National Archives

Cell block at Yuma Territorial Prison today. Once housing 376 men, the prison was abandoned in 1908 and is now a museum.

Courtesy Robert M. Utley, National Park Service

6

San Xavier del Bac Arizona

One of the finest surviving examples of Spanish mission architecture, San Xavier del Bac (ten miles south of Tucson) was northernmost in the chain of twenty-four missions, seven of them in present Arizona, established by Fr. Eusebio Francisco Kino in Pimería Alta around the turn of the seventeenth century. In his diary for the year 1700, the "padre on horseback" describes the founding:

Having arrived at this great rancheria of San Xavier del Bac [April 26] . . . and finding myself with so many Indians . . . and also in view of the many prayers of the natives that I should stay with them, I determined not to go farther. . . . During the seven days that we were here . . . we catechized the people and taught them. . . . On the 27th they gave me five little ones to baptize. . . . On the 28th we began the foundations of a very large and capacious church and house . . . all the people working with much pleasure and zeal, some in digging for the foundations, others in hauling many and very good stones of *tezontle* from a little hill which was about a quarter of a league away.

Fr. Kino died in 1711 and since then the history of *La Paloma Blanca del Desierto* (The White Dove of the Desert) accurately reflects the fluctuating fortunes of the Catholic church in the Southwest. Fr. Kino's successors carried on until the Pima rebellion of 1751, when San Xavier was abandoned. Following the establishment of a presidio at Tubac (*q.v.*), the padres returned and were active until 1767, when the Jesuits were expelled from all Spanish colonies. The Franciscans took their place, only to see the Apaches sack the mission. They began to rebuild in 1772 (probably on the original foundations, since the cruciform plan is Jesuitical rather than Franciscan), and the present church was consecrated in 1797, with many of Fr. Kino's original furnishings and ornaments. Secularization of Church property in 1822 during the Mexican regime again caused abandonment of San Xavier, but it was reoccupied in 1859. Restoration was begun in 1906, and the church is regularly used today.

The mission is notable for its construction and design. Its burned-brick walls are coated with white lime plaster. The baroque entrance façade is adorned with pilasters and panels and enriched with low plaster relief. The interior, with its high altar and side chapels, is embellished with carvings and painted ornaments. Strikingly beautiful in its desert setting, San Xavier is an excellent blending of the Byzantine, Moorish, Spanish, and Mexican Aztec influences that characterize mission architecture in the Southwest.

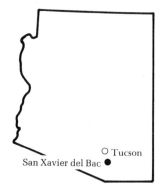

O Tucson
San Xavier del Bac ●

San Xavier del Bac as seen by Albert H. Campbell in 1855. The lithograph is from Volume VII of the Pacific Railroad Reports.

Courtesy University of Oklahoma Library

San Xavier del Bac, restored and once again La Paloma Blanca del Desierto.

Courtesy Arizona Office of Economic Planning and Development

Tucson Arizona

Tucson, a handsome, booming resort city today, received a remarkably bad press in the mid-1800's. The "Tucson bed," which the traveler made by lying on his stomach and covering himself with his back, was a newspaper byword. The Old Pueblo, according to J. Ross Browne, "was a place of resort for traders, speculators, gamblers, horse-thieves, murderers and vagrant politicians. Men who were no longer permitted to live in California found the climate of Tucson congenial to their health. If the world were searched over I suppose there could not be found so degraded a set of villains. . . . Every man went armed to the teeth, and street fights and bloody affrays were of daily occurrence. It was literally a paradise of devils."

Conditions in Tucson got worse before they started to improve. In the spring of 1863, mountain man Joe Walker maintained, "the coyote wolves from the surrounding desert would come and howl at it all night and sneak about its suburbs all day." It was, according to another observer, "a city of mudboxes, dingy and dilapidated, cracked and baked into a composite of dust and filth: littered about with broken corrals, sheds, bake-ovens, carcasses of dead animals, and desolate in the glare of the southern sun. Adobe walls without whitewash . . . baked and dried Mexicans, sore-backed burros, coyote dogs, and terra-cotta children."

In 1867, however, Tucson became Arizona's second territorial capital (until 1877) and began to grow. By 1870 it had a newspaper, a good hotel, a brewery, two doctors, several saloons—and a bathtub. And in 1871, with its first school in operation (and frontier prices ranging from brandy at $40 a gallon to soap at 50¢ a bar, from coffee at $4 a pound to brooms at $6), the town was finally incorporated.

Precise details are lacking, but Fr. Francisco Tomás Garcés is generally credited with founding San José del Tucson on the west bank of the Santa Cruz River about 1775. A walled presidio was soon established on the spot, and the Franciscans built a church and industrial arts school for the near-by Pimas and Papagos. After that, Tucson was probably inhabited continuously, although Apaches made life precarious for another century. Lt. Col. Philip St. George Cooke, with the Mormon Battalion, raised the American flag over the pueblo in 1846. Not until 1856, however (following the Gadsden Purchase of 1853), did U.S. dragoons occupy the town. In December 1858, Fr. Joseph P. Machebeuf (Willa Cather's "Joseph" in *Death Comes for the Archbishop*) described Tucson as "a village of about 800 souls, built around an ancient Mexican fortress."

San José del Tucson Mission, shown in ruins in this photograph taken in the 1870's, was established about 1775. In the early 1800's, its 400-foot-square wall enclosed a mission house, tannery, carpenter shop, soap and candle factory, school, and other buildings.

Courtesy Arizona Pioneers' Historical Society

Tucson in the early 1860's, when J. Ross Browne called it "a paradise of devils." The sketch used here is from Browne's Adventures in the Apache Country.

Courtesy Arizona Pioneers' Historical Society

Tucson's modern San Augustine Cathedral shows the influence of Spanish mission architecture.

Courtesy Tucson News Service

10

Fort Bowie   Arizona

Thanks to the Apaches, the frontier receded slowly in southeastern Arizona. Not until 1886, with Geronimo's capture and exile to Florida, was real peace brought to the region. During the preceding quarter-century, much of the bloodiest fighting centered around Apache Pass—a rough, twisting defile between foothills of the Dos Cabezas on the northwest, the Chiricahuas on the southeast—and Fort Bowie (thirteen miles south of Bowie), established July 28, 1862, to guard the Pass's eastern entrance.

Álvar Núñez Cabeza de Vaca, in 1536, may possibly have been the first white man to see Apache Pass and its welcome Apache Springs. It was the middle of the nineteenth century, however, before California-bound gold seekers, boundary commissions, railroad surveyors, and military columns made the notch a familiar landmark on one of the Southwest's major transportation and communication routes. In 1858 the famed Butterfield Overland Mail Company ran its Concords over the rocky pass, building a stage station near the springs. In the 1860's, when the Apache terror was at its height, stage drivers were sometimes offered triple pay for runs.

The withdrawal of troops during the Civil War aggravated Indian troubles throughout the West. In the Southwest, Confederate activity created an additional problem for the U.S. Army, further decreasing control over the Apaches. Lt. George N. Bascom's attempt to arrest Cochise at Apache Pass in February 1861 had assured the animosity of that important leader. More serious trouble came early in July of 1862 when a strong force of California Volunteers under Brig. Gen. James H. Carleton, marching east against Confederate forces in New Mexico, was surprised in the pass by Apaches under Cochise and Mangas Coloradas. (They were finally repulsed by means of howitzers. "We would have done well," one Indian said, "if you hadn't fired wagons at us."

Fort Bowie was established a few days later—on a hill commanding the strategic springs—to protect Carleton's communications with Tucson and California. This rock and adobe post, only fragments of which are visible today, was replaced in 1868 by a more substantial fort on a slope of Bowie Peak. Both were the hub of military operations against the Chiricahuas. Following the pacification of Cochise in 1872, Chiricahua Agency was located in the pass for a short time, and Fort Bowie became active in the campaigns against Apache renegades under Nachez and Geronimo. Generals George Crook and Nelson A. Miles maintained their headquarters there. Freighters and emigrants continued to use Apache Pass until the railroad reached Arizona in 1881. No longer needed, Fort Bowie was abandoned in 1896.

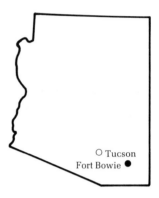

O Tucson
Fort Bowie ●

Fort Bowie in 1890, six years before its abandonment. Guarding the eastern entrance to strategic Apache Pass, it served as the hub of U.S. military operations against the Apaches from 1862 to 1886.

Courtesy National Park Service

The ruins of Fort Bowie as they appear today. Accessible by trail only, they are preserved as Fort Bowie National Historic Site.

Courtesy Robert M. Utley

Tombstone Arizona

"Tombstone," announced the first edition (May 1, 1880) of the *Epitaph,* "is a city set upon a hill, promising to vie with ancient Rome upon her seven hills, in a fame different in character but no less in importance." That her fame was different, no one will deny, but fame it was. The year after Ed Schieffelin's location of the Lucky Cuss silver mine in 1877, the San Pedro Hills of extreme southeastern Arizona were swarming with miners and mining-camp followers. The Tough Nut, Goodenough, East Side, West Side, and other rich mines were promptly located. By 1879, Tombstone was laid out, about a mile from the first Schieffelin camp, and it soon became the most celebrated and widely known boom town in the Southwest.

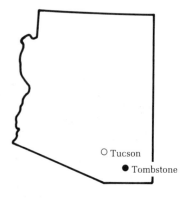

Aside from the richness of its mines (some $80,000,000 in silver before they were flooded), much of Tombstone's fame rests on the admitted lawlessness and violence that marked its 1879–89 decade of prosperity. But the storied Earp-Clanton feud that culminated in the gun fight at the O.K. Corral (October 26, 1881) is only one facet of Tombstone life. The *Epitaph,* in the sprightly, personalized style of the day, recorded them all:

** The ladies of the M. E. church will give an oyster supper at Mining Exchange Hall next Wednesday evening. ** There appears to be an epidemic of sickness visiting Tombstone at the present time. . . . If some of the fossilized, pessimistic, anti-statehood cranks were to die off it would probably do the country some good. ** Full moon last night— also some other things in the same happy fix. . . . ** The Public Library Association . . . will be reopened in a short time. ** Miss Josephine Randall has started a physical culture class among Tombstone young ladies. . . . ** Lovers of vocal music will miss a rare treat if they fail to drop into the Elite theater tonight and hear the exquisite rendering of La Paloma by one of the Ulms sisters. ** A monte game is now in full blast at the Crystal Palace. ** Miss Ella Gardiner, a serio comic vocalist, made her bow . . . at the Bird Cage last night. . . . ** Godfrey Tribolet says that in all his travels he never saw a more efficient fire department than that of Tombstone. . . . ** It won't do any harm to go to church today. Try the experiment anyhow. **

Dating from 1879 to 1882, Tombstone's most important buildings—St. Paul's Episcopal Church, City Hall, Cochise County Courthouse, Schieffelin Hall, the Bird Cage Theatre (now a museum)—are remarkably well preserved today.

Tombstone in the 1880's, at the height of the silver boom. Although its population has dropped from a high of 7,000 in 1881 to 1,600 today, the town remains a picturesque monument to the mining frontier.

Courtesy Arizona Pioneers' Historical Society

The Bird Cage Theatre, where "Miss Ella Gardiner, a serio comic vocalist, made her bow," as it looks today.

Courtesy Phoenix Chamber of Commerce

Fort Smith Arkansas

Thomas Nuttall, the English explorer-naturalist, visited Fort Smith in 1819:

The garrison, consisting of two block-houses, and lines of cabins or barracks for the accommodation of 70 men . . . is agreeably situated at the junction of the Pottoe, on a rising ground of about 50 feet elevation, and surrounded by alluvial and uplands of unusual fertility. The view is more commanding and picturesque, than any other spot of equal elevation on the banks of the Arkansa.

Two years before, in the fall, Maj. William C. Bradford, commanding a company of the so-called Rifle Regiment, and Maj. Stephen H. Long, the topographical engineer, had left St. Louis to establish an Arkansas River post designed to keep peace between the Osages and Cherokees and to protect the settlers beginning to penetrate this area. Shortly before Christmas a stockaded fort had been thrown up at a site, called Belle Point by the French, just below the mouth of the Poteau River.

Despite its picturesque setting and strategic location (until 1820, the westernmost U.S. military post), Fort Smith's fortunes fluctuated wildly. It promptly became the gateway to the Southwest for travelers and the depot for the first forts erected in Indian Territory. (On his way west in 1821, Thomas James tarried a few days at Fort Smith and was received by Commandant Bradford "with the utmost kindness and hospitality." On leaving, he carried along "a large supply of garden vegetables, with a barrel of onions, which we were not to broach until we had killed our first buffalo, when we were enjoined to have 'a general feast in honor of old Billy Bradford.' ") In 1824 most of its garrison had been moved to newly established Fort Gibson (q.v.). Then in 1827 the post was reoccupied, and in 1838 came the decision to construct a more substantial fort around a 450 x 600-foot quadrangle.

The fort was still unfinished in 1841, however, when Gen. Zachary Taylor took command, moving his family into a "plain one-story concern with stone chimneys outside and ample porches in front and rear," and two years later, on his recommendation the rebuilding was halted. Meanwhile, the town of Fort Smith was growing up around the fort. Receiving its post office in 1829, it boasted nearly five hundred persons in 1842. The California gold rush turned the town into a noisy supply point, and in 1858 it became an important stop on the famed 2,391-mile Butterfield Stage route from St. Louis to San Francisco. The military post was finally abandoned in 1871, four years before the arrival of the town's best-known figure: Judge (151 death sentences, 83 hangings) Isaac C. Parker.

Fort Smith

Fort Smith as seen from Indian Territory by H. B. Möllhausen in 1853, when he accompanied Lt. A. W. Whipple's railroad-survey expedition. Josiah Gregg made trips into Indian Territory and Texas from here in 1840 and 1841.

Courtesy University of Oklahoma Library

Restored barracks building and commissary of the second Fort Smith. Note the reconstructed gallows of Judge Parker at the left.

Courtesy Arkansas Department of Parks and Tourism

Restored courtroom of Judge Parker inside the barracks at Fort Smith National Historic Site.

Courtesy Arkansas Department of Parks and Tourism

San Diego   California

San Diego is the oldest Spanish settlement in California. The area was first visited in 1539 by Fr. Marcos de Niza while he was searching, by land, for the Seven Cities of Cíbola. Juan Rodríguez Cabrillo, a Portuguese mariner sailing under the Spanish flag, made the first visit by sea. Sighting Point Loma on September 28, 1542, he sailed his two small vessels, the *San Salvador* and *Victoria,* into a "closed and very good port" that he called San Miguel Bay. The landing was probably near Ballast Point on the east side of Point Loma.

The name was changed to San Diego Bay by Sebastián Vizcaíno, who put his three "well officered" ships into the harbor, "the best in all the South Seas," in 1602. On November 12 the Carmelite friars of his party are generally believed to have celebrated California's first Holy Mass. (This, too, was probably at Ballast Point, where the Spaniards later constructed Fort Guijarros.)

Settlement did not come until 1769, when José de Gálvez, *visitador-géneral* in Mexico City, ordered a full-scale colonizing attempt. From the sea, the *San Antonio* arrived April 11, the *San Carlos* April 29. By land, a column under Fernando de Rivera reached San Diego May 15, while Don Gaspar de Portolá, with Fr. Junípero Serra, arrived July 1. Both expeditions brought a herd of cattle.

On July 16 a crude brushwood shelter was erected and Misión San Diego de Alcalá dedicated. A presidio was also established on the site (present-day Presidio Hill Park, in San Diego's "Old Town"). Six months later, however, when Portolá returned from San Francisco (*q.v.*), little had been done beyond the marking of nineteen new graves. In 1774, to lessen the presidio influence, Fr. Francisco Palou moved the mission six miles inland. An Indian attack on November 4, 1775, caused a brief retreat to the presidio, but the padres returned to the valley in July 1776 and finished work on a temporary church in October. The present mission was dedicated in 1780 and completed in 1813. Restored in 1931, it now contains many relics, including some of Fr. Serra's handwritten records.

San Diego grew up around the presidio. Having become the center of the otter-skin trade by 1834, it was organized as a pueblo. In 1850, under American rule, it was incorporated as a city. "New Town" grew up on the bay to the south, however, and soon became the city's center. Today, Old Town Plaza, surrounded by several adobe buildings dating back to the 1820's, is a Spanish-flavored island in the middle of a modern American city.

O Los Angeles

● San Diego

Misión San Diego de Alcalá in 1853, from a lithograph by Charles Koppel. The first in a chain of twenty-one missions that eventually stretched northward to Sonoma, it was secularized in 1834 and restored in 1931.

Courtesy University of Oklahoma Library

Father Serra Museum in Presidio Park, only a few blocks from San Diego's Old Town Plaza.

Courtesy San Diego Convention and Tourist Bureau

18

Monterey California

Sebastián Vizcaíno discovered Monterey Bay in 1602, although Juan Rodríguez Cabrillo had sighted near-by Point Pinos as early as 1542. After naming it wisely (to honor the Count of Monterey, viceroy of New Spain, who authorized his trip), Vizcaíno proceeded to describe the area in such glowing terms that those who followed him could not recognize it.

So it was that when Don Gaspar de Portolá, with a 64-man colonizing expedition, pushed northward from San Diego through "rocks, brushwood and rugged mountains" and reached Monterey Bay on October 2, 1769, he failed to recognize his objective. He went on to discover San Francisco Bay before returning to San Diego. The following spring, he was more successful, and on June 3, 1770 (before a simple altar under an oak at the site where Vizcaíno had landed 168 years before), he and Fr. Junípero Serra, with ritual and pomp, founded the presidio and the Misión San Carlos de Borromeo.

(In 1771, to shield his acolytes from the soldiers, Fr. Serra moved the mission some five miles south to the Carmel Valley. He died there August 28, 1784, and is buried before the altar. The original mission became the Royal Presidio Chapel and has since remained in continuous use.)

Monterey became the capital of California in 1775, and the town soon expanded beyond the old presidio walls. Foreign trade, although expressly forbidden by the Spanish court, continued to grow. The first U.S. ship, the *Otter,* docked in 1796. And because such essentials as skillets, needles, cotton cloth, and plows were always scarce, subsequent *Yanqui* skippers were seldom turned away. A raid by the Argentinian privateer Hypolite Bouchard in 1818 created a brief flurry of excitement, as did the premature American "conquest," on October 19, 1842, by Com. Thomas Ap Catesby Jones. (Discovering that the United States was not yet at war with Mexico, Jones retired the next day with elaborate apologies.) On April 9, 1822, a delegation of *Californios* met at Monterey to recognize California "from this time . . . as a dependent alone of . . . the Empire of Mexico and independent of the dominion of Spain."

The gracious Spanish mode of life (which Bayard Taylor thought possessed "a natural refinement of manner which would grace the most polished society") continued, even after July 7, 1846, when Com. John D. Sloat sailed into the bay and permanently raised the American flag over the custom house. Today, with many of its handsome old adobe buildings preserved as state historical monuments, Monterey remains a fascinating showcase of Spanish-American culture.

The presidio at Monterey in the 1790's. After Mexico won her independence from Spain in 1821, the first legislature met in Monterey to frame California's first constitution.

Courtesy Library of Congress

The old customhouse, part of which dates back to 1827, is one of eight relics of Spanish-Mexican occupation that constitute the Monterey State Historical Monuments.

Courtesy California Division of Beaches and Parks

San Francisco California

Curiously, the Golden Gate, guarding one of the world's great harbors, was missed by the early Pacific explorers: Juan Rodríguez Cabrillo (*see* San Diego) in 1542, Sir Francis Drake in 1579, Sebastián Rodríguez Cermeño in 1595, and Sebastián Vizcaíno (*see* Monterey) in 1602. It was October 1769 before Sgt. José Ortega, with an expedition headed by Don Gaspar de Portolá, became the first European to see the bay—and that from land. Unimpressed, he failed even to give it a name. (More perceptive was Fr. Juan Crespi, his chaplain: "It is a harbor such that not only the navy of our most Catholic Majesty but those of all Europe could take shelter in it.")

Juan Manuel de Ayala was the first (August 5, 1775) to sail through the Golden Gate, but it remained for explorer-colonizer Juan Bautista de Anza, in 1776, to see the bay as a settlement site. His expedition (30 soldiers and their families, 200 colonists) had marched 1,600 miles from Mexico to Monterey. Scouting ahead, he reached the tip of the peninsula, where, Fr. Pedro Font wrote, they "saw a prodigy of nature which it is not easy to describe . . . the harbor of harbors."

Here on a high mesa (present Fort Point at the Golden Gate Bridge), De Anza set up a cross overlooking the bay's entrance, designating, Fr. Font continues, "the site for the new settlement and fort." About four miles southeast, in "a beautiful arroyo," he located the Franciscan Misión Dolores (now restored). José Joaquín Moraga then brought the settlers from Monterey to establish the presidio (September 17) and mission (October 8).

For seventy years, however, the new colony, called Yerba Buena in 1842, was only an isolated outpost. English Capt. George Vancouver (1792) noted the lack of substantial buildings, Nikolai Rezanov (1806) thought it would be easy to make the area "a corporeal part of the Russian Empire," and American Richard Henry Dana (1835) saw only scattered adobe structures, when "this magnificent bay" seemed destined to become "a place of great importance."

Dana's vision was prophetic, and John C. Frémont supplied an altogether fitting name: "Chrysopylae, or Golden Gate." On July 8, 1846, Capt. John B. Montgomery went ashore from the *Portsmouth* to hoist the Stars and Stripes over the town square (now Portsmouth Plaza), and Yerba Buena became San Francisco. Eighteen months later, gold was discovered at Sutter's Mill (*see* Coloma), and on February 28, 1849, the pennant-bedecked steamer *California* entered the Golden Gate with the first boatload of Forty-niners. Dana returned in 1859 and found San Francisco to be "one of the capitals of the American Republic, and the sole emporium of a new world, the awakened Pacific."

San Francisco in 1812. Sebastián Cermeño supplied the name, although he missed the Golden Gate and his La Bahía de San Francisco *was present-day Drake's Bay.*

Courtesy Library of Congress

A gunport in the north battlements of Fort Point frames the Golden Gate Bridge, which spans both the fort and the mile-wide strait. A museum, open daily, draws visitors to the ancient bastion, now a National Historic Site. The Golden Gate Bridge, completed in 1937, provides a spectacular link between San Francisco and Marin County.

Courtesy Redwood Empire Association

Los Angeles California

"Kansas City to Los Angeles for a dollar!" read the Atchison, Topeka & Santa Fe advertisement one spring day in 1886, and train after train rolled into one-time *El Pueblo de Nuestra Señora la Reina de Los Angeles de Porciúncula* to give the city its biggest, if not gaudiest, real estate boom. But El Pueblo's awakening was long in coming. On September 4, 1781, the scene (just a block from present-day Union Station) was far different.

From near-by San Gabriel Mission (established in 1771) the procession of settlers (11 families, some 44 men, women, and children in all) had marched the final nine dusty miles of their journey under the escort of four soldiers headed by Corp. José Vicente Feliz, the "little father of El Pueblo," who was to rule the colony its first seven years. There was little ceremony. Once beside the Porciúncula, each family moved to its assigned house lot in accordance with the drawing that had taken place at San Gabriel. (Gov. Felipe de Neve had been at the mission since early May, drafting detailed plans for the pueblo and laying out its plaza, lots, and fields. Each family received two plots for corn, a plowshare, a hoe, and an ax.) Earth-roofed huts of willow branches interlaced with tule were erected. A small dam was built, as was an irrigation canal, the *zanjamadre*. By 1784 adobe houses had replaced the makeshift huts, and a chapel had been built. By 1791, El Pueblo's population had climbed to 139; its 29 dwellings, town hall, chapel, barracks, guardhouse, and granaries were surrounded by an adobe wall.

The pueblo site had first been visited on August 2, 1769, by Don Gaspar de Portolá (*see* San Diego) and his party, who found there a Yangna Indian village (probably near the present city hall). Impressed with the fertile valley, they named the river *Porciúncula,* for a chapel in Italy. Fr. Juan Crespi thought the site had "all the requisites for a large settlement." He noted "a large vineyard of wild grapes" and "an infinity of rose bushes in full bloom." Prophetically, he pronounced the soil "capable of producing every kind of grain and fruit."

By 1800, however, the settlement numbered only seventy families, living mainly on grain and cattle. Lawns, sidewalks, and shade trees were unknown. The streets were crooked and ungraded, littered with rubbish and the carcasses of slaughtered animals. Then in 1846 (El Pueblo was a sleepy village of three thousand) came the Mexican War, and by the Treaty of Cahuenga, signed January 13, 1847, at a ranch house in what is now North Hollywood, Los Angeles became American. Soon it was a booming frontier town.

Los Angeles in 1853, from a lithograph by Charles Koppel. Filled with "criminals, murderers, bandits and thieves," according to one contemporary account, "her bowels are absolute strangers to sympathy, when called upon to practically demonstrate it."

Courtesy University of Oklahoma Library

Olvera Street is thought to be Los Angeles's oldest thoroughfare. Named for the residence of Judge Augustín Olvera, who came to Los Angeles from Mexico in 1834, it maintains much of the spirit and charm of the old Spanish pueblo.

Courtesy Greater Los Angeles Visitors' and Convention Bureau

Santa Barbara Mission   California

Santa Barbara, the so-called Queen of the Missions, stands as something of a symbol, both of the idealism that brought the mission system into being and of its essential failure in actual practice. Established December 4, 1786, as the tenth mission in the chain of twenty-one that stretched northward along the California coast to San Francisco and beyond, it escaped secularization in 1834 and is today the only one in which the altar light has never been extinguished. In the early 1800's, when it had more than 1,700 neophytes living in some 250 adobe houses as a prosperous and self-sustaining community, it gave brief promise of fulfilling its primary purpose.

In 1493, Pope Alexander VI issued a bull dividing the New World between Spain and Portugal and enjoining them that each exploratory venture was to be accompanied by "worthy, God-fearing, learned, skilled and experienced men, in order to instruct the inhabitants in the Catholic faith." In practice, however, there was always a disastrous lag between the Bible and the sword. (Civil and military authorities soon set up a system of slavery which threatened the natives with extermination. In one six-year period the Indian population of Hispaniola decreased by nearly one-half.) When Fr. Junípero Serra, a Franciscan, established the first California mission on July 16, 1769 (*see* San Diego), the religious program finally appeared to triumph, but the mission system, with less than seventy years ahead of it, was itself facing extinction. Even in Santa Barbara the mission followed the presidio (founded April 21, 1782, by Capt. José Francisco Ortega) by nearly five years.

The start, however, was propitious. Indians, paid in food and clothing, brought fish and game and assisted in hewing timbers and making adobe bricks. After conversion they worked, under supervision of the padres, to construct dwellings (and the mission itself), cultivate fields, and raise cattle. The first chapel, made of boughs, was replaced in 1789 by a well-constructed adobe church with a red tile roof. Too small within five years, it was replaced by a larger edifice which was destroyed by an earthquake in 1812. Work on the present stone church, begun at once, was completed in 1820. Well preserved, it is a handsome blend of old Spanish and Moorish architecture.

Santa Barbara's influence as a mission declined sharply after 1834. As presidio officers became baronial *rancheros* of vast estates and great herds, the Indian population waned. The profitable seal and otter trade increased American influence, and in August 1846, Com. Robert F. Stockton anchored in the bay, came ashore, and hoisted the American flag.

Santa Barbara Mission, shown here as it looked about 1880, was established in 1786.

Courtesy Southern Pacific Historical Collection

The Queen of the Missions is the only California mission in which the altar light has never been extinguished. Work on the present structure was completed in 1820, and it has since been fully restored.

Courtesy Santa Barbara Chamber of Commerce

26

Fort Ross California

Fort Ross, perched on a ledge above the Pacific a dozen miles northwest of the mouth of the Russian River, represents the deepest Russian penetration of the North American continent. An inadequate food supply in Alaska (where Kodiak had been established in 1745) combined with a growing scarcity of fur animals to prompt the move southward. The Russian-America Company, chartered in 1799 as something of a counterpart to Canada's Hudson's Bay Company, probed the then Spanish-held coast as far south as Bodega Bay in 1809, and several temporary settlements were established in this area.

The move to the more suitable "Colony Ross" site was made in the spring of 1812. The *Chirikov* landed 95 Russians and 40 Aleuts, under the command of Ivan Aleksandrovich Kuskov, at the Kashia Pomo Indian village of Mad-shui-nui. Gifts of trade goods purchased the land. On May 15 construction began, and "in three months, the principal buildings were erected and on the name day of the deceased Tsar Paul I, August the thirteenth, the fort was formally dedicated with the firing of the cannon and small arms, the image of the Savior was placed before the establishment and the settlement was named ROSS."

Fort Ross in 1828, from a lithograph in Auguste Bernard Duhaut-Cilly's Voyage autour du Monde. *The site was purchased for three blankets, three pairs of breeches, two axes, three hoes, and some beads.*

Courtesy Library of Congress

Eventually the site boasted 59 buildings. Inside the twelve-foot-high redwood stockade were the 24 x 31-foot Russian orthodox chapel (built about 1824, with a six-sided tower and rear dome over a round, hollow cupola), the commander's house (1812), barracks, warehouses, shops, and a jail. Outside the blockhouse-guarded enclosure were the huts of Aleut hunters, a bathhouse, a windmill, workshops, a wharf, and farm buildings.

Initially the Russians established a thriving trade with the San Francisco presidio and mission (grain, peas, meat, tallow, and hides for tobacco, sugar, iron, and cloth), but Spanish (later Mexican) officials remained apprehensive. When farming finally proved unsuccessful, as did the experiment in shipbuilding, and fur revenues sagged with near-extermination of the sea otter, the Tsar ordered his subjects to withdraw. In December 1841, Commandant Aleksandr Rotchev sold the entire property to John A. Sutter (*see* New Helvetia *and* Coloma) for $30,000. Included with the buildings, many of which were dismantled and shipped to New Helvetia, were farm implements, 1,700 head of cattle, 940 horses and mules, 9,000 sheep, Mme. Rotchev's prized conservatory, and an arsenal of French weapons salvaged in 1813 after Napoleon's retreat.

The Fort Ross Russian Orthodox chapel, collapsed by the San Francisco earthquake of 1906, has been painstakingly restored as a feature of Fort Ross State Historic Park.

Courtesy Redwood Empire Association

Fort Ross is now a state historic park. The stockade, chapel, blockhouses (one of which is seven sided, the other eight sided), and commandant's house (now a museum) have all been carefully restored.

New Helvetia California

New Helvetia (more commonly, Sutter's Fort) is a study in ironic contrasts. A Swiss barony flying the Mexican flag in a vast wilderness, it became the modern capital of present-day California. Its owner, an autocratic army officer who ruled his enclave in feudal splendor, died impoverished, a victim of his own enterprise. Capt. John Augustus Sutter himself described the situation:

> Agriculture increased until I had several hundred men working in the harvest fields, and to feed them I had to kill four or sometimes five oxen daily. I could raise 40,000 bushels of wheat without trouble, reap the crops with sickles, thrash it with bones, and winnow it in the wind. There were thirty plows running with fresh oxen every morning. . . . I had at the time twelve thousand head of cattle, two thousand horses and mules, between ten and fifteen thousand sheep, and a thousand hogs. My best days were just before the discovery of gold.

The "founder of American agriculture in California," who in 1839 had accepted a 50,000-acre land grant in the rich Sacramento Valley by swearing allegiance to the Mexican flag, had sown the seeds of his own destruction with his decision to build a sawmill on the American River. There, on January 24, 1848, gold was discovered (*see* Coloma). Soon his white retainers would desert New Helvetia for the mushrooming gold camps, and stampeding hordes of Argonauts would overrun his hospitable fort, steal his cattle, drive off his Indians, and eventually take the land itself. (Sacramento, laid out on Sutter's farm in 1840, soon became supply center for the northern Mother Lode. Growing rapidly, it was the state capital by 1854. The Pony Express reached the city in 1860, the transcontinental telegraph in 1861.)

Sutter began work on his fort in April 1840. By 1843, when Swedish scientist G. M. Sandels saw it, New Helvetia had "more the appearance of a citadel than an agricultural establishment. It is protected by an incompleted wall, ten feet high, made of adobes . . . also having a turret with embrasures and loopholes. . . . Twenty-four pieces of different sized ordnance are available for defense. Against the walls, on the inside of the Fort, are erected the storehouses . . . a distillery . . . shops for coopers, saddlers, blacksmiths, carpenters, granaries, and quarters for laborers. An armed sentinel stands on guard at the gateway day and night."

In 1844 and again in early 1846, John C. Frémont visited the fort in preliminary maneuvering against the Mexican government. On July 11, 1846, Capt. Sutter raised the Stars and Stripes over the fort.

New Helvetia (Sutter's Fort) was busy and prosperous in 1846, according to this sketch by J. W. Revere. Throughout the 1840's it was the hospitable goal of covered-wagon emigrants.

Courtesy Library of Congress

Restored New Helvetia, now a state historical monument, is a rich and varied museum of pioneer Californiana.

Courtesy Southern Pacific Historical Collection

Coloma California

In his daily log of events at New Helvetia (*q.v.*), John A. Sutter unwittingly recorded the dawn of a new era in California and the world:

August 27th., 1847. A host of Mormons here to buy provisions and have blacksmith work done. Made a contract with James Wilson Marshall for a saw-mill to be erected on the American Fork.

The next day, Marshall and Peter L. Wimmer "departed early for the Mts . . . with heavily freighted wagons of provisions." Then, five months later, this cryptic note:

January 28th., 1848. Mr. Marshall arrived from the Mts. on very important business.

It remained for the journal of Henry W. Bigler, West Virginia—born Mormon, to fix for history the precise date of the initial discovery of gold at Sutter's Mill: "Monday 24th this day [January] some kind of mettle was found in the tail race that looks like goald first discovered by James Martial, the Boss of the Mill. Sunday 30 clear & has been all the last week our metal has been tride and prooves to be goald it is thought to be rich We have pict up more than a hundred dollars woth last week."

For three days Sutter had pondered (with misgivings which later proved to be entirely justified) the possible consequences of Marshall's find. On February 1 he rode the fifty miles to the millsite to see for himself. A five-day inspection turned up gold all along the river and up tributary ravines and creeks. He called the laborers together, doubled their wages, and pledged them to secrecy. But it didn't work.

"Wittmer returned with two wagons from the mountains," Sutter noted on February 13, "and told everyone of the gold mines there." Word soon reached Samuel Brannan, a San Francisco newspaperman, and on March 15, 1848, the weekly *Californian* first told the world of the discovery. By May 25, just a little more than two months later, Sutter was recording: "Great hosts continue to the Mts." California and the West would never be the same.

Coloma grew up around Sutter's sawmill, the first white settlement in the foothills. It soon boasted a gold rocker and the state's first mining ditch and served as a supply center for the other diggings. Within a decade, however, its placers were largely depleted.

Today the "Queen of the Mines" dozes peacefully, preserved as a state park and surmounted by a hilltop statue of Marshall, who died in poverty in 1885. With his left arm he points down, over the cabin where he lived and the two churches and half-dozen business buildings that remain in the town, to the carefully marked mill and discovery sites.

Sutter's Mill and its tail-race, where the first important gold discovery in California was made on January 24, 1848. Coloma grew up around the sawmill.

Courtesy National Archives

The site of Sutter's Mill today, preserved as part of Marshall Gold Discovery State Historic Park.

Courtesy California Division of Beaches and Parks

Fort Tejón   California

Countless unsolved deaths dot the history of the frontier West, but few are more baffling, or of such long standing, than one described in a cryptic message cut deeply into the wood of an oak in Grapevine Canyon on the future site of Fort Tejón:

Peter le Beck
killed
by
a x bear
Oct. 17
1837

This inscription was first noted in R. S. Williamson's railroad report of 1853. Several ingenious theories have been advanced, one of which holds that the victim was Peter Lebecque, a young Hudson's Bay Company *voyageur,* and that he was killed by a wounded grizzly. But the identity of the slain man has never been definitely established, nor, for that matter, has the slayer, whether animal or human.

Fort Tejón, established August 10, 1854, to guard the strategic pass through the Tehachapi Mountains, also has other facets of interest. For seven of the ten years it existed as a military post, it was "home" to the U.S. Army Camel Corps. This curious experiment in military transportation was ordered by Secretary of War Jefferson Davis, who thought to use the desert animals to supply isolated posts in the arid Southwest and, perhaps, for patrol duty against hostile Indians.

Closely associated with all phases of Fort Tejón's history was Edward F. Beale. Appointed Superintendent of Indians Affairs for California and Nevada in 1852, he had recommended establishment of the post to protect the friendly Indians on near-by reservations. As director of a wagon-road survey party from Texas to California, he brought a 28-camel caravan across the Southwest from near San Antonio to Fort Tejón in 1857. (So well did the camels perform on this five-month trek that Beale recommended wider use of them. The outbreak of the Civil War, however, plus other factors, ended the experiment.) When the fort was abandoned on September 11, 1864, its land and 25 buildings became part of Beale's Tejón Ranch (eventually he owned nearly 200,000 acres).

Though comparatively small (its average complement was 225 troops), Fort Tejón was the chief military, social, and political center of a vast area of central California during the early American occupation period. Fifteen of the officers who served there later became Civil War generals, eight for the North, seven for the South.

Fort Tejón, shown here in an early photograph, was constructed in 1854 and abandoned in 1864. Its land and buildings became part of Edward F. Beale's Tejón Ranch.

Courtesy Tejon Ranch Company

With some of its buildings reconstructed, Fort Tejón is now a state historic park.

Courtesy California Division of Beaches and Parks

El Pueblo   Colorado

The site of present-day Pueblo, at the confluence of the Arkansas River and Fountain Creek, was long a favorite camping spot of Indians, trappers, traders, explorers, and gold seekers. First of these to leave a record was explorer Zebulon M. Pike (*see* Pike's Stockade), on November 23, 1806. His men "cut down 14 logs, and put up a breast work, five feet high on three sides, and the other was thrown on the river." The party remained five days, during which Pike went north and tried unsuccessfully to scale the peak that now bears his name.

Jacob Fowler, trapper and trader, was next to build on the site, in 1822. His three-room log house was apparently well fortified:

We think that a party of Spanierds may be Sent to take us prisnors— for Which Reason Intend makeing a Strong Hous and Hors Pen on the Bank of the River Wheare it Will not be In the Powr of an Anemy to approach us from the River Side—and Shold the Spanierds appeer In a Hostill manner We Will fight them on the Ameraken ground. the River Hear being the line by the last tretey.

Fowler and his men soon moved on, having received word that New Mexico had "de Clared Independence of the mother Cuntry and is desirous to traid With the people of the united States."

The permanent settlement and naming of Pueblo is generally credited to James P. Beckwourth. His party arrived in October 1842 and was soon joined by other free trappers. "We all united our labors, and constructed an adobe fort sixty yards square. By the following spring . . . we gave it the name of Pueblo."

Early visitors were unimpressed. George Frederick Ruxton noted that "no part of the walls [were] more than eight feet high" and that the inhabitants of the "some half-dozen little rooms" lived "entirely upon game, and the greater part of the year without even bread." In 1846, Francis Parkman found "nothing more than a large square enclosure, surrounded by a wall of mud, miserably cracked and dilapidated." The people, he decided, were "as mean and miserable as the place itself."

Indian Agent Thomas Fitzpatrick seemed to agree. In 1847, he reported, Pueblo was "becoming the resort of all idlers and loafers," a depot "for the smugglers of liquors from New Mexico." Utes wiped out the settlement on Christmas Day, 1854. Four years later a party of prospectors from St. Louis concluded that "they could more profitably and easily mine gold by . . . engaging in a good game of 'swap' with the natives." Modern Pueblo was started at last.

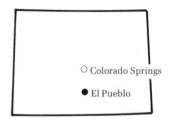

○ Colorado Springs

● El Pueblo

El Pueblo, from a woodcut in Lippincott's Magazine, *December 1880. Francis Parkman thought it a pretty wretched fort in 1846, but he found the view from the gate "a beautiful scene. . . . Tall woods lined the river, with green meadows on either side; and high bluffs, quietly basking in the sunlight."*

Courtesy State Historical Society of Colorado

Along with the model shown here, one of the featured attractions of El Pueblo State Historical Museum in Pueblo is a scaled reproduction of the old fort containing a completely equipped blacksmith shop, trading store, and seven living rooms with crude, early-day furniture.

Courtesy State Historical Society of Colorado

Pike's Stockade   Colorado

After his successful expedition to the Upper Mississippi in 1805, Lt. Zebulon Montgomery Pike was sent, in 1806, to explore the southwestern corner of the Louisiana Purchase, to establish peaceful relations with the Indians, and, perhaps, most importantly, to reconnoiter the Spanish settlements of New Mexico.

The party of twenty-three men, including Dr. John H. Robinson, a civilian volunteer, left St. Louis on July 15. Pushing up the Arkansas to the present site of Pueblo (*q.v.*), it crossed the snowy Sangre de Cristos at Mosca Pass to enter the San Luis Valley — and Spanish territory. Reaching the Río Grande (which Pike believed to be the Red) near present Alamosa, the men dropped south, seeking a supply of timber with which to build a boat. On the Conejos they found it. Here, in February 1807, Pike built a fort as winter headquarters.

The cottonwood-log stockade was thirty-six feet square and twelve feet high, with pickets projecting over the walls. A four-foot ditch was dug around the fort and filled with water. Here in his moated fortress Pike felt secure from the Indians, and on February 7 he sent Dr. Robinson alone to Santa Fe, ostensibly to see about collecting a debt but actually to learn what he could about the country. The Spanish response to this move came on the morning of February 26: a delegation of one hundred troops.

Pike invited the two lieutenants into his stockade. After breadfast, the commanding officer suavely announced: "Sir, the Governor of Mexico, being informed you had missed your route, ordered me to offer you, in his name, mules, horses, money, or whatever you stand in need of, to conduct you to the head of Red River."

"I was induced to consent to the measure," Pike wrote, "by conviction that the officer had positive orders to bring me in." He hauled down his American flag, surrendered the fort, and the party was soon on its way to Santa Fe. He reached that city March 3, was closely questioned by Spanish authorities, and sent the next day, under escort, to Chihuahua. Several weeks later he was taken to the Louisiana border and released.

Unknown today is the exact connection, if any, between the Pike expedition and the schemes of Aaron Burr and Gen. James Wilkinson for an empire in the Southwest. That Pike himself knew nothing of them, however, is generally agreed. He fulfilled a difficult assignment with distinction, and his report supplied the United States with its first authentic information on the Spanish Southwest.

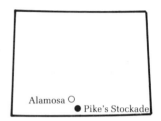

Alamosa ○
● Pike's Stockade

Pike's Stockade on the Conejos, from a latter-day sketch, based on careful research, by Albert Byron Sanford.

Courtesy Denver Public Library Western Collection

Pike's Stockade, five miles upstream from the Río Grande, has been reconstructed. Though occupied but briefly, it played an important role in extending the American frontier into the Spanish Southwest.

Courtesy Colorado Department of Public Relations

Bent's Fort

Along with its famed hospitality, Bent's Fort (Fort William), on the Arkansas River between present-day Las Animas and La Junta, was remarkable for its strategic location, its elaborate construction, its integrity, and its benign influence. Built over the years 1829–32 by William and Charles Bent and Céran St. Vrain, it lay at the crossroads of several historic routes. A number of Plains Indian tribes made it their headquarters, and it was a rendezvous for such mountain men as Old Bill Williams, Uncle Dick Wootton, and Kit Carson (who was post hunter from 1831 to 1842). George Bird Grinnell aptly described it:

> Bent's Old Fort was a stopping-place for all travellers on the Santa Fé trail . . . for Colonel Bent kept open house. On holidays . . . if any number of people were there, they often had balls or dances, in which trappers, travellers, Indians, Indian women, and Mexican women all took part. Employed about the post there was always a Frenchman or two who could play the violin and guitar. On one occasion Frank P. Blair . . . afterward a general in the Union army . . . played the banjo all night.

In size and defenses the 100 x 150-foot structure rivaled the big Upper Missouri posts of the American Fur Company (for whom William started to work, at 15, in 1823). Its 17-foot-high adobe walls, 6 feet thick at their base, were lined with rooms (22 bedrooms alone) that fronted on the bustling *placita* and its robe press and well sweep. Facing north, with a pair of heavy plank doors, the fort boasted two 30-foot-high cylindrical bastions.

Shrewd traders and genial hosts, the Bents were also "the fairest manipulators of Indians in the history of the mountain trade," according to the late Bernard DeVoto, maintaining "an elsewhere unheard-of standard of honor in dealing with them." (William married into the Cheyennes and lived among them peacefully for forty years.) Thanks largely to their influence, the Arapahos and Southern Cheyennes were kept friendly to the whites until well after the Mexican War.

John C. Frémont used the fort as a supply base, Gen. Stephen Watts Kearny rested his Army of the West there in 1846, and Gen. Sterling Price, en route to Mexico in 1847, paused long enough to enlist William as guide. But trade was becoming less and less profitable. Charles had been murdered in 1847 (the year after being appointed first American governor of New Mexico), and St. Vrain withdrew from the partnership a few years later. In 1852, William decided to quit and offered to sell the fort to the U.S. government. When it refused to meet his price, he destroyed the historic post and turned to freighting. The National Park Service has now completely reconstructed Bent's Fort.

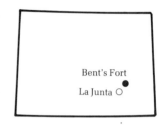

Bent's Fort in 1845, as sketched by Lt. J. W. Abert. The Southwest's biggest and most important fur-trading post, it boasted a pair of cylindrical bastions, a slatted belfry housing two live eagles, and a rare billiard table.

Courtesy State Historical Society of Colorado

Reconstructed Bent's Fort, now Bent's Old Fort National Historic Site.

Courtesy National Park Service

The South Platte Posts Colorado

Furs were being taken in the West from other than Missouri and Columbia waters. While American and British fur companies competed fiercely (first among themselves, then gradually along more national lines) for the rich Northwest, equally hardy mountain men were setting their traps in the Southwest. These free trappers, operating mainly out of Taos (*q.v.*), ranged west across Arizona into Nevada and California and northwest into Utah. For the most part, however, they trapped the mountains of Colorado, making South Park (the famed Bayou Salado), Middle Park, and North Park, working into the headwaters of the North Platte, then looping east and onto the plains for the return to winter rendezvous in New Mexico.

The trappers explored Front Range streams while traveling down the eastern slopes of the Rockies in the mid-1820's, but it was not until the mid-1830's that anyone got around to building a trading post. Then suddenly there were four of them, strung along one fifteen-mile stretch of the South Platte River some forty miles north of present-day Denver.

Lt. Lancaster P. Lupton, who had come west in 1835 with Col. Henry Dodge's dragoons, was apparently the first to visualize the area's commercial potential. Resigning his commission in 1836, he built Fort Lancaster (soon known as Fort Lupton) on the east bank of the river two miles north of the present town of Fort Lupton. His substantial 100 x 150-foot post, northern Colorado's first permanent settlement, was soon prospering. In 1837 he planted the area's first garden (squash, pumpkins, beans, cabbage, and beets), raised chickens and turkeys, and kept pigs and a few milch cows. Outlasting all competitors, he entertained such visitors as Francis Parkman and John C. Frémont—to whom he could offer a hot bath in the wooden tub of his special log bathhouse.

With Lupton flourishing less than a hundred miles from its own big Fort Laramie (*q.v.*), the American Fur Company was instrumental in establishing two rival posts in 1837: Fort Jackson (with Peter A. Sarpy and Henry Fraeb), some six miles down river, and near-by Fort Vásquez (with Louis Vásquez and Andrew Sublette). The following year, to protect themselves, Charles and William Bent and Céran St. Vrain built their own South Platte post, Fort St. Vrain, opposite the mouth of that stream, a crossing site used by such trail blazers as James Purcell (1803), Zebulon M. Pike (1806), and Maj. Stephen H. Long (1820).

None of the posts lasted a decade. Permanent settlement came to the territory with "Pikes Peak or Bust" and subsequent gold rushes in the late 1850's. Today only a reconstructed Fort Vásquez recalls Colorado's once feverish South Platte fur trade.

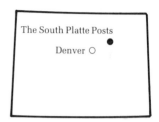

The South Platte Posts

Denver O

The Rocky Mountains as seen in 1820 by Samuel Seymour from the approximate area in which the South Platte trading posts were subsequently built. Seymour, who accompanied Stephen H. Long's expedition to the Rockies, was the first artist in the Trans-Mississippi West.

Courtesy Library of Congress

Reconstructed Fort Vásquez, in the median strip of US 85 some eighteen miles south of Greeley. A brief rival of Fort Lupton, it was one of four trading posts established along the South Platte in the mid-1830's.

Courtesy State Historical Society of Colorado

42

Fort Garland Colorado

If Col. Samuel F. Tappan had not really wanted the heads of the remaining Espinosa Gang members, this in 1863, he should not have offered to pay Tom Tobin for them. The old frontiersman, one of Colorado's most colorful characters, promptly went out and got them. Coming back to Fort Garland, he rode right up to Tappan's quarters, opened a sack, and rolled them out at the commanding officer's feet. "Here, Colonel, I have accomplished what you wished. This head is Espinosa's. The other is his companion's." (Finally, some twenty years later, Tobin collected his reward.)

But life at Fort Garland wasn't always so grim. "There were deer and duck in the vicinity," one officer recalled, "horse racing was a favorite sport, foot races were indulged in. We constructed a primitive gymnasium where we held numerous events. There was much singing . . . considerable card playing." Its officers were renowned for their hospitality to strangers, and its regimental band was "expert in playing the liveliest and latest of popular airs."

Accommodations were plain, of course. On Sangre de Cristo Creek, the Surgeon General reported in 1875, "very fine bathing and swimming arrangements have been established. For winter bathing no arrangements have been made." The water supply, brought by *acequia* from Ute Creek to water boxes at the corners of the parade, was "pure and cold." There was a post garden "of about 6 acres of ground," and the sutler's store was one of the best anywhere.

Fort Garland was built in 1858 to replace near-by Fort Massachusetts (established six years earlier some six miles to the north but abandoned because of its unhealthy location). Constructed primarily of adobe to accommodate one hundred enlisted men and named for the commander of the Department of New Mexico, it was never attacked, but its presence on the frontier kept the restless Utes and Apaches in check. Until it was abandoned on November 30, 1883, it served as a refuge and social center for settlers in the San Luis Valley.

Jim Baker and other frontiersmen lived here from time to time. Kit Carson was post commander in 1866–67; able to speak their language and thoroughly familiar with Indian psychology, he exerted a strong influence for peace in councils with the Utes. "In any dispute," one observer testified, "when violence seemed inevitable, all could be allayed by offering to send for 'Kitty,' as they termed him."

With many of its original buildings intact today, Fort Garland (on the south edge of the town of that name) is a state historical monument.

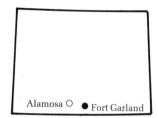

Alamosa ○ ● Fort Garland

Fort Garland about 1868. Built in 1858 and used for a quarter of a century, it was Colorado's most important frontier military post. The sketch is by J. S. Campion.

Courtesy State Historical Society of Colorado

Fort Garland today is remarkably well preserved. A state historical monument, it offers visitors a museum of dioramas and frontier relics.

Courtesy Colorado Department of Public Relations

Denver Colorado

Denver in June 1859 did not impress Horace Greeley (on his way to the gold fields of Gregory Gulch, later Central City). He found "More brawls, more pistol shots with criminal intent in this log city of 150 dwellings, not three-fourths of them completed, nor two-thirds of them inhabited, nor one-third fit to be, than in any community of equal numbers on earth." But the lusty little settlement on the South Platte was on its way. No gold camp itself, it sat astride the roads that led to them, and on the real, if undramatic, need for supplies and services, it came to be the unchallenged metropolis of the Rocky Mountain West.

In 1832 fur trader Louis Vásquez (*see* The South Platte Posts) built a stockade—rude dwelling, trading house, shop, and corral—on Vásquez Fork (now Clear Creek, on the outskirts of North Denver). He moved on four years later, and there was no settlement in the area until September 1858, two months after William Green Russell found a show of gold in Little Dry Creek (in present-day Englewood). A group of Kansans, discouraged by fruitless prospecting around Pikes Peak, then built short-lived Montana City on the Platte's east bank. Rival St. Charles and Auraria were soon established near by, and from the confusion the Denver City Town Company emerged on November 17 at the St. Charles site (the business heart of modern Denver). By year's end it had some twenty cabins, although neighboring Auraria still boasted Colorado's first saloon. Mountain man Richens Lacy "Uncle Dick" Wootton had arrived on Christmas Day, establishing good will by dispensing free Taos Lightning (*see* Taos).

On May 6, 1859, came the important Central City strike. The rush to the Rockies was on. That same month the first two Leavenworth and Pikes Peak stagecoaches arrived after a nineteen-day trip from Kansas. (The first edition of the still published *Rocky Mountain News* had appeared on April 23.) That year also saw the opening of the city's first hotel (the Eldorado) and hospital, the arrival of Baltimore oysters (sixteen dollars a gallon), the founding of the first bank (interest rates: from 10 to 25 per cent a month), and the birth of the first white child (named Auraria). On April 3, 1860, Denver and Auraria joined to become Denver City.

Not until the 1880's, however, with the great silver discoveries at Leadville (*q.v.*), Aspen, Caribou, and Georgetown—and the bonanza kings they produced—was the city's future secure. Moving to the capital to erect their ornate brick and sandstone mansions, they brought along the wealth and business interests that helped to build modern Denver.

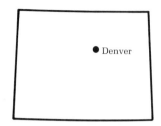

Denver in 1866, with a wagon train on what is now Market Street. Six years earlier, livestock was bothersome enough that one farmer was obliged to warn Rocky Mountain News readers that "eny kows that gits into my medders shal have tale cut off by me, Obadiah Rogers."

Courtesy Denver Public Library Western Collection

Modern Denver, looking west over the Capitol (lower left) and downtown business section toward the snow-covered Rocky Mountains.

Courtesy Colorado Department of Public Relations

Leadville   Colorado

In 1880, A. A. Hays wrote of Leadville's second boom (something denied most mining camps):

[Leadville is] an overgrown mining camp. . . . Along a part of the length of two streets (six inches deep in horrible dust) . . . are seen rows of the typical far Western buildings, some large, some few of brick, one or two of stone, very many small, very many of wood. Outside of these are mines and smelting-works, smelting-works and mines, stumps and log-cabins, log-cabins and stumps, ad infinitum.

The first had come early in 1860, just as Abe Lee and his fellow Georgians, discouraged and blinded by snow, were ready to quit. "We'll try another pan," Lee said, with the prospector's eternal optimism. A few minutes later he yelled: "Boys, I've got all California here in this pan!" California Gulch (just southeast of present Leadville) became one of the state's richest placer diggings, and Oro City, founded that summer, soon boasted a population of five thousand. H. A. W. Tabor ran a store; his wife, Augusta, took in boarders. A few years later the gulch was virtually deserted.

Not until 1875 was the area's real wealth recognized. A metallurgist discovered the heavy red sands that had clogged the gold miners' sluices to be virtually pure carbonate of lead with high silver content. Leadville's second and greatest rush was on.

Once again California Gulch swarmed with miners (erected was one tent hotel which, with three-tier bunks and calico curtains, could sleep 1,000 men), but this time the boom brought more substantial building, and that with incredible speed. Oro City soon merged with near-by Slabtown, and in January 1878, Leadville was incorporated, with Tabor, soon to become one of the most flamboyant "Carbonate Kings" of them all, as mayor and postmaster. By May 1, 1879, a contemporary guidebook credited the camp with "19 hotels, 414 lodging houses, 82 drinking saloons, 38 restaurants, 13 wholesale liquor houses . . . 7 smelting and reduction works, 2 sampling works for testing ores . . . 3 undertakers and 21 gambling houses where all sorts of games are played as openly as the Sunday School sermon is conducted." (However, "the social condition of the city improves every day . . . many ladies of culture and refinement having come in recently to make their home here.")

By 1880 the population reached 14,820 officially (up to twice that unofficially), and even the panic of 1893, which ruined the silver market, failed to kill the self-styled "Magic City." Gold quartz, lead, zinc, manganese, and now molybdenum have given the district—one of the world's most highly mineralized—a century of activity. Still lively, though on a somewhat more subdued scale, it is one of the West's largest and most picturesque mining towns.

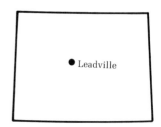

Leadville's Harrison Avenue in the 1870's. The Carbonate Kings were soon to give the booming camp such impressive— and still extant—structures as the Vendome Hotel, Tabor Opera House, and the Healy House (now a state museum).

Courtesy Denver Public Library Western Collection

Leadville, "The Cloud City," with its 10,335-foot elevation, is still some 4,000 feet below the crest of the Continental Divide, which rims it to the west. More than a century of activity has pushed its total mineral production above the $1,000,000,000 mark.

Photo by Steve Emrich, Leadville

Fort Lemhi Idaho

On August 12, 1805, Meriwether Lewis recorded that

at the distance of 4 miles further the road took us to the most distant fountain of the waters of the Mighty Missouri in surch of which we have spent so many toilsome days and wristless nights. thus far I had accomplished one of those great objects on which my mind has been unalterably fixed for many years.

The expedition was atop the Continental Divide (in a gap now called Lemhi Pass, some twenty-five miles southeast of Salmon, Idaho). Hugh McNeal stuck into the ground a pole to which Lewis had fixed a small U.S. flag, a historic "first" for Old Glory. (Two miles back, McNeal "had exultingly stood with a foot on each side of this little rivulet and thanked his god that he had lived to bestride the mighty & heretofore deemed endless Missouri.") Lewis hurried down the other side to "a handsome bold runing Creek" where he "first tasted the water of the great Columbia river."

This "bold runing" stream soon became the short Lemhi River. The expedition followed it a few miles to "a handsome little valley" where, in Sacagawea's homeland, they camped among the friendly Shoshones. Here, from Chief Cameahwait (as Lewis spelled it), her brother, they obtained horses and a guide for the trip to the Pacific.

A half-century later, on June 18, 1855, a party of 27 Mormon pioneers, sent by Brigham Young to teach the Indians "the arts of husbandry and peace according to our gospel plan," established Fort Lemhi (originally Limhi, after King Limhi in the book of Mormon) near the Lewis and Clark campsite. The fort—a timber stockade surrounding 25 cabins, with an adjoining mud-walled corral—was the first attempt at permanent settlement in Idaho and the site of the first irrigation project in the Northwest.

Journal entries of the pioneers tell the mission colony's brief story:

100 Nez Perce Indians . . . appear friendly . . . their chief . . . well pleased with the Mormons [1855]. . . . I commenced to learn the Indian language . . . showed them how to work [1855]. . . . Helped lay off mission garden. Had tooth ache [1856]. . . . Fourteen were baptized [1856]. . . . The grass hoppers have destroyed our crops [1856]. . . . Brother Heber C. Kimball gave us some stray doctrine concerning the marrying of squaws [1857]. . . . George Hill . . . in high spirits telling all he would soon marry the Chief's daughter [1857]. . . . The Indians . . . killed two men and wounded five more . . . in a deplorable condition [February 25, 1858].

The experiment, for complex reasons, had failed. A relief party was sent from Salt Lake City, and in April the Saints abandoned Fort Lemhi.

The spot where Lewis and Clark crossed the continental Divide had changed little by 1853, when John Mix Stanley visited and sketched it. The view here, looking west from the Divide, is what Lewis saw as he descended to the "handsome bold runing Creek" and "handsome little valley."

Courtesy University of Oklahoma Library

Fort Lemhi (shown here about 1900) after it had become a private ranch. Today one of the old irrigation ditches is still in use.

Courtesy Idaho Historical Society

Kullyspell House   Idaho

Kullyspell House, at the eastern end of Lake Pend Oreille near the mouth of the Clark Fork River (near present Hope, Idaho), was the first trading post west of the Rocky Mountains in the United States. David Thompson, the North West Company's remarkable explorer-trader, reached the lake on September 8, 1809. The site was selected two days later. Of the building of the post, he writes:

On the 11th Sept. we made a scaffold to secure the provisions and goods, helved our Tools ready to commence building; our first care was a strong Log building for the goods and Furrs, and for trading with the Natives. . . . On the 23rd we had finished the Store House. To make the roof as tight as possible, which was covered with small Logs, we cut long grass and work[ed] it up with mud, and filled up the intervals of the small logs which answered tolerable well for Rain, but the Snow melting found many a passage; in this manner we also builded our dwelling House; and roofed it, the floors were of split Logs . . . our Chimneys we made of stone and mud.

The Indians (Pend d'Oreilles, or Kalispels, according to the native name Thompson used for the post) were pleased to have traders among them. Their only arms, he noted, "were a few rude lances, and flint headed arrows. These they were now to exchange for Guns, Ammunition, and Iron Headed Arrows, and thus be on an equality with their enemies." He shrewdly used this eagerness to trade to the company's advantage. "I informed them that to procure these advantages they must not pass days and nights in gambling but be industrious in hunting and working of Beaver and other furs."

Before the post was completed Thompson was continuing his explorations. On November 9 he located Salish (Saleesh) House, also on the Clark Fork (near modern Thompson Falls, Montana). The following year he was in present-day Washington establishing Spokane House (q.v.). This important post soon became North West headquarters in the Columbia territory, and the Kullyspell House operations were soon moved to it. The buildings disappeared, and even the site was lost until 1923, when it was definitely identified by an old Kalispel Indian.

Thompson himself left the country for good in 1812, but not before he had made maps of large sections of the Northwest which were "so accurate," acording to Hiram M. Chittenden, "that only the most skillful modern surveys are as good." With sextant and compass, he traveled some 50,000 miles on foot, horseback, and by canoe. The Indians, believing his telescope enabled him to see all things, looked upon him with awe, calling him *Koo-Koo-Sint,* "The Star Man."

Lost for almost a century, the site of Kullyspell House was finally located in 1923 by Alex Kitoo (seated), an old Kalispel Indian, and identified on August 26 of that year by Duncan McDonald (standing), son of early-day Hudson's Bay Company trader Angus McDonald.

Courtesy Idaho Historical Society

All that remains of Kullyspell House today. The stones are probably those of the "Chimneys we made of stone and mud."

Courtesy Idaho Historical Society

Fort Hall Idaho

Fort Hall was officially christened, with the proper frontier blend of patriotism and horseplay, on August 5, 1834, and all because the near-defunct Rocky Mountain Fur Company had refused to take delivery from Nathaniel J. Wyeth of $3,000 in trade goods. Pushing westward from Green River Rendezvous *(q.v.)*, the Boston trader stopped near the junction of the Portneuf and Snake rivers on July 14 and promptly began work on a trading post of his own. Built of cottonwood logs set on end fifteen feet above the ground, with two bastions at diagonal corners, the 80-foot-square fort was completed by August 4. The next day, having "manufactured a magnificent flag from some unbleached sheeting, a little red flannel and a few blue patches," the party "saluted it with damaged powder and wet it in villainous alcohol." All in all, Wyeth concluded, it made "a very respectable appearance among the dry and desolate regions of central America."

Thousand of westbound emigrants were soon to agree. In 1836 the Hudson's Bay Company bought the fort for $8,179.94 and promptly enlarged and reconstructed it with sun-dried bricks. For the next decade and a half its whitewashed walls were a welcome sight to countless wagon trains. Here, 1,300 miles from Independence and with two-thirds of their journey behind them, travelers could catch their breath, repair their wagons, and decide whether to swing southwest across Nevada to California or northwest along the Snake and Columbia into Oregon.

Capt. Richard Grant (Fort Hall's chief trader, 1842–51) tried to discourage travel to Oregon by emphasizing the rigors of the trail, but Dr. Marcus Whitman had taken his two-wheeled cart as far as Fort Boise in 1836 and Joel P. Walker arrived in 1840 with the first wagon. By 1843 the American tide was beginning to roll. The HBC finally gave up the post in 1856. Briefly, in 1859 and 1860, it was occupied by U.S. troops and the Oregon volunteers, charged with protecting the emigrant trains, then abandoned to the weather and repeated floods.

Ironically, one of Fort Hall's most interesting events occurred even before it was properly dedicated: on July 27, 1834, Jason Lee preached the first sermon west of the Rocky Mountains. "The Indians," according to one observer, "sat upon the ground like statues. Although not one of them could understand a word that was said, they nevertheless maintained a most strict and decorous silence, kneeling when the preacher kneeled, and rising when he rose, evidently with a view of paying him and us a suitable respect."

Fort Hall
●
○
Pocatello

Interior view of Fort Hall. Established by Nathaniel J. Wyeth in 1834, it was purchased by the Hudson's Bay Company in 1836 and, as shown here, enlarged and reconstructed.

Courtesy Public Archives of Canada

Today only a marker recalls Fort Hall, destroyed by floods in 1863. Long the only inhabited place between Fort Bridger and Fort Boise, it was the popular rendezvous of thousands of Indians, Spaniards, French Canadians, and Americans, of priests, doctors, missionaries, gold seekers, and homesteaders.

Courtesy Idaho Historical Society

54

Fort Boise   Idaho

Fort Boise (near the junction of the Boise and Snake rivers a few miles west of US 95) was an important milestone in the progress of the wheeled vehicle across the West. To this Hudson's Bay Company post the persistent Dr. Marcus Whitman brought his precious two-wheeled cart (the half of his wagon that remained after the front axle broke east of Fort Hall) on August 19, 1836, thereby pushing the "wheel" frontier several hundred miles west of the Green River, which point Capt. B. L. E. Bonneville of the U.S. Army had reached in 1832. (To a Smith, Jackson and Sublette wagon train, which made a round trip—setting out with ten wagons, two Dearborns, and a milch cow—from St. Louis to the Wind River rendezvous in western Wyoming in 1830, goes the honor of blazing the first wagon trail to the Rockies.)

In 1840, Fort Boise hosted its first wagons, three of them, pushed on across the Snake River to Fort Walla Walla on the Columbia by mountain-men-turned-homesteaders Robert "Doc" Newell, Joe Meek, William Craig, Caleb Wilkins, and C. M. Walker. Three years later, on September 19, 1843, the so-called Great Migration of Oregon-bound emigrants reached the fort (having left the Missouri River at Independence on May 22), and the jovial Francis Payette, veteran Hudson's Bay Company employee, gave them a fittingly hearty welcome. Producing a fiddle, banjo, and accordian, he staged a dance to honor the travel-worn emigrants.

Here, near the twin mouths of the Boise, first John Reed of the Astorians (the Boise was once called Reed's River in his honor) and then Donald McKenzie of the North West Company had tried to establish posts, but the first successful establishment was that of the HBC's Tom McKay, who threw up a crude stockade of cottonwood poles on the site in 1834 as a challenge to Nathaniel Wyeth's newly founded Fort Hall (q.v.). He later replaced his ramshackle post with the more imposing adobe structure he called Fort Boise. As the fur trade declined rapidly after 1840, the fort depended more and more on servicing travelers on the Oregon Trail. An 1845 report speaks of "two acres of land under cultivation . . . 1,991 sheep, 73 pigs, 17 horses, and 27 neat cattle." Some three hundred desert miles from Fort Hall, it was a welcome oasis at the ford of Snake River.

In 1846 the boundary dispute with England was settled and Fort Boise (with Fort Hall) fell under the jurisdiction of the United States. A flood washed away the adobe buildings in 1853, and Indian trouble forced the HBC to abandon the post two years later.

● Fort Boise
○ Boise

Interior view of Fort Boise. Its adobe walls were 400 feet in perimeter, 12½ feet high, and 18 inches thick. Outside were the horse corrals; inside were the dwellings, the blacksmith shop, and stores. Following abandonment by the Hudson's Bay Company, the fort fell into decay and eventually disappeared.

Courtesy Public Archives of Canada

The site of Fort Boise today, beside the Snake River.

Photograph by Marshall Edson, courtesy Idaho Historical Society

Lapwai Idaho

On March 1, 1833, the Methodist *Christian Advocate and Journal* echoed the "Macedonian Call" of the Nez Percés and Flatheads (*see* St. Mary's Mission) and figuratively set fire to the nation's religious press:

No apostle of Christ has yet had the courage to penetrate into their moral darkness. . . . Let the Church awake from her slumbers and go forth in her strength to those wandering sons of our native forests. . . . What can be more worthy of our high estimation than . . . to release immortal spirits from the chains of errors and superstition.

By 1836, Rev. Henry Spalding and his wife Eliza were on their way, with the Marcus Whitmans (*see* Waiilatpu), to Oregon. On November 29 they established Lapwai Mission on Lapwai ("Butterfly Valley") Creek, some ten miles east of present-day Lewiston, Idaho.

"Yesterday reached this desirable spot," Mrs. Spalding wrote in her diary, "where we expect to dwell the remnant of our earthly pilgrimage. As yet our dwelling is an Indian lodge. . . . Blessed be God that we have been spared to accomplish a long & tedious journey."

Work soon began on the first mission building. (In 1838 the Spaldings moved two miles down the creek to the south bank of the Clearwater River, where Lewis and Clark had stopped to trade with the Nez Percés in 1805.) On December 23 they moved into the finished house with its "three windows, four doors, buttery, closet, recess for bed, cedar bedstead and table." Half the 18 x 42-foot structure was to be used for a school, assembly room, and other mission purposes. Until it was finished, Spalding wrote in mid-February 1837, "we assembled for morning and evening prayers and worship on the Sabbath in the open air, and sometimes, before we closed the exercises, our bare heads would be covered with snow. We might as well hold back the sun in his march, as hold back the minds of his people from religious inquiry."

The task wasn't quite that simple. But the Spaldings, in contrast to many well-intentioned Indian missionaries, were tolerant and wise. Along with their religion, they offered instruction in reading and writing, agriculture, and home economics. For present-day Idaho, Lapwai represents its first school and church, planted crops, gristmill, and printing press. One early convert was Old Joseph, father of the Nez Percés famous Chief Joseph, whom Spalding baptized April 12, 1840.

When the Whitmans were brutally murdered in 1847, the Spaldings fled Lapwai. They returned later, however, and Spalding worked among the Nez Percés until his death in 1874. He is buried in a pleasant park on the site.

Photograph of what is presumably the second Spalding cabin on the 1838 site two miles down the Lapwai on Clearwater River.

Courtesy Idaho Historical Society

Spalding Mission Cemetery (on the Clearwater River, ten miles east of Lewiston) contains more than one hundred graves, including those of Henry and Eliza Spalding.

Courtesy *Lewiston Morning Tribune*

Sacred Heart Mission Idaho

Another response to the "Macedonian Call" of the Nez Percés and Flatheads (*see* Lapwai), Sacred Heart Mission was established in December 1842. That spring, Fr. Pierre Jean De Smet had set out from St. Mary's Mission (*q.v.*), which he founded in 1841, for Fort Colville. Along the way he met some Coeur d'Alene Indians:

> I was conducted in triumph to the lodge of the Chief, and there . . . the calumet was brought forth. After it had been handed around several times and smoked in solemn silence the Chief addressed me in the following words: Black Robe, welcome to our country. Long had we desired to see you and be enlightened by your words. . . . I continued to instruct the tribe until far into the night, pausing every half hour to pass around the calumet and give time for reflection. During the pauses, the Chiefs conversed about what they had just heard, explaining it to their subordinates.

Returning to St. Mary's, De Smet sent Fr. Nicholas Point to the Coeur d'Alenes to start the mission. The first site, on the St. Joe River near the southern tip of Lake Coeur d'Alene, was subject to flooding, and in 1846 the mission was moved to a permanent location near the Coeur d'Alene River (along present Interstate 90 some thirty miles east of Coeur d'Alene). Fr. Anthony Ravalli was brought from St. Mary's to build the church.

Work on the 40 x 90-foot chapel (the oldest building in Idaho today) began about 1850. Services, first held in 1853, were conducted regularly until about 1877, when the Coeur d'Alenes were moved to a reservation south of the lake. The church deteriorated steadily until 1925, when restoration was begun.

The chapel is an interesting example of pioneer architecture. Using near-by stone, logs, and mud, wooden pegs in lieu of nails, a minimum of tools, and unskilled Indian labor (only those of exemplary conduct were permitted to work), Fr. Ravalli put together a building of sturdy handsomeness. The six porch columns were hand-planed pine logs. Decorations on the baptismal font and three altars were hand carved, as were the ceiling panels and (by Ravalli himself) the statues of the Virgin Mary and St. John.

In the summer of 1861, Capt. John Mullan camped in the valley while supervising construction of the Mullan Road (*see* Fort Benton). Near-by Fourth of July Canyon immortalizes the party's Independence Day celebration, highlighted by the raising of an American flag to the top of a tall white pine—and much gunfire. (Lurking Indians, thinking the whites had become insane, discreetly withdrew from the forest.) The tree's trunk (some 18 feet of it), bearing the date and the initials *M.R.*, still stands, but the top (141 feet) was blown down in a 1962 storm.

Sacred Heart Mission in 1853, from a lithograph by John Mix Stanley, who accompanied the railroad survey directed by Isaac I. Stevens, first governor of newly formed Washington Territory.

Courtesy Library of Congress

Little used after 1877, Sacred Heart (Cataldo) Mission has nevertheless remained a consecrated church. The chapel, recently restored, is now supervised by Idaho state parks and used for at least one Mass each year.

Courtesy Idaho Travel Council

Silver City Idaho

Idaho, unlike most states, did not develop gradually and consistently from raw frontier to statehood. Familiar enough, to be sure, was the pattern of the first few decades following the entry of Lewis and Clark via Lemhi Pass in 1805. Fur trappers traced out the courses of its streams and crisscrossed its rugged mountain ranges, traders established such important posts as Fort Boise and Fort Hall, and churchmen—Protestant, Catholic, and Mormon—founded missions to introduce the Indian to a side of the white man's way of life he might very well have missed in the mountain men and merchants, but by the end of the 1850's the vast land contained only a handful of whites. Up to the time gold was found in the Clearwater country in 1860, present-day Idaho, in the words of one state historian, "had been for practical purposes entirely given back to the Indians."

Then came the explosion, triggered by successive strikes in the Salmon River and Florence areas, in the Boise Basin, and in the rugged Owyhee country. Almost overnight the trappers' wilderness gave way to a sprawling clutch of lusty mining towns, and in 1863, Idaho Territory was created.

Silver City (high in the Owyhee Mountains, seventy-two miles southwest of Boise) sprang to life in 1863 with the discovery of gold in the headwaters of Jordan Creek, but it was quartz mining, rather than quickly depleted placering, that provided a substantial base for its growth. Today it remains an impressive monument to Idaho's mining industry, a handsomely picturesque ghost of past importance and elegance.

Strikes here were more than ordinarily spectacular: ore assaying $4,000 to $5,000 a ton, massed ruby-silver crystals weighing a quarter of a ton. Silver City soon had its quota of ornate barrooms, a barber shop that advertised baths as a specialty ("Call and be convinced," read the caption under a photograph of an actual bathtub), and a sizable Chinatown.

The Celestials, as in most western mining towns, worked long and hard at jobs few others wanted and received little more for their pains than suspicion and abuse. (The legislature not only prohibited marriages between whites and Chinese but taxed the Orientals four dollars a month to live in the Territory.) Patient and industrious, they reworked quartz reduction-mill tailings and repanned abandoned placers, and until 1885, they were Silver City's water supply. The carrier, shouldering a yoke from which two five-gallon cans swung, delivered one ten-gallon load from near-by mountain springs to the wooden barrel of each patron daily ("with an extra turn on Monday, which was washday") for fifty cents per week.

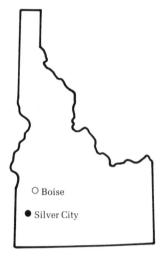

O Boise

● Silver City

Silver City, one of Idaho's most celebrated mining towns, in 1895. At the height of its boom it had several thousand residents.

One word of caution: Access to Silver City today is via a mountain road that would, for sheer ruggedness, rate high in any Guinness record book.

Courtesy Idaho Historical Society

The picturesque ghost of Silver City and its old hillside cemetery (lower left). One memorable Chinese burial featured a hired American band that played "There'll Be a Hot Time in the Old Town Tonight" for the processional and "Down Went McGinty" as the body was lowered into the grave.

Courtesy Idaho Department of Commerce and Development

Council Bluffs Iowa

Council Bluffs, the Iowa city, takes its name from the hills that line the Missouri River in this area. They, in turn, were named for the council held in the vicinity (exact location undetermined, but probably some 12–14 miles north; *see* Fort Atkinson, Nebraska) on August 3, 1804, between the Lewis and Clark party and the Oto and Winnebago Indians. William Clark records the memorable meeting:

Council Bluffs

After Brackfast we collected those Indians under an owning of our Main Sail, in present of our Party paraded & Delivered a long Speech to them expressive of our journey the wishes of our Government, Some advice to them and Directions how they were to conduct themselves. The principle Chief for the Nation being absent, we Sent him the Speech flag Meadel & Some Cloathes. after hering what they had to say Delivered a Medal of Second Grade to one for the Ottos & one for the Missourie.

Under various names, and influences, the area developed slowly for the next half-century. First known as Hart's Bluff, it was settled permanently in 1827 by Francis Guittar, agent of the American Fur Company. The removal of the Potawatomis to this area in 1837 brought with it a temporary military camp, and Fr. Pierre Jean De Smet arrived in 1838 to establish a mission, which he conducted for two years.

The settlement's first boom came with the arrival, on June 14, 1846, of the first Mormons (*see* Winter Quarters). They changed its name to Miller's Hollow, then to Kanesville, and by 1850 almost eight thousand of them lived in the area. Until 1852, when Brigham Young ordered the Saints to Utah (reducing the citizenry by two-thirds), Orson Hyde and an eighteen-member Mormon quorum ran Kanesville by a stern code that permitted neither idleness nor dissipation. After the Mormons departed, the town reorganized as Council Bluffs and was incorporated in 1853.

Final impetus to the city's growth came, it is believed, on August 13, 1859, from a casual conversation on the porch of the old Pacific House. "Dodge, what's the best route for a Pacific railroad to the West?" the visitor asked. Grenville M. Dodge, who in 1852 had made a western survey for the Rock Island, was quick to reply, "From this town out the Platte Valley."

The questioner was the young lawyer Abraham Lincoln, and legend has it that the discussion which followed contributed strongly to his decision, in 1863, as President of the United States, to select Council Bluffs as the eastern terminus of the Union Pacific. By 1870, five other lines had made connections with it and Council Bluffs had become an important middle western city.

A Mormon encampment near Parks Mill, three miles east of Council Bluffs. The painting is by George Simons.

Courtesy Joslyn Art Museum and Mrs. Walter L. Burritt

Abraham Lincoln Monument, commemorating "the visit of Abraham Lincoln to Council Bluffs August 19, 1859." Here he surveyed the Missouri River Valley, leading to his selection, on November 17, 1863, of this city as eastern terminus of the Union Pacific Railroad.

Courtesy *Council Bluffs Nonpareil*

Fort Madison Iowa

"If I understand the Indian character at all," wrote Meriwether Lewis, "I do know that there are but two effectual cords by which the savage arm can be bound, the one is the love of merchandise, and the other the fear of punishment." Fort Madison, the first fort established in Iowa, was intended to provide both cords. For five years it stood on the west bank of the Mississippi River, guarding the frontier and, alternately, trading with the Sauks and Foxes and fighting off their raids.

The cord of fear was represented by a palisaded, five-sided fortress facing the river and guarded by four blockhouses. Although one newspaperman described it (1813) as "a wretched pen, improperly called a fort," it was an adequate and comfortable enough post for its day. Its fatal flaw was not in design, but in location. A ridge behind the fort and a ravine on its west side gave attackers a decided advantage over defenders.

The cord of love was represented by a substantial factory, located just outside the stockade as a safety measure. It was a two-story, 20 x 52-foot, hewn-log building with an eight-foot piazza in front, "the whole under a strong roof of oak shingles." Unlike most posts, its trading staple was not furs but lead. Mines operated by the Sauks and Foxes were located on both sides of the Mississippi in this area. (Credit for the discovery of lead in Iowa is generally given to the wife of Peosta, a Fox warrior. Best known of the deposits: Julien Dubuque's "Mines of Spain," which he began to work in 1788.) At five cents a pound, lead was among the most profitable of all goods handled by the trader. In 1810, Fort Madison collected eighty thousand pounds.

The Indians became increasingly hostile, however, particularly those under Black Hawk. A siege by two hundred warriors was beaten off in 1809, as was another in September 1812, although the factory was destroyed to prevent the besiegers from firing it in a wind and thus destroying the fort itself. In August 1813 the warriors were back, and this time Lt. Thomas Hamilton, the commander, decided to abandon the post. On the night of September 3 the men, carrying what provisions and ammunition they could, crawled on hands and knees through a trench to waiting boats on the river. As the Indians watched from the hills, not realizing what had happened until it was too late, flames shot up from the blockhouses, fired by the last man to escape.

The fort was never rebuilt. The site, however, was marked for years by a lone chimney, now duplicated in stone as a memorial.

Fort Madison in the 1850's. The town was platted in 1835 on the site of the military post burned in 1813.

Courtesy Library of Congress

Lone Chimney Monument on the site of old Fort Madison (1808–13). Settlement in this part of eastern Iowa began in 1833 following the so-called Black Hawk Purchase.

Courtesy W. A. Sheaffer Pen Company

Davenport Iowa

Davenport, established as a fur-trading post, developed into a city by virtue of possession of the first bridge across the Mississippi River, but two near-by islands figured prominently in its early history. Credit Island, to the south, was in 1814 a battlefield for American soldiers under Maj. Zachary Taylor and British soldiers aided by their Indian allies. Rock Island, opposite the present city, was the site of Fort Armstrong, established in 1816 by Col. George Davenport. Much of the activity of the Black Hawk War centered around this military outpost, which, with Fort Snelling (*q.v.*), was an important link in the early chain of western defenses. (It was abandoned in 1836, four years after the Black Hawk Treaty, signed September 21, 1832, just above Rock Island, brought peace to eastern Iowa.)

Col. Davenport left Fort Armstrong after a few years to enter the fur trade with the Indians. In 1833 he replaced his log cabin with a two-story frame house (restored, still standing on Rock Island) in which the city of Davenport was legally founded on February 23, 1836. Meanwhile, on the site of Davenport itself, Antoine LeClaire, one of the city's eight founders, had already built the first house in 1832. A friend of Chief Keokuk and an accomplished linguist, the French halfblood had acted as interpreter during negotiation of the Black Hawk Treaty and had received from the government—at the Indians' request—two sections of land. His house, in 1855, became Iowa's first railroad station.

The westward expansion of the railroads wrote some of Davenport's most exciting history. On February 22, 1854, the Rock Island line became the first to link the Atlantic Ocean and the Mississippi by rail. The previous year, it had broken ground for Iowa's first railroad and organized the Mississippi River Bridge Company. Work on this notable structure, a Howe-truss affair (1,582 feet long, with a 285-foot drawspan), began in 1854, and on April 22, 1856, the *Fort Des Moines* became the first engine to steam across the Mississippi.

On the night of May 6, 1856, in an incident suggestive of sabotage, the side-wheeler *Effie Alton* struck the bridge and burned, destroying the span. Her captain called the bridge "a nuisance and an obstruction," and a suit for damages was initiated (the youthful railroad attorney: Abraham Lincoln). For six years rivermen and the railroads waged bitter court battles, but not until 1862 did the Supreme Court finally give railroads the legal right to bridge navigable streams in their westward path. Seven years later (*see* Promontory), rails would link the Atlantic with the Pacific.

Davenport and Fort Armstrong in the 1850's. Fort Armstrong played an important role in the Black Hawk War, and with the advent of the railroad, Davenport became a bustling commercial center.

Courtesy Library of Congress

Antoine LeClaire's second home in the town he helped to found. Built in about 1856, it is now being restored by the city of Davenport to serve as a community center. LeClaire's (and the town's) first house, built in 1832, was dismantled in the 1960's.

Courtesy City of Davenport

Mount Pisgah   Iowa

The journey of the Mormons from the Mississippi River to their new Zion in Utah (*see* Salt Lake City) is one of the most dramatic episodes in the history of the American frontier. From New York to Ohio to Missouri (*see* Independence) to Illinois the Saints had drifted in search of religious freedom. In Nauvoo, briefly, they thought they had found it. By 1844, with some twelve thousand inhabitants, it was the "most flourishing city" in Illinois. Then on June 27 a mob murdered founder Joseph Smith and his brother Hyrum. Brigham Young assumed leadership of the Church, and in the fall of 1845 he began planning for the last move westward.

The first family of Mormons crossed the Mississippi on February 4, 1846. Young and the Twelve Apostles crossed on February 15. That day, snow began to fall and the thermometer dropped to − 20° F., but the exodus continued. On June 14, four months and three hundred miles later, Young and his party reached the Missouri River (*see* Council Bluffs).

Each halting place of the President in Iowa, fifteen in all, became a "Camp of Israel." At Garden Grove, Elder Orson Pratt recorded (April 24), "we determined to form a small settlement and open farms for the benefit of the poor, and such as were unable at present to pursue their journey further, and also for the benefit of the poor who were yet behind." Fourteen hundred acres were enclosed and planted. Houses and bridges were built, wells dug. "They can stay here and recruit," Young said, "and by and by pack up and come on, while we go a little further."

Mount Pisgah was located (May 18) thirty miles farther west. One of the leading Camps of Israel, it was maintained until 1852. Some eight hundred graves here are poignant reminders of the rigors of the trek.

To the hostility of terrain and weather was added the ever present shortage of food and fuel. Pratt recorded after one torturous day:

The mud and water in and around our tents were ancle deep, and the rain still continued to pour down without any cessation. We were obliged to cut brush and limbs of trees, and throw them upon the ground in our tents, to keep our beds from sinking in the mire. Those who were unable to reach the timber, suffered much, on account of cold, having no fuel for fires. Our animals were turned loose to look out for themselves; the bark and limbs of trees were their principal food.

And in 1856, one of the famous handcart pioneers noted in his journal: "I was never more tired, but God has said as my day my strength shall be." The same might be said for all the Saints on their trek across Iowa—and the West.

O Des Moines

● Mount Pisgah

Mormons on the trail across Iowa. In July 1846 some 15,000 of the Saints were strung out across the state, bringing with them 3,000 wagons, 30,000 head of cattle, horses, and mules, and vast numbers of sheep.

Courtesy Chicago, Burlington & Quincy Railroad

Mount Pisgah Monument. One of the leading Camps of Israel, Mount Pisgah was maintained until 1852.

Courtesy Office of the Historian, The Church of Jesus Christ of Latter-day Saints

Fort Leavenworth Kansas

Fort Leavenworth, on the west bank of the Missouri River some twenty miles northwest of the mouth of the Kaw (present-day Kansas City), was established as Cantonment Leavenworth on March 7, 1827, by Col. Henry H. Leavenworth to protect traffic on the Santa Fe Trail. Huts of logs and bark were erected, along with a loopholed stone wall, as protection against Indians. But in a report dated August 26, 1836, Inspector General George Croghan insisted: "There is about as much propriety in calling this post *Fort* Leavenworth as there would be in calling an armed schooner a line of battle ship. . . . Of defences it has none." (Two blockhouses were added later that year.)

The unmilitary atmosphere had been noted by earlier visitors. "In this delightful cantonment," George Catlin wrote in 1832, the presence of officers' wives and daughters created "a very pleasant little community, who are almost continually together in social enjoyment of the peculiar amusements and pleasures of this wild country . . . riding on horseback or in carriages . . . picking strawberries and wild plums, deer chasing, grouse-shooting, horse-racing, and other amusements."

John Treat Irving, Jr., Washington Irving's nephew, found much the same scene in 1833. To him the post was "a rural look-ing spot—a speck of civilization dropped in the heart of a wilderness. . . . But for the solitary sentinels . . . or the occasion-al roll of the drum . . . we would not have known that we were in the heart of a military station."

Military matters were not forgotten, however. Discipline, often lax in frontier garrisons, was tightened considerably fol-lowing this April 28, 1832 order by Gen. Winfield Scott: "Every soldier or ranger who shall be found drunk or insensibly intoxi-cated after the publication of this order will be compelled, as soon as his strength will permit, to dig his grave at a suitable burying place large enough for his own reception, as such grave cannot fail to be wanted for the drunken man himself or for some drunken companion."

In 1833, by "An Act for the more perfect defence of the fron-tier," Congress established a regiment of dragoons of ten com-panies "liable to serve on horse, or foot, as the President may direct." The First U.S. Dragoons, sent to Leavenworth the fol-lowing year, proved so much more effective than slow-moving infantry in pursuing well-mounted Indians that a second regi-ment was authorized in 1836.

Fort Leavenworth has remained active down to the present. The oldest military post west of the Missouri River, its historic buildings (some dating back to the 1840's) and sites are pre-served, maintained, and marked. There is also an excellent museum.

Fort Leavenworth
Kansas City

An early photograph of the parade ground at Fort Leavenworth. The fort had changed much since John Treat Irving, Jr., de-scribed the "dozen whitewashed cottage-looking houses" that com-prised the barracks and officers' quarters as form-ing three sides of a hollow square. The fourth, open, looked out onto a wide but broken prairie.

U.S. Army photograph

The Rookery, dating to 1832, is the oldest build-ing at Fort Leavenworth. In 1854 it housed the first territorial governor of Kansas.

U.S. Army Photograph

72

Shawnee Mission   Kansas

The letter was dated July 10, 1830:

I have this day been requested by Fish, a Shawnee chief, also Wm. Jackson, a white man, raised with the Shawnees, to make application for the establishment of a mission among them for the education of their children, and I most earnestly solicit your attention to the subject.

The writer was George Vashon, government agent among the Shawnees, removed to the eastern edge of Kansas Territory from Ohio just two years before. The appeal was made to Rev. Jesse Greene, presiding elder of the Missouri District of the Methodist church, and it was promptly heeded.

In September, Rev. Thomas Johnson founded Shawnee Mission (on a wooded bluff of the Kansas River at what is now Fifty-third Street and Mission Road in Kansas City, Kansas), the largest and perhaps most influential religious outpost in the state. (The Baptists and the Friends soon established flourishing missions near by.) By 1836 the mission school had thirty-five children enrolled. "The girls . . . learn to sew, knit, spin, weave, &c. . . . Two of the boys can already make passable shoes, and five others can make good plain chairs, beadsteads, tables, presses, &c. About half . . . can read and write and cypher some."

In February 1839, with start of construction on a "central manual-labor school," Shawnee Mission assumed a broader and even more important role in Indian life. The site this time was to the southeast (off present US 50 just inside the Kansas border, three miles southwest of old Westport, Missouri). Here 400 acres of land were enclosed, with 12 acres in apple trees—the first set out in Kansas—and 170 acres in corn. (From the first, experiments with winter wheat were conducted successfully, though not until the 1870's was this now all-important crop widely accepted.) Missionary Johnson soon had two large buildings under way, along with barns, cribs, granaries, toolhouses, and blacksmith and wagon shops. The school opened in October with 4 teachers instructing 72 children from 10 tribes. By 1842 a visiting churchman hailed the school as "a noble institution which promises to be a blessing to thousands of the red men."

The years preceding the Civil War, however, brought strife to Shawnee Mission, as they did to all of Kansas. In 1854, and again in 1855, as Free Staters and proslavery forces fought for control of the territorial government, Shawnee became the temporary capital, but its influence declined rapidly. The Indians sold their lands and moved away. Shawnee Mission was finally abandoned in 1864. Preserved today by the Kansas State Historical Society are its three principal buildings, recently restored.

Shawnee Mission in the 1850's, at the height of its influence as a "central manual-labor school." The sketch used here is from Henry Howe's Historical Collections of the Great West *(1851).*

Courtesy Kansas State Historical Society

Carefully preserved North Building of Shawnee Mission as it looks today. The former "Dormitory and Boarding School," erected in 1845, became territorial capitol of Kansas on November 24, 1854, when Gov. Andrew H. Reeder moved his executive offices from Fort Leavenworth (q.v.). Proslavery forces made it the capitol again briefly in 1855.

Courtesy Kansas State Historical Society

74

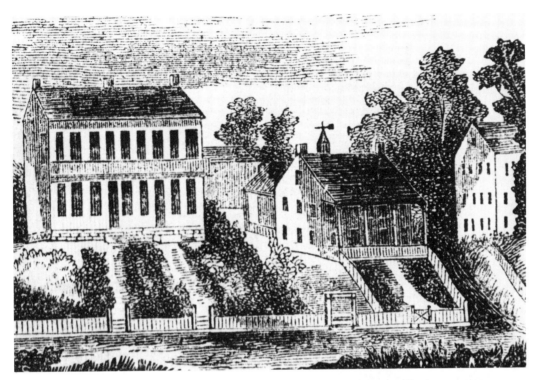

Council Grove Kansas

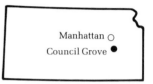

"This point is nearly a hundred and fifty miles from Independence," wrote Josiah Gregg of Council Grove in 1831, "and consists of a continuous stripe of timber nearly half a mile in width, comprising the richest varieties of trees; such as oak, walnut, ash, alm, hickory, etc., and extending all along the valleys of a small stream known as 'Council Grove creek,' the principal branch of the Neosho river."

Council Grove was long a popular rendezvous on the 700-mile-long Santa Fe Trail, particularly for westbound trains. Here, Gregg says, the train's "laborers were employed in procuring timber for axle-tree and other wagon repairs, of which a supply is always laid in before leaving this region." Farther on, timber was scarce and unfriendly Indians more numerous. (By 1865 the trail had become a mighty avenue for western migration. Crossing the toll bridge near Council Grove from May 21 to November 25 were 4,472 wagons, 5,197 men, 1,267 horses, 6,452 mules, 38,281 oxen, 112 carriages, and 13, 056 tons of freight.)

Peace came to Council Grove, as well as its name, on August 10, 1825, when U.S. commissioners, making an official survey of the Santa Fe Trail, signed a right-of-way agreement with the Osage Nation guaranteeing unmolested passage for the traders. Council Oak Stump (two blocks east of the river on Main Street) marks the site. (The first white men in this area were probably those of the Coronado party in 1541. The following year, Fr. Juan Padilla, a Franciscan, returning to convert the Quivirans, was killed in this vicinity, it is believed by many, to become the first Christian martyr in the United States.)

In 1846 a treaty with the Kaw Indians gave them the Council Grove area. Seth M. Hays became the first white settler in 1847, establishing his home and trading post in a log cabin just west of the Neosho on the north side of the trail; a government blacksmith arrived the following year. The town of Council Grove was incorporated in 1858.

The 1846 treaty obligated the United States to make an annual payment of $1,000 to advance the education of the Kaws. A contract was made with the Methodist Episcopal Church South (which had maintained a missionary to the tribe since 1830) to establish a mission and school at Council Grove. Construction began in September 1850. Kaw Methodist Mission was completed in February 1851, and school began in May under the direction of Thomas Sears Huffaker. But the Kaws were unresponsive to the work of the Church. Classes for Indian children were held until 1854, when the school was closed. Reopened that same year, it became one of the first for white children in Kansas Territory.

Kaw Methodist Mission at Council Grove a few years after it was built. Constructed of native stone, its eight rooms accommodated up to fifty boarding students, as well as teachers, missionaries, farmers, and other mission workers.

Courtesy Kansas State Historical Society

Kaw Methodist Mission today. Now state owned, it is operated as a museum by the Kansas State Historical Society. Council Grove has developed a useful tour map of historic sites in the area.

Courtesy Kansas State Historical Society

76

Fort Scott   Kansas

Fort Scott, as well as the Fort Leavenworth–Fort Gibson military road which served it, were direct results of the Indian Removal Act of 1830, which committed the government to relocate all eastern tribes to land west of the Mississippi River. By 1835 more than thirty thousand Indians had been settled in territory immediately west of Missouri and Arkansas, and the need for more military posts, along with improved communications between them, was immediately apparent. On July 2, 1836, President Andrew Jackson approved the enabling act that provided for this expanded frontier defense and patrol system.

The Fort Leavenworth–Fort Gibson leg of the authorized military road—designed to extend north to Fort Snelling (*q.v.*) on the Mississippi and south to Fort Jesup on the Red River in Louisiana—was surveyed in 1837. Fort Scott, on the south bank of the Marmaton River five miles west of the Missouri border and approximately halfway between Leavenworth and Gibson, was located April 9, 1842. The First U.S. Dragoons reached "Camp" Scott on May 30. Before the end of the year the temporary log quarters were being replaced by permanent buildings laid out around the "Plaza." By December 1844 most of these buildings (officers' quarters, barracks, stables, a hospital, and a guardhouse) were completed, all facing the parade ground. Surrounding the fort itself was a twelve-foot-high stockade of heavy timbers. An iron gate to the west provided the only opening.

Meanwhile, the 286-mile military road had been surveyed in the fall of 1837 (by blazing timber in the wooded sections and erecting mounds at one-mile intervals in the prairie country) and much of it built by 1840. A Quartermaster General's report in December 1844 admitted that it had been damaged considerably the past year by excessive rains, but there was no question as to its military importance: "Being the only direct route from the northwestern part of Missouri and Iowa to Arkansas and Texas, it has been much traveled. . . . I recommend that the bridges be replaced, and the road repaired."

Fort Scott was garrisoned until 1855, when the rapidly westward moving frontier caused its abandonment, but the outbreak of the Civil War created a new frontier, that between Missouri, with Southern sympathies, and Free State Kansas. Reestablished, Fort Scott served as a military supply depot for Union forces from 1862 to 1865. Again during a later period, 1869 to 1873, it was an army headquarters.

With many of its permanent buildings now restored as Fort Scott National Historic Site, the old post, on the edge of the town's business district, is a picturesque reminder of the early frontier.

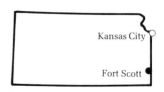

Early-day Fort Scott, with the officers' quarters (left) facing the parade ground.

Courtesy Kansas State Historical Society

The seventeen-acre Fort Scott National Historic Site includes the post headquarters, officers' quarters, barracks, hospital, bakery, and guardhouse. There is a museum. Interpretive and living history programs are presented on summertime weekends and special occasions.

Courtesy Fort Scott Area Chamber of Commerce

Fort Riley Kansas

Fort Riley, a sprawling, still-active military reservation south-west of Manhattan near the point where the Smoky Hill and Republican rivers join forces to become the Kansas River, was located (as Fort Center) in the fall of 1852 and established and renamed (in honor of Bennet Riley) in 1853. That year and in 1854, a few buildings, most of them temporary, were erected. The post, then garrisoned by infantry, became a center for protecting settlers during Indian wars, drilling troops for frontier duty, and supplying other western forts.

In 1855, Congress appropriated money for converting Fort Riley into a cavalry post by erecting new quarters, stables, and storehouses. (The Cavalry School was organized at Riley in 1891 and maintained until November 1, 1946.) Plans called for construction with stone, taken from quarries in the vicinity. Finishing woodwork, hardware, and glass were shipped from the East by boat to Fort Leavenworth. From here the materials, along with contracted workmen, were transported by wagon to Fort Riley.

"With fifty six-mule teams," recalled Percival G. Lowe, wagonmaster at Leavenworth, "I met, on the Fort Leavenworth levee, about 500 men, mechanics, laborers, etc., just landing from steamboats. . . . Without incident . . . we arrived at Riley . . . work in all branches commenced the first week in July. Excavations for foundations, quarrying rock, burning lime, making brick, cutting wood for burning them, hauling rock, sand, wood, etc., burning charcoal—in short, in a few days all the gangs of mechanics and laborers were adjusted to their work and everything was moving as smoothly as possible. . . . By the end of July a kiln each of brick, lime and charcoal had been burned, one two-story stone building finished, except hanging the doors and putting in the windows, and a number of others well under way. This completed building was taken possession of for offices, and two iron safes containing the funds for paying the men were put in the front room."

The most important early building remaining on the reservation is the first territorial capitol, a two-story limestone structure erected in 1855 at the now extinct town of Pawnee. In it the first territorial legislature met July 2–6, 1855, before the proslavery majority unseated the Free Staters and adjourned to Shawnee Mission (*q.v.*). The proslavery administration in Washington made the site of Pawnee part of the military reservation, thus disposing of the boom town which Andrew Reeder, first governor of Kansas and a Free Stater, was promoting for territorial capital. Now restored and furnished as it was in the 1850's, the old capitol is a state-owned museum.

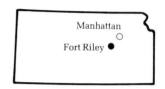

Fort Riley in 1878, from a pen drawing by L. Leduc, Sixteenth Infantry Band. The Seventh Cavalry, which rose to fame under George A. Custer, was organized here in 1866. Custer himself was briefly second in command at the post.

Courtesy National Archives

The first Kansas capitol, built in 1855, is now on the Fort Riley reservation. Completely restored, it is operated as a museum by the Kansas State Historical Society.

Courtesy Kansas State Historical Society

80

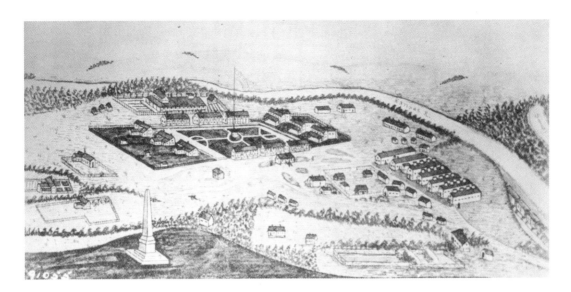

Fort Larned **Kansas**

Fort Larned was established in 1859 to protect Santa Fe Trail commerce and to serve as a centralized distribution point for treaty annuities to the Plains Indians. The location of the original "Camp on the Pawnee Fork"—at the base of Lookout Hill (now Jenkins Hill) about three miles west of the Arkansas River and present-day Larned, Kansas—was the choice of William Bent. To control the Indians, he felt, "it is essential to have among them the perpetual presence of a controlling military force."

Preliminary construction began October 22. Plans, according to Capt. Lambert Wolf's diary, "are made for the horse and cattle stable, also for officers' and company quarters, all of which are to be built of sod, cut with spades by members of our company." By midsummer of 1860, at a new location three miles to the west, the original sod-roofed adobe structures were erected, and it was not until the summer of 1864 that more permanent construction was ordered.

The buildings, nine of which still stand today, were erected over the next four years around a 400-foot-square parade. Of sandstone quarried at Lookout Mountain, they included officers' quarters to the west, barracks on the north, bakery and hospital on the east, and stables and quartermaster building (its two-foot-thick walls pierced by wedge-shaped gun slits) enclosing the south. Also erected at this time was the pride of the post commander: a 100-foot flag pole.

Water, always a problem, was hauled from the Pawnee Fork and stored in huge barrels adjacent to the barracks. A tunnel, to be used in time of siege (of which there were at least three), was dug from the fort to the creek bed. (Perhaps the shortage of water encouraged the consumption of whiskey. An 1864 report stated that "Dissipation, licentiousness and venereal diseases prevail . . . to an astonishing extent.") Despite Indian scares, however, Fort Larned enjoyed dances, full-dress dinner parties, quiltings, taffy pullings, and cock fights. "Guard mounting, inspection, and dress parade are announced by the familiar sounds of the fife and drum," Henry M. Stanley noted in 1867. "The officers are affable with their equals and gracious toward their subordinates."

By 1870, however, the arrival of railroads in western Kansas marked the end of the Santa Fe Trail and greatly reduced the need for a military post. Fort Larned's garrison was moved to Fort Dodge on October 28, 1878, and the post was officially abandoned on August 4, 1882. Preserved today as the Fort Larned National Historic Site, it has a visitors' center and special interpretive programs. A dozen miles to the northeast is 100-foot-high Pawnee Rock, a state monument, one of the famed landmarks of the Santa Fe Trail.

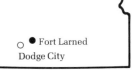

Fort Larned in 1867, when the post was, according to Henry M. Stanley, "a model of neatness."

Harper's Weekly, June 8, 1867

Fort Larned today. One of the most important frontier posts along the Santa Fe Trail, it is also one of the best preserved. Every building in the original quadrangle still stands and may be visited.

Courtesy Kansas Industrial Development Commission

Fort Dodge   Kansas

Fort Dodge, strategically located between the Cimarron and Mulberry Creek crossings of the Arkansas River (on present US 154, four miles southeast of Dodge City), was one of the most important of the posts located along the Santa Fe Trail to protect travelers, stagecoaches, wagon trains, and railroad survey and construction parties. The fort was established in 1864 by Grenville M. Dodge and named for his uncle, Col. Henry I. Dodge. The site was a favorite campground for wagon trains on the road to Santa Fe (westward the trail forked to become Cimarron Cutoff to the south, the Arkansas River Route to the north) and freight outfits operating between Fort Hays and Camp Supply, Indian Territory. Army officers of note who held posts here include Nelson A. Miles, George A. Custer, and Phil Sheridan.

The Fort Dodge area witnessed much of the action in two of the frontier West's most stirring dramas, both related in part to the arrival of the Santa Fe Railroad from the east in 1872. The destruction of the free-roaming buffalo, to be sure, began long before. As early as 1835, Josiah Gregg mentioned their slaughter (for the hide and tongue) and guessed that unless the practice were stopped, they would soon be extinct. (In 1852, St. Louis received some 100,000 buffalo robes.) Yet as late as 1870 estimates of the population of the vast herds ranged from 6,000,000 to 25,000,000. Then the slaughter began in earnest—5,373,730 of them in the Southwest from 1872 to 1875 according to Gen. Miles. The kill was even greater in 1877 and 1878, the Santa Fe shipping out 750,000 hides in one year, and by 1880 the southern herd was almost extinct. (In one three-year period at the end of the century the Santa Fe carried away, to fertilizer plants in the East, 1,350,000 tons of buffalo bones.)

As buffalo moved off stage, cattle moved on. Near-by Dodge City—started in 1871 with the sod house of government teamster H. L. Sitler and laid out the following year when the railroad arrived—soon became the shipping center of the Southwest. By 1875 most cattle trails led to Dodge, and in 1884, Texas drovers alone brought in 106 herds numbering 300,000 head. For ten years the town was the largest cattle market in the world, and for fifteen years it was one of the wildest spots on the frontier. As a rendezvous at one time or another for hunters, trappers, cowboys, soldiers, railroad builders, bullwhackers, Indians, saloonkeepers, dancehall girls, gamblers, and outlaws, Dodge City came as close as any, perhaps, to the vice- and violence-ridden cowtown of legend. Fort Dodge, its role finished, was abandoned in 1882.

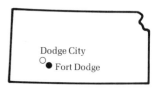

Dodge City
Fort Dodge

Fort Dodge in 1867. The first buildings were of sod and adobe, although some of the troopers lived in dugouts.

Harper's Weekly, May 25, 1867

Fort Dodge is now a state soldiers' home. Two of the original buildings, veneered with stone, still stand, along with the commandant's quarters and another structure that was built in 1867.

Courtesy Kansas State Historical Society

Fort Hays Kansas

"Before General Custer left," wrote Elizabeth B. Custer, "he removed our tents to a portion of that branch of Big Creek on which the post [Fort Hays] was established. He selected the highest ground he could find, knowing that the rainy season was not yet over." Custer had foresight, but he underestimated the ferocity of spring storms on the Great Plains.

Fort Fletcher had been established on October 11, 1865, fourteen miles southeast of what is now Hays, Kansas, to guard the Smoky Hill Trail to Colorado and to protect construction camps of the Kansas Pacific Railroad. Abandoned May 5, 1866, and reoccupied October 11 of that year, the post was renamed on November 11 for Gen. Alexander Hays, killed in the Battle of the Wilderness. Then on June 7, 1867, disaster struck.

The rains were accompanied by a terrific lightning display — "the heavens seemed to shower down fire upon the earth," as Mrs. Custer described it. They had barely returned to their soggy beds when the flood alarm sounded. She and Eliza, her Negro maid, crept to the opening of the tent, and "to our horror, the lightning revealed the creek — which we had last seen, the night before, a little rill in the bottom of the gully — now on a level with the high banks." The two women got out their clothesline and managed to rescue three soldiers, but "seven men were drowned near our tent, and their agonizing cries, when they were too far out in the current for us to throw our line, are sounds that will never be stilled."

The men were caught while camped temporarily on the creek above the fort. The post itself — of log and adobe, and poorly built — was soon awash, and a wagon bed was converted into an improvised ferry. "The post was thus emptied in time to prevent loss of life. First the women, then the sick from the hospital, and finally, the drunken men; for the hospital liquor was broken into, and it takes but a short time to make a soldier helplessly drunk."

Fort Hays was relocated July 4 on the south edge of what soon became Hays City, a typical post town attracting scouts, farmers and cattlemen, pleasure-bent soldiers, and desperadoes. (The deputy U.S. marshal in 1868 was James Butler "Wild Bill" Hickok.) The new buildings were of frame construction, except for the limestone blockhouse and guardhouse (still standing). The post was headquarters for the Indian campaigns of Gen. W. S. Hancock in 1867 and Gen. Phil Sheridan in 1868. Custer's Seventh Cavalry was quartered there from 1867 to 1870. By 1889 the frontier had long since passed and Fort Hays was abandoned.

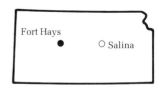

Fort Hays in 1875. Its first troops were so-called Galvanized Yankees — former Confederate prisoners of war.

Courtesy National Archives

The original blockhouse (now a museum) at old Fort Hays. Of sturdy limestone, it and a guardhouse remain of the post, relocated and rebuilt following the 1867 flood.

Courtesy Kansas State Historical Society

Fort Snelling Minnesota

Fort Snelling, constructed 1820–23 on a 100-foot-high bluff overlooking the St. Peter's (later Minnesota) River a half-mile above its mouth, was a thorough bargain. Lt. Zebulon M. Pike, sent to explore the Upper Mississippi Valley in 1805, arrived on the site September 21, purchased it from the Sioux two days later. "They gave me . . . about 100,000 acres, equal to $200,000. . . . I gave them presents to the amount of about $200, and . . . I allowed the traders to present them with some liquor, which, with what I myself gave, was equal to 60 gallons." Soldiers built the post for 15¢ a day above their regular $5.00 per month. With this minimum investment, the United States acquired effective control over the northern reaches of the Louisiana Purchase, secured its exploitation for American traders, and paved the way for eventual settlement.

Fr. Louis Hennepin in 1680 and Pierre Charles Le Sueur in 1700 were probably the earliest white men to visit this strategic river junction. After them came French trappers and traders, then the English fur companies, whose influence remained strong, even after the Treaty of Ghent (1814) prohibited their activities. Finally, Lt. Col. Henry H. Leavenworth was sent north in 1819 to establish a fort, which he located near present Mendota (*q.v.*). After a miserable, scurvy-ridden winter at "Cantonment New Hope," he moved across the river to "Camp Coldwater" near the bluff. In August 1820, Col. Josiah Snelling took over, began construction of Fort St. Anthony atop the bluff. It was occupied in 1822, completed in 1823, and officially renamed in January 1825 (on the recommendation of Gen. Winfield Scott) "as a just compliment" to its builder.

Charles J. Latrobe approached "the long looked-for Fort with its towers and imposing extent of wall" in 1833. That evening he ascended one of the bastions to "listen to the roar of the Great Falls [on the Mississippi in the heart of present Minneapolis] rising on the night air at a distance of seven miles." The fort had, he felt, "much more pretension both to regularity of design and picturesque situation than any of its fellows along the frontier." The view to the east he found "highly romantic. To your left lies the broad valley of the Mississippi . . . to the right and in front, the St. Peter's. . . . A more striking scene we had not met with in the United States."

The establishment of other forts after 1858 turned Fort Snelling into a supply station, but military forces were not withdrawn until October 14, 1946. The Veterans Administration now uses the vastly expanded facility. The historic section, however, is maintained as a state park.

Fort Snelling in 1838, as painted by Seth Eastman. A strategic outpost of military strength and government for more than three decades, it strongly influenced the development of the Northwest.

Collection of John Gordon Campbell, Frick Art Reference Library photograph

This round tower is one of the "towers and imposing extent of wall" seen by Charles J. Latrobe in 1833. Now a museum, it, the commandant's house (built in 1820), and other buildings and fortifications of the original post are preserved in 320-acre Fort Snelling State Historical Park.

Courtesy Minnesota Department of Economic Development

Mendota Minnesota

Mendota, but for the fact that government mills, like those of the gods, grind slowly, might well have grown into the sprawling metropolitan area which the twin cities of Minneapolis and St. Paul comprise today. The first permanent settlement in Minnesota, it sprang up opposite Fort Snelling (*q.v.*) in the early 1820's, but its strategic location at the confluence of the Minnesota and Mississippi rivers (Mendota is derived from a Sioux word meaning "meeting of the waters") had made it a familiar site to trappers and traders long before that. While St. Anthony and Pig's Eye, the Twin Cities' progenitors, squatted unimpressively beside the Mississippi on either side of Fort Snelling, Mendota was the focal point of the Red River fur trade (*see* Pembina) and the busiest community in the Northwest.

Important to the American, Columbia, and Fort Factory fur companies, the town (also known as St. Peter's until 1837, for the earlier name of the Minnesota River) became the meeting place for traders and trappers under the guidance of Maj. Lawrence Taliaferro (long-time Indian agent at Fort Snelling), Henry H. Sibley, Jean Baptiste Faribault, and others. Faribault moved to the site in 1822 (his house, built in 1837, has now been restored). Taliaferro arrived in May 1823 aboard the *Virginia,* first steamboat to navigate the Mississippi to this point. With him were Minnesota's first slaves (whom he later freed, one to marry the now well-known Dred Scott). Sibley came to Mendota in 1834 as factor for the American Fur Company. Later the state's first governor, he made the settlement a pioneer center of business and cultural activities. In his home (also restored) he entertained such early celebrities as John C. Frémont, George Catlin, Joseph Nícollet, and Seth Eastman. Protestant missionaries visited Mendota as early as 1829.

The settlement grew up on government land, and by the time legal ownership was transferred to Mendota, the fur trade was shifting to St. Paul, where, by 1841, whiskey merchant Pierre "Pig's Eye" Parrant, the only resident in 1838, had been displaced by Fr. Lucian Galtier and his log chapel consecrated to St. Paul. Meanwhile, a squatter's cabin had appeared at St. Anthony's Falls (now the heart of Minneapolis), where Col. Snelling's soldiers had begun construction of a gristmill and sawmill in 1821. (The nature of their first businesses produced the quip that "while Minneapolis was conceived in water power, St. Paul was born in whiskey.") Mendota, its chance for greatness gone, carried on as a small trading center. Today it is a picturesque reminder of preterritorial days.

Mendota in 1848, as painted by Seth Eastman. The view is from the north.

Collection of Dr. H. B. Zimmermann, St. Paul

The home of Henry H. Sibley, built in 1835. Now restored by the Sibley House Association, it is open to the public from May through October.

Courtesy Minnesota Department of Economic Development

St. Louis Missouri

Edmund Flagg wrote of St. Louis in 1838:

The finest point from which to view the little "City of the French" is from . . . the opposite bank of the Mississippi. . . . The city, retreating as it does from the river's bank—its buildings of every diversity of form, material, and structure, promiscuously heaped the one upon the other, and the whole intermingled with the fresh green of forest-trees, may boast of much scenic beauty. The range of white limestone warehouses, circling like a crescent the shore, form the most prominent feature of the foreground.

Six years before, Washington Irving had also noted diversity: "St. Louis—mixture of French & American character—French billiard room—market-place where some are speaking French, some English." And it was the same with the business leaders themselves, Americans like William Ashley, William Sublette, and Robert Campbell working and competing with Frenchmen like Pierre Chouteau, Jr., Michael Silvestre Cerré, and J. P. Cabanné, but there was one unifying factor: furs. Many of the warehouses along the river contained pelts from the vast frontier to the west; others were filled with the trade goods needed to secure more. Few businesses in the city failed to have some connection with the fur trade.

The situation was logical enough. Pierre Lacléde had selected the site as a trading post in December 1763, announcing that he "intended to establish a settlement which might hereafter become one of the finest cities in America." Work on the post, supervised by the youthful Auguste Chouteau, began in February 1764. Within five years Lacléde's fur business amounted to more than eighty thousand dollars annually. The new settlement below the mouth of the Missouri River had become the center of the western fur trade, a position it never relinquished.

From its original five streets facing the river (now largely cleared as part of the Jefferson National Expansion Memorial), St. Louis expanded with the West, for which it was the natural gateway. Here the formal ceremony of transfer of Upper Louisiana to the United States was made on March 9, 1804, and from here, that same year, Lewis and Clark departed on their epochal expedition, to return in triumph in 1806. It was also here, in 1809, that the famed Missouri Fur Company (William Clark, Manuel Lisa, Pierre [Sr.] and Auguste P. Choteau, Sylvester Labadie, and others) was organized. And at the St. Louis water front on August 2, 1817, the *Zebulon M. Pike* docked to become the first of a giant flotilla of steamboats soon to serve the city. The warehouses which caught Flagg's eye in 1838—including that of Lisa—were being built to serve them. St. Louis and the West were on the eve of tremendous development.

St. Louis in 1832, as painted by Leon Pomarede. The unchallenged center of the western fur trade, it saw the average annual value of its furs rise from $200,000 for the period from 1788 to 1804 to $300,000 for the forty years after the Louisiana Purchase.

Courtesy the City Art Museum and the Paget Studio, St. Louis

This two-story stone warehouse beside the Mississippi was built by Manuel Lisa in 1818, the year after the first steamboat reached St. Louis. It was dismantled in 1959 and is now partially reconstructed as an exhibit of the Jefferson National Expansion Memorial.

Courtesy Massie, Missouri Division of Commerce and Industrial Development

The 630-foot Gateway Arch in St. Louis has become one of America's best-known travel landmarks. Keystone of the Jefferson National Expansion Memorial, the Arch celebrates the city's role as Gateway to the West in the days of America's frontier expansion.

Courtesy of Walker, Missouri Division of Tourism

St. Charles Missouri

On May 16, 1804, William Clark described the "french Village 7 leags. up the Missourie" that was to be the last inhabited white settlement the expedition was to see for more than two years:

we arrived at St. Charles at 12 oClock a number spectators french & Indians flocked to the bank to See the party. This Village . . . about one mile in length, Situated on the North Side of the Missourie . . . contns. about 100 houses, the most of them small and indefferent and about 450 inhabitents Chiefly French, these people appear Pore, polite & harmonious

On September 21, 1806, he noted the triumphant return:

at 4 P M we arived . . . we saluted the Village by three rounds from our blunderbuts and the Small arms of our party . . . the inhabitants of this village appear much delighted at our return and seem to vie with each other in their politeness to us all. . . . the banks of the river thinly settled &c. (*some Settlements since we went up*)

Louis Blanchette built the first cabin, perhaps as early as 1769, and was soon joined by other French-Canadians. Auguste Chouteau surveyed *Les Petites Côtes* (The Little Hills) in 1787. Four years later, when its church was blessed and the village became *San Carlos del Misuri,* it counted no more than a dozen houses. But newcomers were pushing into the valley. Two years before Clark's first visit, Perrin du Lac had sensed the coming change. St. Charles was an important and altogether pleasant settlement, he noted, "but notwithstanding the beauty of its situation, the salubrity of its air, and the richness of its soil [the residents] have not been permitted to enjoy these advantages long." Americans were crowding into the country, "which already contains about four hundred families." Among the best known of these early settlers were Daniel and Rebecca Boone.

By 1817 the tide of Anglo-American immigration was running strong. The town was "crowded with the refuse of Kentucky," Timothy Flint observed in disgust. "Fighting, maiming, the most horrid blaspheming, thieving & every species of riot & outrage [were] the order of the day & night." On June 9, 1819, the *Missouri Gazette* observed that "never has . . . an influx of people . . . been so considerable."

In 1832, Maximilian, Prince of Wied, noted about three hundred houses, a massive church, and "many European fruit trees in blossom." Heavy German emigration was giving the region yet another atmosphere—and the frontier was moving westward (*see* Independence). By the time it became an incorporated city in 1849, St. Charles (the temporary capital of Missouri from 1821 to 1826) had already played out its brief role of importance in the development of the West.

St. Charles about 1840, when it was near the peak of its development. "A long line of neat edifices . . . along the shore," Edmund Flagg noted in 1834, "beyond these, a range of bluffs rear themselves proudly above the village." J. C. Wild and Lewis F. Thomas included this view in their Valley of the Mississippi Illustrated.

Courtesy Missouri Historical Society

These brick buildings, which served as the Missouri capitol from 1811 to 1826, are now preserved as a state historic site. St. Charles boys once slipped into the second-story assembly chamber and wrote above the speaker's chair: "Missouri, forgive them. They know not what they do."

Courtesy Walker, Missouri Division of Tourism

94

Jefferson Barracks Missouri

Jefferson Barracks, like St. Louis (*q.v.*), was a gateway to the West. In the length and importance of its service to the expanding frontier, it has few peers. Established in July 1826 on a 1,702-acre wooded site a dozen miles below St. Louis ("amid gentle rolling hills and commanding an unusual view of the river," according to one observer), it remained an active military post until after World War II. For many decades it funneled men and munitions to frontier garrisons throughout the West, and on its officer rolls were many of the noted military figures who explored the frontier, who pacified the Indians, who won—and lost—the Civil War.

Lt. Jefferson Davis, following his graduation from West Point in 1828, came to the Barracks with a Negro slave as body servant. After the Black Hawk War (*see* Davenport) he brought Chief Black Hawk here as captive and in 1855, as Secretary of War, organized the famed Second Cavalry, which furnished Generals Albert Sidney Johnston and Robert E. Lee to the Confederacy (Lee was post commander in 1855), Generals George H. Thomas and George Stoneman to the Union. Other Civil War generals from the Barracks include Ulysses S. Grant (sent to the post in 1843 as a lieutenant), W. T. Sherman, Don Carlos Buell, W. S. Hancock, John C. Frémont, James Longstreet, Joseph E. Johnston, G. B. Crittenden, D. M. Frost, A. A. Pope, and J. B. Hood. Post commander from 1827–32 was General Henry Atkinson, leader of the famed 1819–20 Yellowstone Expedition. Here, too, some years later, was organized the First U.S. Dragoons.

Not the first U.S. military post in the Louisiana Purchase, Jefferson Barracks was nonetheless associated closely with it. Under Spain, troops stationed in St. Louis occupied the "Fort on the Hill." In 1804 this area formally became American and two years later, U.S. troops were moved to Fort Bellefontaine, on the Missouri River north of the city. The fort was abandoned in 1827 after the garrison had been transferred to the newly established post, appropriately named for the man who had negotiated the purchase.

Despite the acknowledged beauty of its setting, Jefferson Barracks was a rather crude post during the first dozen years of its existence. To save money, inexperienced soldiers were used for most of the construction. Not until 1837 were the gray limestone buildings that lined three sides of the parade (the river side was left open) finally completed—at a modest cost of seventy thousand dollars.

Jefferson Barracks as it looked in 1841, some fifteen years after it was established. This scene is from J. C. Wild's The Valley of the Mississippi

Courtesy Missouri Historical Society

Laborer's house at Jefferson Barracks Historical Park. Built in 1851 for the use of civilian workmen at the ordnance depot, it has been furnished with items from the 1850–65 period in Missouri. The building was restored from original plans and specifications discovered in the National Archives.

Courtesy St. Louis County Department of Parks and Recreation

Fort Osage   Missouri

Fort Osage, first U.S. outpost in the Louisiana Purchase and the only government trading factory west of the Mississippi River, was established in September 1808 on the south bank of the Missouri River at a spot marked "Fort Point" on the Lewis and Clark map of 1804. Gen. William Clark himself selected the spot in 1808 while on his way to negotiate a treaty with the Osages. Also called Fort Clark, the post was occupied intermittently until 1827, when it was officially abandoned.

President Thomas Jefferson promised the Osages a fort and trading station in 1804. Construction was authorized by the War Department on May 17, 1808. On the same day, George C. Sibley was appointed Indian agent with compensation fixed at "800 dollars a year salary and 365 dollars annually, in lieu of subsistence, with an allowance of 200 dollars as an outfit for the purchase of domestic utensils."

Distinguished visitors in 1811 included John Bradbury and Thomas Nuttall, English naturalists traveling with Astorian Wilson P. Hunt. On April 8, Bradbury noted, "we came in sight of the Fort . . . were saluted by a volley as we passed on to the landing place." Naturalist Henry M. Brackenridge, keelboating up the Missouri with Manuel Lisa, arrived two weeks later. "The Fort," he wrote, "is handsomely situated about one hundred feet above the level of the river which makes an elbow at this point giving an extensive view up and down the river."

Temporarily abandoned during the War of 1812, Fort Osage was re-established in 1816. On August 1, 1819, the *Western Engineer,* first steamboat to ascend the Missouri this far, arrived with the Yellowstone Expedition. Major Stephen J. Long described the post as "a stockade of an irregular, pentagonal form . . . two block-houses are placed at opposite angles. There is also a small bastion at a third angle. Within are buildings for quarters, store-houses, etc."

Boon's Lick Trail, Missouri's first east-west highway, reached Fort Osage that same year, and regular stage service was extended from St. Charles (*q.v.*) in 1821. Fur-company opposition caused abandonment of the U.S. factory system the following year, however, and on "Satterday, 6 July, 1822," Maj. Jacob Fowler, passing this way, commented on "the Shattered Setuation of Every thing We See." The garrison, he noted, "Was Commanded by one officer of the united States armey—Haveing two men under His Command Both of them Haveing disarted a few days ago and Carryed off all His amenition."

Largely restored today (some twenty-seven miles east of downtown Kansas City), Fort Osage is an impressive memorial to the early American frontier.

Fort Osage, as re-created by George Fuller Green. (No contemporary picture of this first U.S. outpost in the Lousiana Purchase has ever been found.) From this area on May 1, 1832, Capt. B. L. E. Bonneville departed with 110 men and 20 wagons, crossing South Pass (q.v.) on July 24. To him and his men belongs the credit for taking the first wagon across the Rocky Mountains.

Courtesy Jackson County Park Department

Fort Osage, reconstructed through the cooperation of the Jackson County Court and the Native Sons of Kansas City, stands today as a memorial to the Louisiana Purchase. A museum in the "factory," or trading house, illustrates the trading post operation.

Courtesy Missouri Division of Tourism

98

Franklin Missouri

A Mrs. Frizzell aptly described the importance of the Missouri River in her book *Across the Plains to California in 1852:*

From this river is time reconed & it matters not how far you have come, this is the point to which they will all refer, for the question is never, when did you leave home? but, when did you leave the Mississouri river?

Franklin, platted in 1816 on the Missouri's north bank some 150 miles above St. Louis, had virtually disappeared by Mrs. Frizzell's time. But after September 1, 1821, the day a small trading party headed by William Becknell left for Santa Fe (arriving there November 16) to pioneer commerce over the famous trail to the southwest, the town was, for a time, a river point to be "reconed" with. In the fertile Boon's Lick country, where good farmland brought a remarkably high four to twelve dollars an acre, it attracted settlers with such legends as "If you plant a tenpenny nail there at night, hit'll sprout crow bars by mornin.'"

In 1818 the Jockey Club of Franklin was holding regular three-day race meetings, and a library was organized in 1819, the year artist George Caleb Bingham's family arrived. A road led up from the river to a two-acre public square lined "in tolerable compact order" by "thirteen shops for the sale of merchandize, four taverns, two smiths' shops, two large team-meals, two billiard-rooms." Although it possessed few "elegant buildings," the town boasted "an agreeable & polished society" (a society, however, from which the young Kit Carson, an apprentice in David Workman's saddle shop, gladly ran away in 1826 to join a Santa Fe–bound wagon train).

Franklin remained the most important town west of St. Louis until 1828, when it was nearly washed away by the rampaging Missouri. The new Franklin, two miles back from the river, never regained its former importance, but for a decade or more it played its role in the westward expansion of a growing nation, the courage and determination of its first settlers a worthy model for those who followed.

As Benjamin A. Cooper of near-by Cooper's Fort wrote Gov. Benjamin Howard at the time of the War of 1812:

We have maid our Hoams here & all we hav is here & it wud ruen us to Leave now. We be all good Americans, not a Tory or one of his Pups among us, & we hav 2 hundred Men and Boys that will Fight to the last and we have 100 Women & Girls whut will tak there places wh. makes a good force. So we can Defend this Settlement wh. with Gods help we will do. So if we had a fiew barls of Powder and a hundred Lead is all we ask.

This Victor Higgins lunette in the Capitol at Jefferson City shows the arrival of the first steamboat, the Independence, *at Franklin on May 28, 1819. Ironically, it was the steamboat, soon to bypass the town with its west-bound passengers and freight, which helped to kill Franklin.*

Courtesy Walker, Missouri Division of Commerce and Industrial Development

Arrow Rock Tavern, built about 1834 a few river miles above Franklin, was an important site long before the town developed (ferry service began about 1817). It was here in 1821 that William Becknell crossed the Missouri on his first successful trading expedition to Santa Fe.

Courtesy Walker, Missouri Division of Commerce and Industrial Development

THE FIRST STEAM BOAT ON THE MISSOURI. THE INDEPENDENCE ARRIVING AT FRANKLIN
MAY 28, 1819.

Westport Landing Missouri

"Mosquitoes and Ticks are noumerous & bad," Lewis and Clark reported on June 26, 1804, and flooding in the bottom land where the Kaw River flows into the Missouri was a problem, too, as Pierre Chouteau, Jr., could attest. His trading post, established in the spring of 1821 at "French Bottoms"—where the *coureurs des bois* had traded with the Indians as early as 1700—was swept away about 1830. Undaunted, he moved it a few miles east to what is now the foot of Grand Avenue, where Peter Roy had established a ferry in 1828. Here in the town of Kansas, popularly known as Westport Landing, and in Westport itself (laid out by John C. McCoy in 1834 four miles to the south) were planted the twin roots of present-day Kansas City.

The inland settlement—by eliminating twelve miles of trail and the undependable Blue River ford—soon rivaled Independence(*q.v.*) as eastern terminus of the Santa Fe Trail. McCoy opened a general store (at what is now Westport Road and Pennsylvania Avenue) and offered free lots to prospective businessmen. When the capricious Missouri destroyed the steamboat landing at Independence, Westport's future was assured—with McCoy as the town's first postmaster!

The American Fur Company's 1837 expedition to the Rocky Mountains, accompanied by Sir William Drummond Stewart and artist Alfred Jacob Miller, made its final preparations at Westport. Other famous figures to visit the town included John C. Frémont (1843) and Francis Parkman (1846), who is reported as believing that "whiskey circulates more freely in Westport than is altogether safe in a place where every man carries a loaded pistol in his pocket."

Meanwhile, Westport Landing was gaining both people and trade with the opening to settlement in 1836 of the Platte Purchase in northwestern Missouri. Arkansas River traders Céran St. Vrain and William Bent began hauling their freight directly to the landing in 1845, establishing a pattern followed by others. By 1846, with increasing Santa Fe Trail traffic, the town's population reached seven hundred, and despite a serious cholera epidemic in the early 1850's (which conbined with the arrival of the railroads in the 1860's to ruin Westport), Westport Landing incorporated itself as "the City of Kansas" on February 22, 1853.

A few years later, New York *Tribune* reporter Albert D. Richardson found the levee "a confused picture of immense piles of freight, horse, ox, and mule teams receiving merchandise from the steamers, scores of immigrant wagons, and a busy crowd of whites, Indians, half-breeds, Negroes and Mexicans." The town's population was two thousand, and, he added prophetically, it "had unbounded, unquestioning faith that there was *the* City of the Future."

Kansas City

Westport Landing

"The City of Kansas" in the mid-1850's, when the Santa Fe trade filled the streets with spenders, gamblers, and roistering herders, piled the levee with groceries, cotton goods, Indian trade items—and whiskey. The engraving is from Charles A. Dana's The United States Illustrated.

Courtesy Library of Congress

On this site at the corner of Westport Road and Pennsylvania Avenue John C. McCoy built his one-story log cabin in 1833–1834 to trade with westbound travelers. It was lot no. 1 in Westport, the first to be developed commercially in Kansas City, Missouri.

Courtesy Convention & Visitors Bureau of Greater Kansas City

102

Independence Missouri

Francis Parkman described Independence in 1846 as the town fought desperately to hold its trading position:

The town was crowded. A multitude of shops had sprung up to furnish the emigrants and Santa Fe traders with necessaries for the journey; and there was an incessant hammering and banging from a dozen blacksmiths' sheds, where the heavy wagons were being repaired and the oxen shod. The streets were thronged with men, horses and mules.

That year, a rock road was laid to the Missouri River, a few miles to the north, and as westbound cargo piled up along the riverbank—crates of sugar, dry goods, bacon, rice, and glassware; barrels of Kentucky liquor—a railroad was built to the town, with trains of flatcars drawn by mules over hand-hewn hardwood rails. In the 1850's, however, river traffic turned to the new City of Kansas to the west, and Independence soon lost its commercial importance.

Settlers began to reach this area in 1825. Two years later, Independence was platted as the seat of Jackson County. Samuel Weston opened a blacksmith and wagon shop, and the new town succeeded flood-plagued Franklin (q.v.) as outfitting point for travelers going west. Early visitors, however, were not overimpressed. Although Independence was "full of promise" in 1832, Charles J. Latrobe found it to be like most of the towns springing up in the West, towns that "consist of nothing but a ragged congeries of five or six rough log-huts, two or three clap-board houses, two or three so-called hotels, aliases grogshops." As late as 1839, Victor Tixier found the best hotel "a poorly enclosed dormitory where eight large beds were strewn about so as to accommodate sixteen travelers."

In May 1846, Independence was excited by the departure of the first overland-mail stagecoach for Santa Fe. In 1850, Samuel H. Woodson established monthly mail service to Salt Lake City, and summer service to California was extended the following year. In the 1860's the Butterfield Stage was leaving Independence each day. These coaches, reported the *Missouri Commonwealth,* were "in elegant style, each arranged to convey eight passengers. The bodies are beautifully painted and made watertight, with a view of using them as boats in ferrying streams."

Then came the decline. Today, the town is overshadowed by its onetime rival, Kansas City. Long a popular gateway to the West, it is perhaps best known as headquarters for the Reorganized Church of Jesus Christ of Latter Day Saints, established in 1852 after dissension arose in the Mormon church. (Independence expelled the Mormons in 1834, when as many as three hundred of their homes were burned.)

Independence Courthouse in the 1850's. Work on this brick structure began in 1836. It replaced Jackson County's first courthouse, built in 1827 of white-oak and walnut logs cut by a slave and still preserved. The engraving is from Charles A. Dana's The United States Illustrated.

Courtesy Library of Congress

Memorial to Samuel Weston, who helped to bring prosperity to Independence with his blacksmith and wagon shop.

Courtesy Massie, Missouri Division of Commerce and Industrial Development

104

IN MEMORY OF
1783 · SAMUEL WESTON · 1846

FOUNDER, IN 1827, AT INDEPENDENCE,
MISSOURI, OF THE WESTON BLACKSMITH
AND WAGON SHOP, FROM THAT TIME
THE STARTING POINT OF WAGON TRAINS
OVER THE SANTA FE, OREGON, AND
CALIFORNIA TRAILS.
BORN IN NORTH IRELAND, IMPRESSED
INTO THE BRITISH NAVY IN 1812,
RESCUED BY UNITED STATES NAVY
AND JOINED THEIR FORCES.
CAME TO JACKSON COUNTY IN 1824
FROM GREEN COUNTY, KENTUCKY.
FIRST COUNTY JUDGE BY ELECTION 1827
ASSISTED IN BUILDING OUR FIRST
COURT HOUSE

ERECTED BY CITIZENS OF INDEPENDENCE
1948

Samue Weston
1846

St. Joseph **Missouri**

St. Joseph represents another early trading venture that "met with success." Joseph Robidoux first visited the site in 1799, then returned in 1827 to establish a post for the American Fur Company. He bought the establishment (for five hundred dollars) in 1834, the year Maximilian, Prince of Wied, noted that it consisted of two white-painted houses and "extensive fields of maize protected by fences, and very fine cattle grazing the plain." Three years after it was platted (1843), Fr. Pierre Jean De Smet found St. Joseph in a "most prosperous condition," with "350 houses, two churches, a city hall, and a jail."

But it remained for a then unknown and unnoted visitor (a member of an 1844 wagon train of some eight hundred persons) to give the town its greatest stimulus for growth. He was James W. Marshall, the itinerant wheelwright whose 1848 discovery of gold at Sutter's Mill (*see* Coloma) was to boom "St. Joe" the next year. By the middle of February 1849, several thousand California-bound adventurers had streamed into the town. The westward spread of cholera, which had already reached the downstream settlements of Independence and Westport, reinforced the boom and helped to make St. Joe a major supply point and wagon-train stop. An average of twenty river steamers a day were pouring emigrants and gold seekers into the town. Between April and June, 1849, some fifteen hundred prairie schooners crossed the Missouri there to begin the trek westward. Thousands more crossed on ferries above and below the town.

"The city was packed so full of people," Swiss artist Rudolph Kurz noted, "that tents were pitched about the city and along the opposite bank of the river in such numbers that we seemed besieged by an army." When Eleaser Ingalls wrote his *Journal* (1850–51), the boom was apparently at its height:

St. Joseph is quite a village, and doing quite a great deal of business at this time; but the way they fleece the California emigrants is worth noticing. I should advise all going to California by the Overland Route to take everything along with them that they can, as every little thing costs three or four times as much here as at home. The markets are filled with broken down horses jockeyed up for the occasion, and unbroken mules which they assure you are as handy as sheep. It is the greatest place for gambling and all other rascality that I was ever in.

After that, "Uncle Joe" Robidoux's driving of the golden spike to complete the Hannibal & St. Joseph Railroad on February 13, 1859, and Johnny Fry's dash for the Missouri River ferry with the first pouch of westbound Pony Express mail on April 3, 1860, were almost anticlimactic.

St. Joseph in 1850. Two years earlier, Rudolph Kurz noted the many bourgeois, clerks, and engagés of the various fur companies who crowded the streets and public houses and concluded: "St. Joseph is for them now what St. Louis was earlier—their rendezvous."

Courtesy Chicago, Burlington & Quincy Railroad

Robidoux Row, as recently restored. Probably the oldest house in St. Joseph, it is where the town's founder, Joseph Robidoux, died on May 27, 1868.

Courtesy St. Joseph Chamber of Commerce

Three Forks Montana

These historic instructions were part of an equally significant letter:

The object of your mission is to explore the Missouri river, & such principal stream of it, as, by it's course & communication with the waters of the Pacific Ocean, may offer the most direct & practicable water communication across this continent, for the purposes of commerce. . . .

Given under my hand at the city of Washington, this 20th day of June 1803

Th. Jefferson
Pr. U.S. of America

"Meriwether Lewis, esquire," to whom the letter was addressed, led his party out of St. Louis on May 14, 1804, spending that winter among the Mandans (*see* Fort Mandan). At midmorning on July 27, 1805, some 2,475 miles from the Mississippi, he fulfilled his first objective, arriving "at the junction of the S. E. fork of the Missouri" (the Gallatin), where the country opened "suddonly to extensive and beautifull plains and meadows which appear to be surrounded in every direction with distant and lofty mountains." He rightly concluded that this was "the three forks of the Missouri."

Along with its beaver—and Lewis' "trio of pests . . . mosquetoes eye knats and prickly pears"—the Three Forks region contained implacably hostile Blackfeet. Near here in 1807, John Potts, a member of the Lewis and Clark expedition, was killed in the famous episode that saw John Colter stripped of his clothes and given the chance to run for his life.

In 1810 came the first tragically brief attempt to establish a Missouri Fur Company post at Three Forks. Pierre Menard and thirty-two trappers arrived April 3 and promptly built a stockade, but on April 21, Menard wrote Pierre Chouteau, Jr., in St. Louis: "A party of our hunters was defeated by the Blackfeet on the 12th Inst. There were two men killed. . . . This unfortunate affair has quite discouraged our hunters, who are unwilling to hunt any more here." George Drouillard, the Lewis and Clark party's best hunter, was killed in May. The post was abandoned a few months later. Another attempt in 1832 by Henry Vanderburgh of the American Fur Company and by Jim Bridger of the rival Rocky Mountain Fur Company also failed.

In 1840, Fr. Pierre Jean De Smet worked briefly in the region. No attempt at settlement was made until 1864: Gallatin City was short lived. Only with the arrival of the railroad in 1908 did the near-by town of Three Forks come into existence.

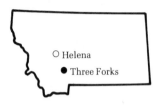

Charles M. Russell's model for Lewis and Clark and Sacagawea, photographed at Three Forks.

Courtesy Historical Society of Montana

Aerial view of the Three Forks, today as much a landmark as it was when Lewis and Clark first saw it on July 27, 1805.

Courtesy Montana Travel Promotion Bureau

Gates of the Mountains Montana

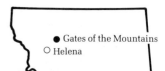

On July 19, 1805, Meriwether Lewis described in detail one of the most memorable natural sights his expedition encountered in its two and a half years of exploration:

this evening we entered much the most remarkable clifts that we have yet seen. these clifts rise from the waters edge on either side perpendicularly to the hight of 1200 feet. every object here wears a dark and gloomy aspect. the tow[er]ing and projecting rocks in many places seem ready to tumble on us. the [Missouri] river appears to have forced it's way through this immence body of solid rock for the distance of 5¾ Miles and where it makes it's exit below has th[r]own on either side vast collumns of rocks mountains high.

the river appears to have woarn a passage just the width of it's channel or 150 yds. it is deep from side to side nor is there in the 1st 3 Miles of this distance a spot except one of a few yards in extent on which a man could rest the soal of his foot. Several fine springs burst out at the waters edge from the interstices of the rocks. it happens fortunately that altho' the current is strong it is not so much so but what it may be overcome with the oars for there is hear no possibility of using either the cord or Setting pole. it was late in the evening before I entered this place and was obliged to continue my rout untill sometime after dark before I found a place sufficiently large to encamp my small party; at length such an one occurred on the lard. side where we found plenty of lightwood and pich pine. this rock is a black grannite below and appears to be of a much lighter colour above and from the fragments I take it to be flint of a yellowish brown and light creem-coloured yellow. from the singular appearance of this place I called it the *gates of the rocky mountains.*

William Clark, with three men of the party, had scouted ahead. He, too, commented on the "Cream Coloured flint," but his reaction was somewhat more personal: "my feet is verry much brused & cut walking over the flint, & constantly stuck full [of] Prickley pear thorns, I puled out 17 by the light of the fire to night Musqutors verry troublesom."

Everyone who traveled the Upper Missouri country was memorably impressed by its multitude and variety of scenery and rock formations, and many of the more literate visitors recorded what they saw. George Catlin noted that "in many places . . . there is one continued appearance . . . of some ancient and boundless city in ruins—ramparts, terraces, domes, towers, citadels and castles may be seen—cupolas, and magnificent porticoes, and here and there a solitary column and crumbling pedestal, and even spires of clay which stand alone." Sunlight and shadows cast "a glory over the solitude of this wild and pictured country, which no man can realize unless he travels here and looks upon it."

Gates of the Mountains (ten miles north of Helena), as seen by A. E. Mathews a half-century after Lewis and Clark described it.

Courtesy Historical Society of Montana

Gates of the Mountains today is essentially unchanged. Only the access is easier. In summer an excursion boat makes regular trips into the "dark and gloomy" gorge. One can picnic, and camp, where Lewis did in 1805, but the rugged mountains on either side of this Missouri River are preserved as a primitive area.

Courtesy Historical Society of Montana

Pompeys Pillar Montana

If, as some believe, a man's life can be read in the lines of his face, then perhaps the history of a physical landmark can be similarly interpreted. In the case of Pompeys Pillar, the first of these lines to be dated, July 25, 1806, were scratched by Capt. William Clark of the Lewis and Clark expedition:

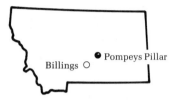

> at 4 P. M. arived at a remarkable rock situated in an extensive bottom of the Star. Side of the river & 250 paces from it. This rock I ascended and from it's top had a most extensive view in every direction. This rock which I shall call Pompy's Tower is 200 feet high and 400 paces in secumpherance and only axcessable on one Side. . . . The nativs have ingraved on the face of this rock the figures of animals & near which I marked my name and the day of the month & year . . . and opposit to a large Brook I call baptiests Creek.

It now seems reasonably certain that Clark intended to honor, in rock and creek, Sacagawea's infant son, "Jene Baptiest," born at Fort Mandan (*q.v.*) the winter before. He nicknamed the boy "Pomp"—Shoshone for chief or first-born—and became so attached to him that he later paid for his education in St. Louis.

Since then the one-time signal tower of the Indians has had many visitors, famous and obscure. Manuel Lisa and John Colter undoubtedly saw it in 1807 as they set about establishing the Yellowstone fur trade. "Derick and Vancourt, May 23, 1834," immortalizes the visit of two now unknown figures. In 1860 the pillar served Lt. Henry E. Maynadier as an observation point from which to study an eclipse of the sun.

Gold seeker James Stuart noted Clark's signature in 1863 and decided somewhat unimaginatively that the landscape probably looked then "precisely the same as it does now." Capt. Grant Marsh inscribed "Josephine, June 3, 1875," to mark the visit of his steamer and the Lt. Col. James W. Forsyth expedition studying navigation conditions on the river.

For comic relief (and perhaps an ominous warning?) there is the 1873 Indian ambush of George A. Custer and several hundred of his men while they were swimming and playing in the river. No one was even wounded that time, but three years later the outcome was far different. Writing of the ill-fated Sioux expedition of 1876, Gen. John Gibbon recalls that he climbed Pompeys Pillar on April 17 of that year. While his men hewed their names on the rock, he stared over the "precipice of perpendicular rock . . . toward the mouth of the Little Big Horn, afterwards to play so prominent a part in the history of our campaign."

St. Mary's Mission Montana

St. Mary's Mission (at present-day Stevensville, thirty miles south of Missoula) represents a number of significant "firsts" for Montana: first permanent settlement (1841), first agricultural crops (oats, wheat, and potatoes, 1842), first gristmill (1845, with millstones shipped from Belgium to Fort Vancouver and brought overland from there). But its importance is underscored by an even more unusual fact.

History contains many accounts of missionaries roaming the earth in pursuit of converts, but rarely does it record the demand by would-be converts for religious instruction. It remained for the Nez Percés and Flatheads (*see* Lapwai) to ask for missionaries, and then, ironically, they had to send four delegations to St. Louis—in 1831, 1835, 1837, and 1839—before both tribes were satisfied. The Protestants were the first to respond, reaching the Nez Percés in 1836. Five years later the Jesuits sent "Black Robes" to the Flatheads.

The missionaries left Westport Landing (*q.v.*) in May 1841, guided by Thomas Fitzpatrick, one of William H. Ashley's mountain men. The party, which arrived at Fort Hall (*q.v.*) August 15, included three priests (Pierre Jean De Smet, Nicholas Point, and Gregory Mengarini) and three lay brothers. Twenty Flatheads escorted them from here to Montana. The story of their arrival and the establishment of the mission is recorded by Fr. Mengarini:

Our five months journey was ended that the toil of a missionary life might begin . . . we soon set to work to erect a log cabin and a church and built around them a sort of fort, protected by bastions. The earth was already frozen and the trench for foundations had to be cut with axes; trees had to be felled and trimmed in the neighboring forest. . . .

Let not my readers, accustomed to grander buildings, sneer at the first church and missionary residence among the Rocky Mountains. The walls were of logs interlacing one another, the cracks being filled with clay; the partitions between the rooms were of deerskin; the roof was of saplings covered by straw and earth; the windows were 2 x 1 ft. and deer skin with the hair scraped off supplied the place of glass.

Fr. Anthony Ravalli took over direction of the mission in 1845. The next year, visiting Fr. De Smet was delighted to find "the little log church we built five years ago about to be replaced by another which will bear comparison with those of civilized countries." This new church remains today, a monument to the long service of Fr. Ravalli, who worked there intermittently (*see* Sacred Heart Mission) until his death in 1884. The old church improvements, however, were sold (for $250) to Maj. John Owen on November 5, 1850.

St. Mary's Mission in 1848. This sketch was made by Fr. Nicholas Point, one of the original party of Jesuits who went to the Flathead Indians in 1841.

Courtesy Historical Society of Montana

A restored building at Fort Owen (St. Mary's Mission). The fort is now a state historical monument.

Courtesy Montana Highway Commission

Fort Benton Montana

Fort Benton was established by the American Fur Company (as Fort Lewis) in 1846, rebuilt of adobe and renamed (for Senator Thomas H. Benton of Missouri, who often served as the company's advocate in Washington) in 1850. By this time the beaver was almost extinct and other furs were hard to come by, so the post's primary importance for the next four decades (until completion of the Great Northern Railway in 1889) was that of a trade center at the head of Missouri River navigation.

On July 2, 1860, the AFC-built *Chippewa*, first stern-wheel steamboat to penetrate the Upper Missouri, reached Fort Benton (farther from the sea by a continuous water course than any other steamboat had previously been). Two years later, with gold discovered at Bannack (*q.v.*), four steamers disgorged passengers and cargo and the boom was on. Supplies—food, clothing, powder and ball, tobacco, and whiskey—were freighted out "by means of ox teams and profanity." As one early observer described the scene, "perhaps nowhere else were ever seen motlier crowds of daubed and feathered Indians, buckskin-arrayed half-breed nobility, moccasined trappers, voyageurs, gold seekers and bull drivers . . . on the opening of the boating season."

In 1866, thirty-one boats steamed into Fort Benton (the count reached thirty-nine the following year), seven of them being tied up at one time in June. For the season they brought in some two thousand passengers and six thousand tons of freight valued at six million dollars. Beyond, the trails forked: southwest to the Montana gold camps, west over the Mullan Road to Washington, and north into Canada.

In 1858–62, John Mullan had surveyed for and supervised the construction of a military route between Fort Benton and Walla Walla, Washington, the first wagon road over the northern Rockies. (Only a crude trail, its 624 miles required 47 days for loaded wagons, no less than 35 days for pack animals. In 1864 it even accommodated a camel train.) A bit later came the Whoop-up Trail to Canada. (When the federal government outlawed the selling of whiskey to Indians, Fort Benton traders established themselves across the boundary in Canada. The trail was named, according to the story, when someone asked a merchant how business was going and he answered, "Oh, they're damn well whoopin' it up.")

The American Fur Company closed out its business at Fort Benton in 1870, leasing the post to the government. The Seventh Infantry was garrisoned there briefly. Today, the fort is a picturesque ruin.

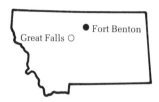

Fort Benton, as depicted by John Mix Stanley in 1853 before the arrival of the first steamship. Before establishing this post, the American Fur Company operated out of Fort McKenzie and Fort Piegan, both a few miles down the Missouri.

Courtesy University of Oklahoma Library

The old trading post today (at the east edge of the Fort Benton business district), the loopholes of its remaining blockhouse still guarding the now placid Missouri. Near by is a historical museum.

Courtesy Montana Highway Commission

Butte Montana

The speaker was Cornelius F. Kelley, who rose from dollar-and-a-half-a-day water boy to head of the giant Anaconda Copper Company:

There it rises—a tiny particle of granite measured by the expanse of this earth's crust, yet nowhere else has there been a spot known to man in which the hidden forces of nature contrived to concentrate the wealth of mineral that it contained and that its fissured mass still embraces.

The "tiny particle of granite" he referred to was Butte Hill. His observation was, in part, the wisdom of hindsight, for in 1858 the hill's vast mineral wealth was far less apparent.

Caleb E. Irvine camped that year on the site of present-day Butte with a pack train of Indian trade goods. He found an old pit, about five feet deep, which had been dug sometime before. Later it came to be known as the "Original Lode"—but Irvine was no miner.

It was 1864 before G. O. Humphrey and William Allison arrived from Virginia City to find gold in Silver Bow Creek (below Butte Hill on the south). They sank a shaft into the Original Lode and washed their dirt along the creek where short-lived Silver Bow Town sprang up. Butte City itself began on the naked slope of the hill, but its growth was slow until 1874. In that year William L. Farlin, one of the area's first prospectors, returned from Idaho and quietly claimed several outcrops of quartz from which he had previously taken samples for assay. As word spread that Butte's black ledges were rich in silver, the boom was on. (The opening by Joseph Ramsdell, in August 1866, of what is now credited as the first body of commercial copper ore in Butte had received scant notice.) Production rose rapidly the following year, when the town's population reached four thousand. To the end of the decade, Butte's mines were famed only for their silver.

Perhaps the most important event in Butte's history, however, occurred on a crisp October morning in 1875. Michael Hickey, a former Union soldier, staked a claim on the hill overlooking Butte and named it the Anaconda (having just read a Civil War account that said "Grant encircled Lee like a giant anaconda"). From that original hole in the ground eventually sprang the Anaconda Company. The following year brought to Butte young Marcus Daly, the immigrant who, at fifteen, had "landed in America with nothing in his pockets save his . . . Irish smile." Anaconda and Daly grew up together, playing a key role in the development of Butte and Montana.

Butte Hill in 1882. The Moulton (left) and Alice (right) mines dominate the skyline above Walkerville, now a northern suburb of Butte. These were silver mines then. Copper king Marcus Daly managed the Alice after coming to the district in 1876.

Courtesy The Anaconda Company

The World Museum of Mining in Butte is larger today than even its founders could have dreamed. With Anaconda gone and the copper industry pretty much a memory in Montana, the Anaconda-Butte area itself resembles a sprawling mining museum.

Courtesy Travel Promotion Unit, Montana Department of Commerce

Bannack Montana

Two miles southwest of present-day Dillon, where Rattlesnake Creek joins Beaverhead River, there was a crude signpost in 1862. On one side of a roughhewn board was daubed, in axle grease:

> Tu grass Hop Per digins
> 30 myle
> Kepe the trale nex the bluffe

On the other side was:

> To Jonni Grants
> one Hundred & twenti myle

The "grass Hop Per digins" was Bannack, Montana's oldest town and first important gold camp; Jonni Grant was a rancher in Deer Lodge Valley. The presence of gold in Gold Creek, west of Helena, was known as early as 1856, but it was not until July 28, 1862, that John White, William Eads, and a small party of prospectors from Colorado hit a placer bonanza on Willard's (Grasshopper) Creek. Bannack, named for the Bannock Indians, sprang up overnight and soon had a thousand people living in tents, shacks, and crude log cabins.

In September 1863, Sidney Edgerton, the Ohio lawyer who had been appointed chief justice of newly created Idaho Territory, arrived with his family, en route to Lewiston. The difficulty of wintertime travel in the mountains caused him to stay in Bannack. Returning to Washington the following spring, he advocated the creation of a new territory. Congress did just that, establishing Montana Territory on May 26, 1864. President Lincoln named Edgerton its governor, Bannack the temporary capital, where on December 12, 1864, the Territory's first legislative assembly met. In the meantime, however, the placers played out and most of the town's miners had deserted it for near-by Virginia City (*q.v.*). The legislature did the same thing.

In addition to serving as base of operations for the notorious Henry Plummer (*see* Robbers' Roost) and giving Montana its first capitol, hotel, and jail (now a state monument), the camp provided the Territory with one of its first schools. "Bannack," wrote Lucia Darling, Gov. Edgerton's niece, "was tumultous and rough, the headquarters of ... highwaymen, and lawlessness and misrule seemed the prevailing spirit.... But ... many worthy people ... were anxious to have their children in school. I was requested to take charge." She opened her school (in her home) in October 1863 with twenty pupils, who used whatever books their families owned or could borrow, attended until late fall, then started again in the spring. The following summer, Bannack built a log schoolhouse.

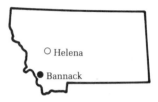

Bannack in the 1860's, with a Fourth of July parade in full swing. Here in January 1864 the vigilantes hanged Henry Plummer, the town's highwayman sheriff, and two of his chief deputies to end a year-long reign of terror in the southwestern Montana gold fields.

Courtesy Historical Society of Montana

Overgrown with weeds, the once-famous Hotel Meade (the county courthouse before the county seat was moved to Dillon) stands deserted at Bannack, Montana's first territorial capital and now a state monument.

Courtesy Montana Travel Promotion Bureau

Virginia City Montana

Few gold camps have had their birth chronicled so explicitly (and lightheartedly) as has Montana's Virginia City. Six miners, led by young Bill Fairweather, left the Madison River to cross a sharp ridge. Late in the afternoon of May 26, 1863, they dropped down into a shallow valley. Henry Edgar, a member of the party, continued the story in his *Journal.*

"Fairweather and I were to make camp and stand guard. The other four proceeded up the gulch . . . prospecting. About sundown Bill went across the creek to picket the horses. 'There is a piece of bedrock projecting,' said Bill, 'and we had better go over and see if we cannot get enough money to buy a little tobacco.'"

While Edgar washed the first pan of dirt, Fairweather "scratched around in the bedrock with his butcher knife and . . . called: 'I've found a scad!' I had the pan about half washed down, and I replied: 'If you have one I have a thousand.' And so I had."

Together they washed $12 in gold from three pans. The following day, the six of them panned out about $180. "We spent the next morning measuring the ground and staking it off. . . . 'What shall we call the Gulch?' I asked. 'You name it.' Barney Hughes said. So I called it Alder Gulch on account of the heavy clump of alders along the . . . creek."

Agreeing to say nothing of their find, they went to Bannack (*q.v.*) for supplies, but the secret was written on their faces. "Friends on every side," Edgar wrote. 'Bob Dempsey grabbed our horses and cared for them. Frank Buff got us to his cabin. Salt Lake eggs, ham, potatoes, everything! Such a supper!"

When the prospectors headed back for Alder Gulch, this on June 2, the trail was crowded. A meeting was called and a set of rules to govern claims was agreed upon. On June 6 the caravan had reached Alder Gulch. "This is the creek," Edgar shouted, and the rush was on. The name "Virginia" was a compromise with Southern sympathizers, whose preference for Varina (the wife of Jefferson Davis) was overridden.

Its extreme isolation (the only stage route was the one to Bannack) helped create the camp's greatest problem (assuring safe shipment of Alder Gulch gold to the outside) and led directly to its dramatic solution. Here the storied Vigilantes were organized. Their activities, which soon spread to the other camps (*see* Robbers' Roost), culminated in the multiple hanging (at the present corner of Wallace and Van Buren streets) of George Lane, Boone Helm, Frank Parrish, Haze Lyons, and Jack Gallagher on January 14, 1864.

Virginia City in the 1860's, when it was perhaps the richest and toughest camp in Montana Territory. Ten-mile-long Alder Gulch then supported a half-dozen communities with an estimated population of ten thousand.

Courtesy Historical Society of Montana

Virginia City today is something of a museum in situ. *Extensively restored, with its sister camp of Nevada City to the west, it is an interesting exhibit of mining town life a century ago.*

Courtesy Montana Travel Promotion Bureau

Robbers' Roost Montana

Thomas J. Dimsdale, an educated Englishman and one-time Oxonian, prefaces his celebrated defense of the vigilantes of Montana, as follows:

There can scarcely be conceived a greater or more apparent difference than exists between the staid and sedate inhabitants of rural districts, and the motley group of miners, professional men, and merchants, thickly interspersed with sharpers, refugees, and a full selection from the dangerous classes that swagger, armed to the teeth, through the diggings, and infest the roads leading to the newly discovered gulches, where lies the object of their worship—Gold.

"The administration of the *lex talionis* by self-constituted authority is, undoubtedly, in civilized and settled communities, an outrage on mankind," he agreed. But Virginia City (where he moved in mid-1863), Bannack, and other "newly discovered gulches" were, obviously, not civilized and settled communities. Here "civil law is as powerless as a palsied arm."

The propriety of vigilante action, then, boiled down to this question: "Is it lawful for citizens to slay robbers or murderers, when they catch them, or ought they to wait for policemen, where there are none, or put them in penitentiaries not yet erected?" The vigilantes answered the question with twenty-four hangings between December 20, 1863, and February 5, 1864. And Dimsdale approved. Organized robbery and murder promptly ceased.

Robbers' Roost (two and one-half miles north of Laurin) was built in 1863 by Pete Daly as a roadhouse. A rambling two-story log structure with full-length porch and upstairs veranda facing west, it sat astride the ninety-mile stage route between Virginia City (*q.v.*) and Bannack (*q.v.*). A bar and a gambling room occupied most of the first floor. The undivided second floor served as a dance hall. Here—as well as at Rattlesnake Ranch, Dempsey's Cottonwood Ranch, and hide-outs in both Virginia City and Bannack—Henry Plummer and his "Innocents" (after their celebrated password, "I am innocent") planned their crimes. Corresponding in cipher, they marked men and coaches for plunder, making frequent use of stage stops along this well-traveled road.

Weather-beaten, its old hitching rail intact, if unused, Robbers' Roost rests comfortably today in a fenced grove of old trees, a picturesque reminder of stagecoach travel in the frontier West. One of hundreds of similar rude establishments strung beadlike along the early-day trails, it is unusual for its size, its surprisingly good state of preservation, and the caliber of the outlaws it sheltered in its first year.

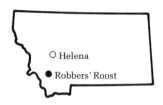

Robbers' Roost, which served as a hangout for Henry Plummer and his gang of road agents in 1863. Plummer came to Bannack in November 1862 and had his band organized by the following April. On May 24, two days before gold was discovered at Virginia City, he was elected sheriff.

Courtesy Montana Travel Promotion Bureau

Robbers' Roost stands firm today, much as it did when built more than 120 years ago. But this latter-day sign noting the historical details has, ironically, succumbed to the elements.

Courtesy Montana Travel Promotion Bureau

124

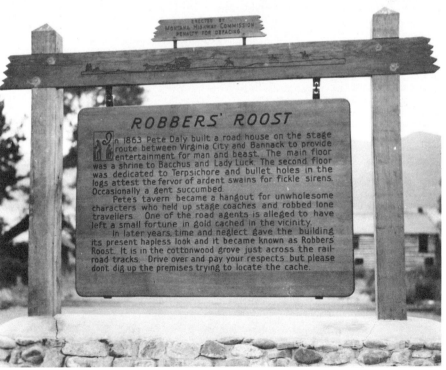

ROBBERS' ROOST

In 1863 Pete Daly built a road house on the stage route between Virginia City and Bannack to provide entertainment for man and beast. The main floor was a shrine to Bacchus and Lady Luck. The second floor was dedicated to Terpsichore and bullet holes in the logs attest the fervor of ardent swains for fickle sirens. Occasionally a gent succumbed.

Pete's tavern became a hangout for unwholesome characters who held up stage coaches and robbed lone travellers. One of the road agents is alleged to have left a small fortune in gold cached in the vicinity.

In later years, time and neglect gave the building its present hapless look and it became known as Robbers' Roost. It is in the cottonwood grove just across the railroad tracks. Drive over and pay your respects but please dont dig up the premises trying to locate the cache.

Last Chance Gulch Montana

Important gold discoveries became an annual affair in Montana in the 1860's. In 1862 it was Grasshopper Diggings (Bannack); in the following year came the strike at Alder Gulch (Virginia City); late in the summer of 1864 it was Last Chance Gulch's turn. The exact discovery spot in the narrow, rocky canyon is now covered by the seven-story Montana Club, at the corner of Sixth Street and Fuller Avenue in modern Helena.

As word of the strike spread, miners poured into the area, throwing up the usual hodgepodge of tents, shacks, and crude business buildings. The winding trail up the gulch, used by bull and mule-team freight outfits entering the camp, became Main Street. By October the name "Last Chance Gulch" was no longer deemed suitable, and "Helena"—with the accent on the second syllable—was adopted. (The name was suggested by one John Somerville as a fitting tribute to his home town in Minnesota.) To most of the miners, however, "h-e-l" spelled *hell*. The accent was promptly switched to the first syllable, and so it has remained, along with twisting Main Street and, in the older section of the city near the head of the gulch, the weather-beaten old frame buildings that are scattered here and there among the boulders.

Far tamer than her two sister gold camps to the south, Helena experienced very little vigilante activity. The townsite obtained a patent in 1870. Subsequent discoveries of rich placer gold in the gulches east of the Missouri, of quartz gold to the south and around Marysville to the west, and of silver and lead at Rimini to the southwest helped the town grow steadily. In 1875, Helena wrested the honor of being the territorial capital from Virginia City.

The following year, James H. Bradley was quite impressed to find that "many of the buildings are of a substantial and expensive character. The people are unusually intelligent, moral, industrious, and enterprising. The best illustration of this is the fact that they support ten newspapers, two of which publish daily editions, all thriving, well-conducted, and very readable. Such is the community . . . in the heart of a desert with hundreds of miles of uninhabited wilderness stretching away on every side of it, dissevering it from the rest of the civilized world as completely as though it were on an island in mid-ocean." After such an appreciative endorsement, winning the right to be state capital in 1894—over Anaconda, after two bitterly contested elections—must have come as something which was to be expected.

● Last Chance Gulch (Helena)

Bridge Street, Helena, in 1865. The tents, shacks, and crude stores of the early rush have been replaced with considerably more substantial structures.

Courtesy Historical Society of Montana

Last Chance Gulch when gold was discovered in 1864, now Helena, the capital of Montana is a delightful blend of the old and the new.

Courtesy Montana Highway Commission

Custer Battlefield Montana

First word of the tragedy came on June 27 to those on the steamer *Far West,* waiting on the Big Horn about a half-mile above the mouth of the Little Big Horn. The Indian who brought it was recognized as Curly, George Armstrong Custer's Crow scout. Promptly taken aboard, he gave way at once to violent demonstrations of grief.

Capt. Stephen Baker gave him paper and pencil and showed him how to use them. The Crow began to draw and to gesture in sign language.

Baker was the first to speak: "We're whipped!" he said hoarsely.

The full impact of these words was felt when two messengers from Gen. Alfred H. Terry arrived to confirm Curly's report. The battle had been fought on the afternoon of June 25. The army had been overwhelmed by at least 2,000 and possibly by as many as 5,000 warriors, mostly Sioux. Custer's resistance had lasted perhaps an hour. There were no survivors. His last message, signed by his adjutant ("Benteen—come on—big village—be quick—bring packs. W. W. Cooke. P. S. Bring packs."), went unheeded as Maj. Marcus A. Reno and Capt. Frederick W. Benteen were hard pressed to avoid a similar defeat for their own commands. The fight had cost the lives of 265 officers and men.

Custer died as he had lived: with a flamboyant flourish. His body, though stripped, was neither scalped nor mutilated. Most of his men seem to have fared little worse, although there is still much controversy about this. Lt. James H. Bradley scouted the battlefield on June 27. Beyond "scalping, in possibly a majority of cases, there was little mutilation," he reported. "Many of the bodies were not even scalped, and in the comparatively few cases of disfiguration it appeared to me rather the result of a blow than a knife." Other reports conflict with this. Perhaps the full story of what happened at the Little Big Horn will never be known.

As for the Indian, what did he hope to gain? (Ironically, the battle, one of the Indian's greatest victories, came near the end of a war he had already lost.) Of course the whites had broken the solemn treaty signed in 1868, and their pretext for this campaign was highly questionable. But it was Custer himself who perhaps best expressed the mood of the Sioux:

If I were an Indian, I often think that I would greatly prefer to cast my lot among those of my people who adhered to the free open plains, rather than submit to the confined limits of a reservation there to be the recipient of the blessed benefits of civilization, with its vices thrown in without stint or measure.

Custer and Crazy Horse spoke the same language.

A portion of Montana artist J. K. Ralston's After the Battle. Historian K. Ross Toole has called the painting "the most authentic portrayal of the battle yet painted."

Courtesy Mr. and Mrs. Don C. Foote

Aerial view of Custer Battlefield National Monument. In the left foreground can be seen the Custer monument and the fenced-in area where Custer and his men made their stand. The National Cemetery is shown at the top. Lectures on the Custer battle are given at the museum building by National Park Service personnel hourly during the summer.

Courtesy Montana Highway Commission

Bellevue Nebraska

Bellevue (on the Missouri River six miles below Omaha) is the oldest existing town in Nebraska and was, during the fur-trade era, its largest community, yet its early history is obscure. A trading post may have operated here as early as 1810, although the records of John Bradbury (1811) and Maj. Stephen H. Long (1819) do not mention it. (Manuel Lisa, said to have named the site for its fine river view, established his own Fort Lisa nine miles north of present Omaha in 1812. Near-by Cabanné Post, founded as early as 1823, was moved to Bellevue by the American Fur Company in the mid-1830's with Peter A. Sarpy in charge.) Hiram M. Chittenden believes the first traders were Ramsay Crooks and Robert McLellan. In 1823, Andrew Drips of the Missouri Fur Company was operating a log post about a mile to the north, and that same year, Maj. Joshua Pilcher moved the agency of the Omaha, Oto, Missouri, and Pawnee Indians to Bellevue from Fort Atkinson. In 1831 the federal government bought Drips' post as headquarters for Agent John Dougherty.

George Catlin visited Dougherty (in 1831 or 1832) and hailed the agency as "a lovely scene . . . doubly so to the eye of the weather-beaten *voyageur* [who] finds himself a welcome guest at the comfortable board of the Major." He was pleased to see again "a civilized habitation . . . surrounded with corn-fields, and potatoes, with numerous fruit-trees, bending under the weight of their fruit—with pigs and poultry, and kine."

Bellevue was also an important center for Indian missionary work. Baptist Moses Merrill arrived November 19, 1833, and worked in Bellevue for two years before moving some ten miles southwest to establish his Merrill Mission. Presbyterian mission work under John Dunbar began in 1834. In 1854, Francis Burt, first territorial governor, took his oath of office in Bellevue. He died two days later, however, and his successor ended the settlement's political future by favoring the younger community of Omaha.

The exact location of the Sarpy post is unknown, but its busy wharf, one of the best on the Missouri in the 1840's, was the scene of many a battle of wits as the American Fur Company sought each year to smuggle its trade whiskey up the Missouri. After army inspection at Fort Leavenworth, the greatest danger to the traders was the Indian agent at Bellevue. In 1843 the successful ruse was loading the liquor on cars of the *Omega's* narrow-gauge tramway, pushing them along the darkened hold just out of sight of the inspector. The next year, the liquor was put into barrels of flour marked "P. A. S." (for Peter A. Sarpy), and these were rolled onto the wharf before inspection and put aboard again just before the *Nimrod* steamed away that night.

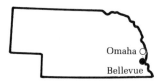

John Dougherty's Indian agency at Bellevue as seen by Karl Bodmer in 1833. Fellow artist George Catlin considered Dougherty "one of the oldest and most effective agents of our frontiers."

Courtesy Library of Congress

A chimney of one of the buildings is all that remains today of Merrill Mission, southwest of Bellevue. Moses Merrill worked in Bellevue two years before moving to this site.

Courtesy Sarpy County Historical Society

130

Fort Atkinson Nebraska

On August 3, 1804, William Clark noted:

> The Situation of our last Camp Councile Bluff or Handsom Prarie . . . appears to be a very proper place for a Tradeing establishment & fortification.

Fort Atkinson (on Council Bluffs, up the Missouri some fourteen miles above present-day Omaha) was established in September 1819 as Camp Missouri (at the river's edge), the winter encampment of the Yellowstone Expeditionary Force under Col. Henry Atkinson. In June 1820 flood waters destroyed the cantonment, which was then moved to the top of the bluff, its name changed to Fort Atkinson.

Two other Yellowstone expeditions probed the Missouri country in subsequent years. In 1823, Col. Henry H. Leavenworth led an expedition against the Arikaras. In 1825, Atkinson pushed beyond the mouth of the Yellowstone. These expeditions had at least three primary objectives: to overawe the Indians with U.S. military power, to counteract British influence along the frontier, and to establish a chain of forts along the Upper Missouri. But Atkinson, finding the British no serious threat, considered additional military posts unnecessary. His recommendation, plus an awakening interest in the Southwest, kept the government from advancing beyond Council Bluffs at this time and led to the abandonment of Fort Atkinson on June 27, 1827.

Fort Atkinson had prospered briefly in its new position atop the bluff. Teamsters, laborers, traders, hunters, trappers, and Indians—in addition to "The Fighting Sixth" Infantrymen—gave the post, Nebraska's first town, a population of about one thousand. In 1822, Prince Paul, Duke of Württemberg, reported that the "good-looking white-washed buildings of the fort could be seen at a considerable distance." The complex included eight ten-room log houses, a council house, brickyard, limekiln, sawmill, gristmill, rock quarries, bakery, school, and a library with five hundred books. As for the "agricultural enterprise," Prince Paul found it splendid. "A considerable stretch of land along the Missouri . . . had been converted into excellent garden land. I saw . . . cabbage, beans, onions and melons of excellent quality."

This area saw its first steamboat, the *Western Engineer,* in 1819, when Maj. Stephen H. Long's exploratory expedition to the Rockies (via the Platte River) established Long's Camp on the Missouri several miles below the bluffs. The craft, its dragon's-mouth bow emitting smoke, fire, and steam, completely amazed the watching Indians. "White man, bad man," they explained, "keep Great Spirit chained, built fire under him to make him paddle their boat."

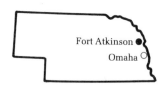

Ruins of Fort Atkinson, painted by Karl Bodmer in 1833. Prince Maximilian, whom Bodmer accompanied, described the fort as "a quadrangle, with a bastion or blockhouse, in two of the angles. At present there were only the stone chimneys, and, in the centre, a brick storehouse under roof."

Courtesy Nebraska State Historical Society

Reconstructed barracks mark the west wall of old Fort Atkinson at Fort Atkinson State Historical Park.

Courtesy Fort Atkinson State Historical Park

Scotts Bluff Nebraska

Scotts Bluff, a welcome landmark and a favorite camping spot on the continent's most important overland trail, is a symbol for the seekers of a century ago. Past this striking erosional remnant of the ancient Great Plains came those seeking homes in Oregon, souls in Idaho and Washington, furs in Wyoming and Montana, gold in California, religious freedom in Utah. Short on physical goods, for the most part, they (those, at least, who survived) were long on determination, courage, resourcefulness, and faith. Theirs was a way of life, a faith in American democracy that was, says the National Park Service, "nurtured, tempered, and re-vitalized by the rigors of the trail. Freedom of thought and action, and equality of opportunity inspired the pioneers who followed the Oregon trail, and it was they who extended these principles of Americanism beyond the Rocky Mountains."

These travelers, of course—on the Oregon Trail as well as the Mormon Trail, which followed the opposite (north) bank of the North Platte River—were relative late-comers. Artifacts of the area, a traditional Cheyenne, Arapaho, and Sioux hunting ground, indicate this valley has been an important corridor for human migration for at least ten thousand years.

In the mid-nineteenth century, Scotts Bluff witnessed the passing of most of the makers of western history. Following the Astorians, who spent the winter of 1812–13 in the vicinity ("The Hills on the south . . . are remarkably rugged and Bluffy and possess a few Cedars."), and mountain men William Ashley, Jim Bridger, Tom Fitzpatrick, and Jedediah Smith came pioneer relogous figures like Jason Lee (in 1834, the first mission-ary to the Northwest), Samuel Parker and Marcus Whitman (Presbyterians, in 1835), Henry Spalding with his wife, Eliza, and Narcissa Whitman (in 1836, the first white women to see Scotts Bluff), and Fr. Pierre Jean De Smet (1840). After them came John C. Frémont (1842), Stephen W. Kearny (1845), and Francis Parkman (1846). Brigham Young arrived in 1847 as the herald of thousands of Mormon refugees.

Today the buffalo have disappeared. (In 1843 one party noted that "it took the herd two entire days to pass, even at quite a rapid gait.") And deer are not too common. Otherwise the mod-ern traveler might be inclined to see the site as James Clyman did in 1844:

encamped in the midtst of Scotts blufs By a cool spring in a romantic & picturisque vally surroundded except to the E. by high & allmost im-passably steep clay cliffs of all immagenary shapes & forms supped on a most dlecious piece of venison.

Scotts Bluff, as it was first drawn in 1837 by Alfred Jacob Miller. To him it had the appearance of "an immense fortification with bastions, towers, bat-tlements, and ambra-zures."

Courtesy Walters Art Gallery

Now a national monu-ment (just off US 26), Scotts Bluff offers the motorist an impressive view of southwestern Nebraska—if not what one awed 1862 visitor de-scribed as "a scene sel-dom vouchsafed to mor-tals."

Courtesy Union Pacific Railroad

Chimney Rock   Nebraska

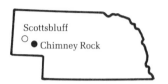

Chimney Rock, an "inverted funnel" to Fr. Pierre Jean De Smet in 1841, is a slender 100-foot-high column atop a conical base twice that height. Geologically, it is composed of Brule clay with interlayers of volcanic ash and Arickaree sandstone. Historically, it is the most commented-on landmark along the "trunk line" of the Oregon Trail (*see* Fort Kearny). The Astorians (*see* Fort Laramie), perhaps the first white men to see the rock (1813), ignored it, ironically enough. Of the estimated quarter of a million people who traveled this route in covered wagons from 1843 to 1869, however, few of those who kept journals and diaries (and there were literally hundreds of them) failed to describe the rock.

The first recorded use of the name "Chimney Rock" was by Joshua Pilcher in 1827. (The Indians, unfamiliar with the white man's chimney, called it "The Tepee" or "The Wigwam.") Warren A. Ferris (1830) referred to it as the "Nose Mountain," but admitted it was more commonly called "Chimney," going on to exclaim that it "appears at the distance of fifty miles shooting up from the prairie in solitary grandeur, like the limbless trunk of a gigantic tree." Subsequent travelers, equally impressed, expressed their wonderment in many different ways.

It was "a work of art" to Nathaniel J. Wyeth (1832), "among the curiosities of the country" to Capt. B. L. E. Bonneville (1832), "singular and interesting" to John Bidwell (1841), "picturesque" to Richard F. Burton (1860), and "a wonderful display of the eccentricity of Nature!" to Rufus B. Sage (1841). Others made more fanciful comparisons. The rock reminded Charles Preuss (1842) of "a shot-tower in Baltimore," Philip St. George Cooke (1845) of "the pharos of a prairie sea," Elijah White (1842) of the Washington Monument, and Rev. Samuel Parker (1835) of Beacon Hill. More prosaic emigrants saw "a potato hole" or "a haystack with a pole through its top."

As for Fr. De Smet, he was but one of many to be deceived by the Chimney's apparent fragility. When he saw it for the first time in 1840, he felt "a few years more and this great natural curiosity will crumble away and make only a little heap on the plain." Yet a near-by spring made it a popular campsite, and in the 1860's it sheltered a Pony Express station, then a telegraph and stage station. Today, as a National Historical Site (just south of US 26 and the North Platte River some twenty-three miles east of Scottsbluff), Chimney Rock is the same strikingly impressive landmark it was in yesteryear.

Chimney Rock, as painted by Alfred Jacob Miller in 1837. Of the twenty-one early travelers on the Oregon Trail known to have sketched the rock, Miller was the first. He called it a "remarkable formation."

Courtesy Walters Art Gallery

Chimney Rock today. It did not, as Fr. De Smet thought it would, "crumble away and make only a little heap on the plain."

Courtesy Nebraska Game and Parks Commission

Winter Quarters Nebraska

Winter Quarters (a north-side suburb of modern Omaha) was a temporary settlement founded in September 1846 by emigrant Latter-day Saints, under Brigham Young, on their way to their new home in the Great Salt Lake Basin. Well organized, as was the entire trek, the settlement was laid out in uniform blocks, then divided into 22 wards, each presided over by a Bishop. By December the Saints had provided a water supply, erected 631 houses (548 of logs, 83 of sod), a gristmill, and a council house. Pickets filled the gaps between the closely spaced houses to form a crude stockade. The population was 3,483. "Although observers found their general condition to be pitiful," one historian admits, not without pride, "their mutual dependence made it far from hopeless."

This interdependence expressed itself in many ways. "Seeing so many boys and girls running about the street," recalled Emmeline B. Wells, a schoolteacher convert from Massachusetts, "I decided I could best be of help . . . by opening a school. We had only a big log house with a dirt floor and a dirt roof, and rough benches. There weren't many books; and the mice ate up some of those we did gather. Yet we had a good time and learned our lessons even in the midst of hardships."

More significant as a collective enterprise was the celebrated Mormon Battalion. The U.S. government, having rejected all Church pleas for help in moving west, finally agreed to accept five hundred young Mormon recruits for duty in the Mexican War. An advance of forty-two dollars was paid each recruit as a clothing allowance, and most of this went into a common fund. From it and the pay checks that followed the Church collected more than fifty thousand dollars. The money remaining after the soldiers' families were cared for went to finance the journey to the West.

The exodus itself, of course, was delayed, but the military battalion enabled five hundred Saints to explore much of the Southwest at government expense and to return as disciplined soldiers ready for the troublesome years ahead. As Brigham Young himself put it, "the Mormon Battalion was organized from our camp to allay the prejudices of the people, prove our loyalty to the government of the United States, and for the present and temporal salvation of Israel."

The delayed hegira began in April 1847 with the advance company of 143 men, 3 women, and 2 children (*see* Salt Lake City). This was followed in July by what is sometimes called "the First emigration." It consisted of 1,553 persons, 566 wagons, 2,213, oxen, 124 horses, 887 cows, 358 sheep, 35 hogs, and 716 chickens (the Saints were notable statisticians). By mid-1848, Winter Quarters was abandoned.

George Simons' sketch of the steamer Omaha *landing Mormons at Florence, Nebraska, 1854. Eight years before, following their expulsion from Nauvoo, Illinois, thousands of the Saints had streamed across Iowa. As many as sixteen thousand exiles wintered in the Missouri Valley, most of them at Winter Quarters and at Kanesville (now Council Bluffs), Iowa.*

Courtesy Council Bluffs Free Public Library

This Arvard T. Fairbanks bronze in Mormon Cemetery, at the site of Winter Quarters (now Omaha), commemorates the six hundred emigrants buried in this vicinity during the hard winters of 1846–47 and 1847–48.

Courtesy Nebraska State Historical Society

138

Fort Kearny Nebraska

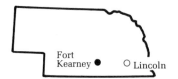

The Oregon Trail, according to National Park Service Historian Merrill J. Mattes, "is largely a term of literary convenience." Poetically, it may very well be the "Path of Destiny" of Jesse Applegate (leader of the famed "Cow Column" of the 1843 Great Migration) or Howard R. Driggs' "Trail of American Homebuilders" that stretched from the Missouri to the Columbia to make the expanding United States a two-ocean nation. Ezra Meeker called it "America's Greatest Trail," and it is undoubtedly that, too—and the "Whiteman's Big Medicine Road" of the Indians, who never ceased to be amazed at the stream of covered wagons that snaked their way over it year after year.

Practically, however, the Oregon Trail is not so easy to define. In some ways it resembled a giant rope thrown across the Trans-Mississippi West, a rope frayed at both ends. Strands from its eastern end touched such Missouri River points as Westport, Independence, St. Joseph, Bellevue, and Council Bluffs. Western strands stretched into Idaho, Montana, Utah, Nevada, and California, as well as into Oregon. But the "trunk line," according to Mattes, can be traced more precisely. It started at Fort Kearny on the Platte, into which all of the feeder routes led, and followed the Platte, North Platte, and Sweetwater to South Pass (q.v.) in southwestern Wyoming.

Fort Kearny (seven miles southeast of present-day Kearney, Nebraska) was established to protect Oregon-bound emigrants from the Indians. Lt. Daniel P. Woodbury came to the site in June 1848 with 175 men and promptly started construction of the post. Adobe blocks were made first, then a sawmill was set up and sod stables erected. Plans drawn in 1852 show two two-story blockhouses (never constructed) of heavy timbers, powder and guard houses, a lookout accessible by ladder, and officers' quarters. Barracks and other facilities were added later.

Until the coming of the Union Pacific ended the use of wagon trains (Fort Kearny was abandoned in 1871) the post was an important source of supplies and services. M. Powell, California bound in 1848 (with forty-two thousand other emigrants, according to Hubert Howe Bancroft), comments appreciatively on the blacksmith shop: "The venerable descendant of Vulcan, with his assistants, seems to be in great demand."

In this area in 1847, a year before the fort was established, the Mormon pioneers saw their first herds of buffalo. They spent so much time chasing them that Brigham Young finally called the camp together and, in the words of Appleton Harmon, "said that thair should be no more game killed until such time as it should be needed for it was a Sin to waste life & flesh."

Fort Kearny, the eastern terminus of the "trunk line" of the Oregon Trail, was established in 1848, the year Oregon Territory became a part of the United States. This C. C. Mills photograph was made ten years later, in 1858.

Courtesy Library of Congress

Fort Kearny State Historical Park, on the south bank of the Platte River. The stockade wall and several buildings have been reconstructed by the Nebraska Game and Parks Commission, which administers the once important site.

Courtesy Fort Kearny State Historical Park

Homestead National Monument Nebraska

The Homestead Act, heralded as "the greatest democratic measure of all history," was signed by President Abraham Lincoln on May 20, 1862. Becoming effective January 1, 1863, it entitled every qualified claimant—any citizen (or alien declaring his intention of becoming a citizen), twenty-one years of age or the head of a family—to file on "one-quarter section of unappropriated Government land"; only a small filing fee was required. Title was granted after five years if the claimant had lived on the land and completed certain requirements with regard to cultivation.

Within sixty years the government had given to more than one million individual claimants an acreage nearly equivalent in size to that of Texas and Louisiana combined. Vast areas of the West had been settled, and countless waves of European immigration had been absorbed. Free land and expanding industrialization had joined to double the nation's population from 1860 to 1900.

Daniel Freeman was, in many ways, typical of most homesteaders, especially in his resourcefulness. In 1862 he arranged for a squatter's claim to the piece of land he desired, a quarter-section on Cub Creek about four miles northwest of Beatrice, Nebraska. To make sure he could keep it, he sought out the Land Office agent in Brownville, who was at a New Year's Eve party (1862), and persuaded him to go to his office and let him file his claim shortly after midnight. The patent on Freeman's land (granted September 1, 1869, by the General Land Office) bears the designation: "Homestead Certificate No. 1, Application 1" (this for the Brownville office).

Freeman's "proof paper," dated January 20, 1868, and signed by two of his neighbors, swore

that we have known Daniel Freeman for over five years . . . that he is the head of a family consisting of wife and two children . . . that the said Daniel Freeman entered upon and made settlement on said land on the 1st day of January 1863, and has built a house thereon part log and part frame 14 by 20 feet one story with two doors two windows shingle roof board floors and is a comfortable house to live in.

Homestead National Monument was established March 18, 1936, as a memorial "emblematical of the hardships and the pioneer life through which the early settlers passed in the settlement, cultivation and civilization of the great West." Comprising the original homestead, it preserves a homesteader's log cabin (not Freeman's) erected in 1867. In it are furnishings and tools of the type used by eastern Nebraska pioneers.

The "Original Freeman Homestead Cabin," built by Daniel Freeman in 1867. This photograph (taken About 1869) shows Mrs. Freeman and her daughter, Eliza (center), flanked by hired man and hired girl. Freeman moved into a more comfortable house in 1876, living in it until his death in 1908.

Courtesy National Park Service

Homesteader's cabin at Homestead National Monument. Living history demonstrations are a summer feature at the site.

Courtesy National Park Service

Fort Robinson

May 6, 1877, was a great day in the life of Camp Robinson. (Established, somewhat reluctantly, in March 1874 as the military arm of the Red Cloud Agency of the Sioux, the post did not become a fort until January 1878.) The Sioux War—the Crook-Mackenzie and Miles campaigns to punish the Indians for the Custer disaster—was drawing to a close, and now Crazy Horse, with his band (217 men and 672 women and children with some 2,000 ponies and 117 guns and pistols), was on his way to turn himself in. W. P. Clark, the officer who met the hostiles, describes the impressive surrender march:

When the Sioux Chief Crazy Horse came in . . . he formed all of his warriors in line, in advance of the women and children; then, in front of this line, also mounted, he had some ten of his headmen; and then in front of these he rode alone. I had been sent with Indian scouts to meet him. He sent me word requesting a similar formation on our part, and asked that I should ride on in advance alone. Then we were to dismount and first shake hands, while seated on the ground, *that the peace might be solid.* After all this had been done his headmen came up, the peacepipe was produced, and we solemnly smoked. One of his headmen put a scalp-jacket and war-bonnet on me, and presented me the pipe with which peace had been made.

Peace, for Crazy Horse, lasted less than four months. Shortly before midnight on September 5 he died, bayoneted to death by a soldier attempting to put him in the guardhouse. The tragic death of the important Sioux leader—the first to break Custer's line, the last to surrender—is a complex event. Eyewitness descriptions and reconstructions of it vary in detail. The truth, of course, will never be known. But the death itself is somehow symbolic. Eventual defeat for the Indians in their struggle with the encroaching whites was fully as inevitable as the personal defeat of Crazy Horse.

Red Cloud Agency (two miles west of present-day Crawford, Nebraska) was located among the Sioux in the summer of 1873. A 949-man garrison set up Camp Robinson near by in March 1874, then moved the post a mile and a half to the west two months later. Here, in a highly picturesque valley protected on the north by a wall of castle-like cliffs rising an almost sheer 1,000 feet, the garrison set about building the permanent camp.

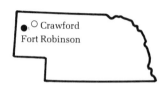

Fort Robinson's log barracks in 1883. In 1919 the post became a quartermaster remount depot, growing eventually into the world's largest remount station.

Courtesy Nebraska State Historical Society

Now a 22,000-acre state park, Fort Robinson offers historical interpretation as well as guest accommodations like this former barracks.

Courtesy Nebraska Game and Parks Commission

Mormon Station Nevada

The leader of a small group of Utah traders describes business at Mormon Station (in the Carson River Valley near the east shore of Lake Tahoe) in the summer of 1849:

Flour . . . was worth $2.00 a pound, fresh beef $1.00, bacon $2.00. A friend of mine went over the mountains and left a yoke of cattle with me, and one day I got a thousand dollars for one of those oxen in the shape of beef. . . . One time a captain of a train of emigrants came along and wanted to buy five hundred pounds of flour at $2.00 a pound, but I refused him, not having sufficient to deal out in such large amounts. . . . For a few loaves of bread I could get a good horse.

That April, when the future of the Salt Lake colony itself was in doubt, a group of fifteen Mormons had traveled west to California. Here along the Humboldt Road seven had stopped to establish a supply station, the first permanent settlement in that part of western Utah which is now Nevada. Trade with California-bound travelers was brisk, and when the Mormons returned to Salt Lake Valley that fall, they took with them about one hundred head of horses, along with much-needed coin and other valuables.

A roofless stockade built by H. S. Beattie in 1849 was apparently the settlement's only structure for two years. In 1851, Salt Lake City merchant Col. John Reese arrived to establish a more formal trading post. A log cabin was erected, as was (at a cost of two thousand dollars) a stockade to enclose more than an acre of land. A fine crop of turnips was raised that first year— and sold at one dollar a bunch. By November 12 enough settlers had arrived to justify the establishment of an informal squatter government. Orson Hyde, one of the Twelve Apostles, arrived in 1855, made Mormon Station the seat of recently created Carson County, and changed its name to Genoa. Here, on December 18, 1858, appeared the state's first newspaper, the weekly *Territorial Enterprise* (now published at Virginia City), this at a time when the entire Nevada region boasted less than a thousand people.

Not until 1858, however, when Nevada's true wealth was discovered—the incredibly rich silver hoard of the Comstock (*q.v.*)—did Genoa really prosper. Then, as California gold seekers stampeded back across the Sierra Nevadas, the town acquired a telegraph line, stagecoach station, gristmill, and sawmill. By August 1859 the frontier had receded to the point where flour was selling in Genoa at twenty cents a pound.

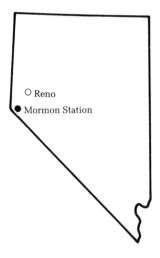

O Reno
● Mormon Station

Mormon Station. When built, in 1851, this was probably the only house in present-day Nevada.

Courtesy Nevada Historical Society

Genoa in its early years. The Territorial Enterprise *began publication here on December 18, 1858.*

Courtesy Nevada Historical Society

Reconstructed Mormon Station is now a museum.

Courtesy Sierra Press Bureau

Las Vegas Fort Nevada

The year is 1844 and the writer is John C. Frémont:

May 3 . . . we encamped in the midst of another very large basin, at a camping ground called Las Vegas—a term which the Spaniards use to signify fertile or marshy plains. . . . Two narrow streams of clear water, four or five feet deep, gush suddenly, with quick current from two singularly large springs. . . . The taste of the water is good, but rather too warm to be agreeable; the temperature being 71D in the one, and 73D in the other. They, however, afforded a delightful bathing place.

In a region where water and life are synonymous, *Las Vegas* was almost destined for settlement. ("This oasis," wrote Gwinn Harris Heap in 1853, "deserves the name of The Diamond of the Desert, so beautiful and bright does it appear in the centre of the dreary waste that surrounds it.") And Jefferson Hunt, logically enough, felt it should be Mormon. In 1847, while en route to California to buy seed grain for the Church's Utah settlements, he camped at Las Vegas Spring, recommended it favorably on his return. Eight years later, Brigham Young agreed.

Thirty young men, under William Bringhurst, were detailed "to go to Las Vegas, build a fort there to protect immigrants and the United States mail from the Indians, and to teach the latter how to raise corn, wheat, potatoes, squash, and melons." The party left Salt Lake City on May 10, 1855, arriving June 14 and 15. Contemporary accounts detail their experiences.

Las Vegas, they found, was "a nice patch of grass about half a mile wide and two or three miles long." Mesquite was cleared, crops planted. They "in general look well," one colonist reported on September 11, "the melons are just beginning to get ripe." Timber prospects were "not very flattering." (Logs had to be hauled twenty miles from the Charleston Mountains: "15 miles hard road—gravel and rocks—and the rest sand.") But there was always adobe. "Our fort, 150 feet square is now progressing rapidly; the walls are of adobe and are to be 14 feet high. . . . Houses are going up and we will soon begin to live quite comfortably." The next year, lead was smelted from outcroppings which had been discovered at Cottonwood Springs to the southwest.

In January 1857 the settlers were "released" from the mission, and by 1858, Las Vegas was entirely abandoned. Overland Mail carriers continued to stop at Vegas Springs and during the Civil War troops were stationed there at short-lived Fort Baker, but not until May 1905, with the coming of the railroad, was Las Vegas settled permanently.

Las Vegas Fort

This crude sketch of Las Vegas Fort, drawn for Church President George T. Smith by John Steele, shows the "Tooly grass," the "Musquete," and the "Carell."

Courtesy Office of the Historian, The Church of Jesus Christ of Latter-day Saints

Las Vegas Fort, restored in 1980, is on property owned by a Las Vegas fraternal club and may be visited.

Courtesy Las Vegas News Bureau

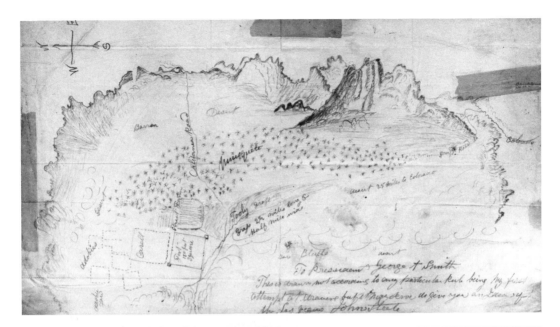

Lake's Crossing   Nevada

From California gold-rush days (and before; here, in 1846, the ill-fated Donner party lingered one day too long) down to the present, Truckee Meadows has been a pleasant tarrying place for the overland traveler. Whether seeking relief from the surrounding deserts, supplies with which to make a personal assault on near-by Comstock Lode, wealth from the legally operated gaming tables, or simple surcease from an unwanted marital partner, the visitor has liked the valley of the Truckee River, its accommodations, its activities (the notable Jackson-Jeffries fight in 1910), and its services.

First settler on the site was C. W. Fuller. In 1859, the year of the Comstock rush, Fuller's Crossing consisted of a dugout dwelling on the south bank of the river. The following year, Fuller added a crude toll bridge made of logs. Then in 1863 he sold out to M. C. Lake, who put up a small building to serve as store and stopping place.

As Lake's Crossing, on the Peavine Toll Road to booming Virginia City, the site continued to prosper. It became Reno (for Gen. Jesse Lee Reno) on May 9, 1868, when the Central Pacific Railroad, then pushing eastward for its historic "meet" at Promontory (q.v.), held a public auction of real estate. Two hundred lots (the first brought six hundred dollars) were sold the first day. One hundred houses were thrown together the first month, and the success of this initial boom was assured in 1870 when the seat of Washoe county was wrested from near-by Washoe City. (Founded in June 1854 by Orson Hyde, this Mormon settlement flourished briefly as a score of sawmills cut mine timbers for the Comstock.)

Lake grew with the town, even helped to mold it, despite the fact it was no longer his namesake. When his store burned, he built the first Riverside Hotel, a three-story frame affair with a wide veranda. Each time his bridge washed away, he promptly replaced it, continuing to collect tolls (a dollar a head on Virginia City-bound cattle) until his charter finally expired. And to keep business south of the river, he donated land, plus fifteen hundred dollars, and saw the courthouse built next to his hotel.

At the turn of the century the Riverside was moved back (to become a barn), and an ornate, becupolaed structure of red brick took its place. When this, in turn, was destroyed by fire in 1923 (about the time the present concrete bridge was put across the Truckee), the first section of the present Riverside Hotel was erected.

● Lake's Crossing
(Reno)

This oil painting of Lake's Crossing in 1863 shows the first accommodations for travelers available in what is now Reno. In the foreground is M. C. Lake with Chief Winnemucca.

Courtesy Nevada Historical Society

Reno today, looking west. The third and latest Riverside Hotel on the site of Lake's Crossing (to the left of the two upper bridges on the Truckee) makes this the only spot in Nevada that has served as a hostelry continuously for a century.

Courtesy Reno News Bureau

Comstock Lode Nevada

The Comstock Lode, perhaps the world's richest deposit of silver ore, was discovered in 1859 on the naked slope of Sun Mountain (later called Mount Davidson). By the end of the century it had produced hundreds of millions of dollars in silver, laid the foundation for a score of personal fortunes (Hearst, Mackay, Fair, Flood), helped turn San Francisco into a fashionable metropolis, lent a hand in paying the Civil War debt, and financed the laying of the Atlantic telegraph cable. In the process, it spawned a dozen mining towns, queen of which was Virginia City, able to boast in its heyday of twenty-five thousand people, a hundred saloons, twenty theaters and music halls, and several imposing hotels.

Aside from silver, however, the Comstock had little else. There were no forests. "A more barren-looking and forbidding spot could scarcely be found elsewhere on the face of the earth," it seemed to J. Ross Browne in 1859. "The whole aspect of the country indicates that it must have been burned up in hot fires many years ago and reduced to a mass of cinders, or scraped up from all the desolate spots in the known world, and thrown over the Sierra Nevada mountains in a confused mass to be out of the way. . . . It is inconceivable that this region should ever have been designed as an abode for man."

The wind was "the most villainous and persecuting" that ever blew. And the water—what little there was of it—was "the worst ever used by man." Only by "correcting it," that is, mixing "a spoonful of water in half a tumbler of whisky," could it be drunk at all.

As for the city itself, Browne found it a predictable reflection of climate and terrain. "Frame shanties, pitched together as if by accident; tents of canvas, of blankets, of brush, of potato-sacks and old shirts, with empty whisky-barrels for chimneys; smoky hovels of mud and stone; coyote holes in the mountain side . . . pits and shafts with smoke issuing from every crevice . . . dotted over with human beings of such sort, variety, and numbers, that the famous ant-hills of Africa were as nothing in the comparison."

Yet the Comstock developed impressively. Thousands of claims were consolidated into a score of big, economically operable mines. Water-hungry mills, a dozen or more of them, sprang up along the Carson River. Needed timber was V-flumed from the mountains to the Washoe Valley and floated by river to the mills. The 20,000-foot Sutro Tunnel was drilled to drain the deeper mines. Today, after a half-century of semipermanent ghosthood, the Comstock is still an impressive monument to the mining frontier in the West.

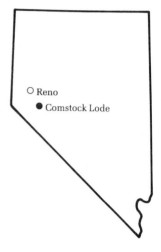

Virginia City in 1861, from a lithograph by Grafton T. Brown. Two years earlier, it was described as "speckled with snow, sagebushes, and mounds of upturned earth, without any apparent beginning or end, congruity or regard for the eternal fitness of things."

Courtesy Library of Congress

Virginia City today. Among its other reminders of past greatness is the still-published Territorial Enterprise. *The state's first newspaper (begun at Genoa on December 8, 1858), it moved to Virginia in 1860, once employed such frontier writers as Samuel L. Clemens (Mark Twain), William Wright (Dan DeQuille), and Fred Harte (Bret Harte's brother).*

Courtesy Nevada Department of Economic Development

Fort Churchill   Nevada

Fort Churchill, the first and most important military post established in Nevada, probably owes its founding to a couple of Bannock Indian women. The 1859 silver rush into the Washoe country led inevitably to the killing of game and the destruction of pine-nut trees, both of which, in this desert area, affected adversely the Indians' food supply. Driven from their accustomed spots, the Bannocks, Paiutes, and others became restless and resentful. The kidnaping by white men of several young Bannock women is believed to have been the fatal spark. The Indians, in retaliation, recaptured the women, then burned the trading post of James Williams (about twenty-five miles east of Carson City) and killed five whites for good measure. The war scare that resulted led to Special Order No. 67, Department of California, authorizing establishment of a post on the Carson River.

Capt. Joseph Stewart, heading "The Carson River Expedition" against the Indians, received his orders July 13, 1860. The site was selected July 20, and work began at once. With the threat of the Civil War and the Secessionist movements in near-by Virginia City and Carson City, the fort's original three companies were strengthened with a fourth (to an average strength of about two hundred men). Throughout the war the outpost served as a main supply depot for the Nevada military district, as well as a base for troops patrolling the east-west and north-south overland trails. After the war, its importance diminished sharply and it was finally abandoned on June 15, 1871. Ironically, the public-auction sale of the post buildings realized only $750.

The coincidence in history of the so-called Paiute War and the short-lived Pony Express gave the latter much of its almost legendary heroics. News of such events as Lincoln's election, his first inaugural, the firing on Fort Sumter, and the defeat at Bull Run all went west in the *mochilas* of intrepid Pony Express riders. Fort Churchill figured in two of these exploits. Robert H. "Pony Bob" Haslam—who, with William F. "Buffalo Bill" Cody and Johnny Fry (*see* St. Joseph), was one of the three best-known riders—made one epochal ride of 380 miles (in 36 hours) through this territory at the height of the Paiute uprising. He is also credited with carrying the 1860 election returns from Smiths Creek westward to Fort Churchill (and the first telegraph station), a total of 120 miles, in 8 hours and 10 minutes.

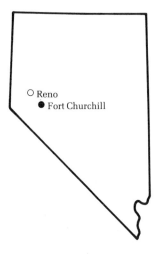

○ Reno
● Fort Churchill

Fort Churchill, looking north to the two-story officers' quarters. Barracks flank the west side of the parade and post headquarters, commissary, store, hospital, and laundry the east. The guard-house, bakery, stables, and corrals close the square on the south.

Courtesy Nevada Historical Society

In Fort Churchill State Park (just west of US 95-A near Weeks), adobe walls on stone foundations still guard the Nevada desert more than a century after the last Pony Express rider surrendered his dispatch-filled mochila.

Courtesy Nevada Department of Economic Development

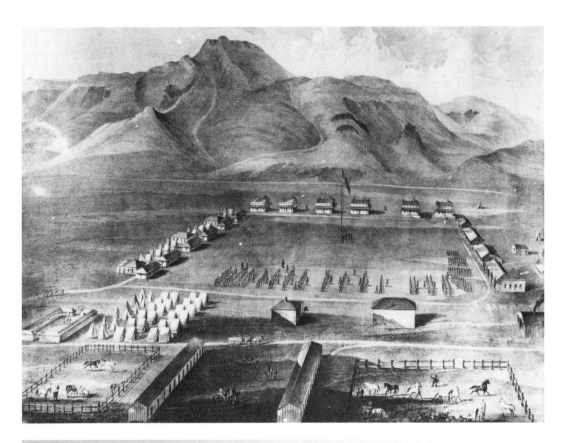

Tiguex New Mexico

When Francisco Vásquez de Coronado's expedition was making its fruitless search for gold across the southern Plains, Tiguex consisted of twelve pueblos scattered along the west bank of the Río Grande. At one of them, from 1540 to 1542, Coronado established his headquarters. (Precise identification is impossible today. Coronado State Monument, with its giant Kuaua Pueblo excavated and one kiva reconstructed, has long been the "traditional" site. Most authorities now, however, favor a near-by site believed to have been the pueblo Coronado named *Puaray.*) And here, more than four centuries ago, were brought together the three facts most influential in shaping the culture of today's New Mexico: the Indian, the Conquistador, and the Church.

Hernando de Alvarado, in 1540, was the first white man to visit Tiguex. Coronado, recovering from his wounds at Zuñi (and his disappointment at finding Cíbola merely an adobe pueblo "all crumpled together"), had sent him eastward with a scouting party. He paused at the Tiguex pueblòs long enough to recommend them as an excellent wintering place, then continued his explorations. Meanwhile, Fr. Juan de Padilla reportedly made converts so fast that Indians "even climbed on the backs of others to reach the arms of crosses and decorate them with feathers and roses."

Disillusionment came quickly. An advance guard for Coronado under García López de Cárdenas requisitioned one of the pueblos and most of its contents for housing and food. When Coronado arrived in September, he sent soldiers through the pueblos for clothing and, according to Pedro de Castañeda, "there was nothing the natives could do except take off their own cloaks and hand them over."

Full-scale warfare erupted when a Spaniard, having ordered an Indian to hold his horse, "ravished or had attempted to ravish his [the Indian's] wife." Outraged, the Tiguex people revolted, killing some horses. Cárdenas besieged one pueblo with smudge pots, forced the defenders to surrender, then ordered "that 200 stakes be driven into the ground to burn them alive." After it was all over, Castañeda reports, "none escaped alive except a few who had remained concealed in the pueblo." Major fighting had ended by April 23, 1541, when Coronado left to search for Quivira, but on his return, the Tiguex and Pecos Indians were still hostile. In early April 1542, after a winter of discouragement and dissension, Coronado departed for New Spain.

Fr. Luis de Escalona, Fr. Juan de la Cruz, and Fr. Padilla remained behind to become the southwest's first martyrs (*see* Council Grove). Two years of cruelty, treachery, and rapine had set a grim pattern for Spanish-Indian relations for centuries to come.

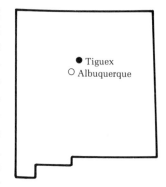

Religious murals discovered in a kiva (ceremonial chamber) at the ruined Kuaua Pueblo, overlooking the Río Grande, a few miles northwest of Bernalillo.

Courtesy New Mexico Department of Development

Excavated and partially restored, the ancient Kuaua Pueblo is now Coronado State Monument. The building at lower left is the museum, which contains many Tiguex Province artifacts. The custodian's residence is just behind it.

Courtesy New Mexico Department of Development

Taos New Mexico

"Darn the white diggins, while thar's buffler in the mountains. Whoopee! Are you for Touse? This hos is thar in one sun, wagh!" The sentiment was that of John Hatcher (as recorded by Lewis H. Garrard), but it was shared by George Frederick Ruxton, and by most mountain men, a hearty crew that counted such stalwarts as Old Bill Williams, Uncle Dick Wootton, the Robidoux brothers, Kit Carson, Milt Sublette, Jean Baptiste La Lande, the Bents (William, Charles, George, Robert), Céran St. Vrain, Jedediah Smith, Ewing Young, Lucien Maxwell, Jim Beckwourth, and many others. American trappers wandered into Taos after 1800 and made the congenial old Spanish-Indian pueblo their headquarters for half a century. With the decline of the fur trade in the mid-1830's, many married and retired to the Taos area. Kit Carson married a New Mexican heiress, became a landowner, businessman, and colonel in the U.S. Army. Charles Bent married an older sister of Carson's wife, was appointed governor of New Mexico by Gen. Stephen Watts Kearny, and was scalped alive, then murdered, at his home in Taos during the bloody Pueblo insurrection of 1847.

Hernando de Alvardo (*see* Tiguex) first visited multistoried Taos Pueblo in 1540. Francisco de Barrionuevo arrived in 1541, Juan de Oñate in 1598. Franciscans built San Gerónimo de Taos next to the pueblo before 1617. Destroyed and rebuilt once before the Taos-directed Pueblo Revolt of 1680 (when it was again razed), San Gerónimo became a completely new church in 1706. Then in 1847, following Gov. Bent's murder, Col. Sterling Price bombarded it with his artillery, killing 150 of its 700 barricaded defenders. San Gerónimo was reduced to ruins.

The village of Don Fernando de Taos grew up slowly around its traditional plaza—"a league away" from Taos Pueblo, at the Indians' request—but the exact date of its founding is unknown (Spanish settlers drifted into the area in the early seventeenth century). Indian raids were a constant threat, and in 1760, Comanches carried away fifty women and children (never recovered), after which the rear walls of the houses were connected to form a rectangular fortress. In the eighteenth century its annual trade fair, attracting Indians, traders, and settlers from the entire Southwest, made Taos the busiest village in the province.

Never a manufacturing town, Taos did produce one important and far-famed frontier commodity: Taos Lightning. "The first house we passed," noted Garrard on entering the town in 1847, "was a distillery where the 'mountain dew' of New Mexico—*aguardiente de Taos,* is made; and such is the demand, it is imbibed before attaining a very drinkable age, by both foreigners and residents, with great avidity."

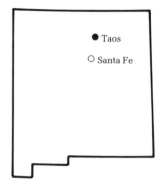

● Taos
○ Santa Fe

Taos Pueblo, looking today much as it did in 1540 when Alvardo first saw it but for the horses, the one contribution to his culture the Indian truly appreciated. Near by are the ruins of San Gerónimo, one of New Mexico's first missions.

Courtesy New Mexico Department of Development

The parlor of Kit Carson's home in Taos. On the wall is a portrait of Kit's friend, business partner, and brother-in-law, Gov. Charles Bent, who was murdered in the 1847 uprising.

Courtesy New Mexico Department of Development

158

El Morro   New Mexico

"Pasó por aqui," begins the inscription on what historian Erna Fergusson calls New Mexico's great stone autograph album. "There passed by here the Adelantado Don Juan de Oñate, from the discovery of the Sea of the South [the Gulf of California], the 16th of April of 1605." And thus two years before the founding of Jamestown, fifteen years before the Pilgrims landed at Plymouth Rock, El Morro, a 200-foot-high sandstone mesa-point some fifty-three miles southeast of Gallup, received the first of more than five hundred decipherable names and inscriptions.

Nor was this the first visit by white men. Oñate himself had already seen the headland in 1598. Fr. Bernardino Beltrán and Capt. Antonio de Espejo saw it in 1583. (It was referred to as *El Estanque del Penol* in Pérez de Luxán's journal of the expedition.) Fr. Agustín Rodríguez and Capt. Francisco Chamuscado probably saw El Morro in 1581, but the first white visitors were undoubtedly soldiers of the Coronado expedition, which captured the near-by Zuñi pueblo of Hawikúh (Cíbola) in 1540.

Before the proud Spanish, of course, came the Indians. Around the base of the mesa are hundreds of petroglyphs. Their precise meanings are tentative, but their age probably coincides with that of the two large pueblos built on top of the mesa. The larger, Atsinna, is thought to date from about 1175 to 1425.

Then there is the Mission Period. In 1629, Gov. Francisco Manuel de Silva Nieto scratches for posterity his role in carrying the Faith to the Zuñis. Three years later there is this inscription: "They passed on March 23, 1632, to the avenging of the death of Father Letrado.—Lujan" Thus was recorded the rejection of Christianity by the Zuñis. Other notable Spanish inscriptions: Don Diego de Vargas (1692, following the collapse of the Pueblo Revolt), Gov. Don Féliz Martínez (1716, on his unsuccessful campaign against the Hopis), and the Bishop of Durango (1737, on his way to the Zuñis). The latest surviving dated Spanish inscription is marked 1774.

Following Gen. Stephen Watts Kearny's conquest of Santa Fe (*q.v.*), Americans began moving westward in increasing numbers. Few failed to record their passing. First to visit El Morro were Lt. James H. Simpson and the artist Richard H. Kern in 1849. One of the most curious expeditions to pass was certainly that of Edward F. Beale and his camel caravan in 1857. "It is a most singular formation," May Stacy noted on August 23. "The rock covers an area of about four to five miles. It is rather circular in formation and upon the top it is, in places, level."

Inscriptions stopped in 1906 when El Morro National Monument was established by President Theodore Roosevelt.

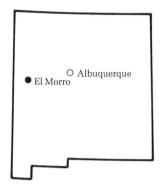

Pasó por aqui. . . . The inscription of Oñate in 1605 is the oldest of more than five hundred still decipherable at El Morro National Monument.

Courtesy New Mexico Department of Development

El Morro, a stone history book from which the knowing observer can read a nearly eight-century-long chronicle of life—Indians, Conquistadors, friars, emigrants, traders, Indian agents, soldiers, surveyors, and pioneer settlers—in this arid corner of the Southwest.

Courtesy New Mexico Department of Development

Santa Fe New Mexico

"Los Americanos! Los Carros! La entrada de la caravana!" Josiah Gregg heard the excited cries as he led his wagon trains into Santa Fe, the Spanish village at the end of eight hundred miles of trail from Missouri. The Americans responded in kind: "Each waggoner must tie a brand new 'cracker' to the end of his whip ... to outvie his comrades in the dexterity with which he flourishes this favorite badge of authority."

Yet dramatic *entradas* were not new to Santa Fe's *plaza pública,* even in 1843, when Gregg reported that 230 wagons hauled in $450,000 in merchandise. William Becknell, the "Father of the Santa Fe Trail" (*see* Franklin), had pioneered the overland trade with his arrival on November 6, 1822 (he sold his $150 worth of goods for $700). An even more important entry had been made a century before, in 1692, when Don Diego de Vargas, the newly appointed Spanish governor, marched peacefully into the city. And even this was a re-entry, a reassertion of Spanish rule after the Pueblo Revolt of 1680.

The first *entrada* was in the winter of 1609–10(?), when Don Pedro de Peralta founded *La Villa Real de la Santa Fé de San Francisco.* Almost immediately he started construction of *El Palacio Real,* the Palace of the Governors, which until 1909 continuously housed Spanish, Indian, Mexican, and American governors. (Today, after three and a half centuries of damage, repair, reconstruction, and restoration, the block-long adobe, its full-length portal shading the busy sidewalk along the north side of the square, contains the excellent Museum of New Mexico.) In its dungeon were entertained such Americans as Zebulon M. Pike (1807), James Baird and Robert McKnight (1812), Auguste P. Chouteau (1817), and David Meriwether (1818). And here, too, on August 19, 1846, Gen. Stephen Watts Kearny came "to take possession of New Mexico . . . in the name of the government of the United States."

If Santa Fe was a symbol of excitement to some (Gregg doubted that "the first sight of the walls of Jerusalem were beheld with much more tumultuous and soul-enrapturing joy"), it was just a nondescript mud village to others. In 1807, Pike saw only "a fleet of flat-boats moored at the foot of a mountain." George Frederick Ruxton (1846) compared its "wretched" mud houses to "a dilapidated brick kiln or a prairie-dog town" (whose "miserable, vicious-looking" inhabitants were obviously "worthy of their city"). Dr. Frederick A. Wislizenus found the streets "irregular, narrow, and dusty" and noted that the "so-called palacio . . . exhibits two great curiosities, to wit: windows of glass, and festoons of Indian ears." As for Col. J. F. Meline (1867), he was impressed most by the burros: "I am never tired of looking at their picturesque ugliness," he wrote.

The original Palace of the Governors, an all-purpose fortress with walls five feet thick, was flanked by two towers, the one on the east (right) housing a chapel, the one on the west an arsenal, with dungeon attached. To the north, surrounded by a wall, the Palace grounds extended two blocks and included a patio, soldiers' barracks, woodsheds, and outbuildings.

Courtesy Museum of New Mexico

Santa Fe's Palace of the Governors as restored in the twentieth century from a plan of the original found on an old map in the British Museum. Here, when he was territorial governor (1878–81), Lew Wallace wrote the last three parts of Ben Hur.

Courtesy New Mexico Department of Development

Albuquerque New Mexico

The year was 1706. The site was "a goodly place of pasturage" beside the *Río Bravo del Norte* ("Fierce River of the North"), as the Río Grande was then known. Don Francisco Cuervo y Valdés, twenty-eighth governor and captain-general of New Mexico, his secretary, and a few witnesses picked up stones and bunches of grass and threw them to the four points of the compass, shouting, "Long live the King!" Then, to honor his patron saint, Francisco Xavier, and the Duke of Alburquerque, viceroy of New Spain, he named the new settlement San Francisco de Alburquerque. (Two and a half centuries and 350,000 settlers later, it is still the "Duke City." The Viceroy, however, realizing that the villa had been founded without consulting King Philip V of Spain, diplomatically changed its official name to San Felipe de Alburquerque. Indifferent spellers dropped the first *r* and it became, finally, *Albuquerque*.

The locality was first seen by white men in 1540 when a party of Coronado's soldiers under Hernando de Alvarado visited many of the Río Grande Indian pueblos (*see* Tiguex). Other explorers followed, and after Juan de Oñate's time (1598), haciendas developed in this vicinity. These were destroyed in the Pueblo Revolt of 1680, and not until 1706, with the return of the Spanish colonists from their twelve-year exile in El Paso, did Gov. Cuervo y Valdés order thirty families of settlers to move down the river from Bernalillo to the shady ford where Albuquerque was founded.

Fr. Manuel Moreño started work almost immediately on the Church of San Felipe de Nerí (northwest corner of the plaza). Except for a remodeled façade and other minor changes, it stands today much as it was built. (Designed to withstand firebrands and battering rams, its adobe walls are more than four feet thick, its windows twenty feet from the ground. Parish records indicate it has not missed a Sunday service since 1706.) The original church convent (northeast corner) was built soon afterward, housing Franciscan missionaries for more than a century. The plaza, originally surrounded by an adobe wall, was the center of life (and defense) in the villa, which by 1790 had a population of 5,959.

An important military post during both Spanish and (after 1821) Mexican regimes, Albuquerque became an American outpost following Gen. Stephen Watts Kearny's occupation in 1846. (A fourth flag was added during the Civil War, but the Confederacy's brief control of New Mexico ended March 26–28, 1862, with defeats at Apache Canyon and Glorieta Pass.) The arrival of the Santa Fe Railroad in 1881 resulted in the founding of New Albuquerque, two miles to the east. Today, engulfed by this vigorously growing rival, "Old Town" plaza clings stubbornly to her ancient adobes and mellow charm.

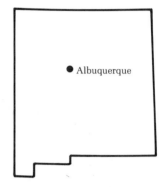

Albuquerque, treeless and dusty in the 1850's. W. W. H. Davis describes it in his El Gringo (1857): "In the centre is a plaza of some two or three acres in extent, and into which the principal streets lead. The houses are generally grouped about without order, and the best are but indifferent mud buildings. . . . As a place of residence it is far less pleasant than Santa Fe. At some seasons high winds prevail. . . . Then there are flies and musquitoes."

Courtesy University of Oklahoma Library

Casa de Armijo, on the east side of Albuquerque's "Old Town" plaza, from a south-side portal. Although the front section has been remodeled from time to time, much of the old building is about two centuries old. It served as headquarters for both Union and Confederate officers during the Civil War.

Courtesy New Mexico Department of Development

Fort Union New Mexico

In 1856, five years after its establishment by Col. E. V. Sumner, Fort Union was no summer resort. "The entire garrison covers a space of about eighty or more acres," Assistant Surgeon John Letterman noted, its scattered buildings, unprotected by stockade or blockhouse, presenting "more the appearance of a village . . . than a military post." Construction was of unseasoned, unhewn, and unbarked pine logs. Rapidly decaying, these afforded "excellent hiding places for that annoying and disgusting insect the cimex-lectularius, so common in this country." (The bedbugs resulted in the men's "almost universally sleeping in the open air when the weather will permit.") His conclusion: "Badly laid and badly built, it is now essential that the post be rebuilt."

The Civil War, plus Gen. Henry H. Sibley's invasion of New Mexico from Texas, prompted construction of ditches, parapets, and bombproofs a mile to the east. This threat quickly collapsed, however, following Union victories around Glorieta Pass in March 1862. From 1863 to 1866 an extensive construction program was carried out on the new site.

For forty years Fort Union played a key role in shaping the destiny of the Southwest. Its troops protected settlers and travelers on the Santa Fe Trail from Indian attack and mounted campaigns that penetrated the homeland of the Apaches, Utes, Navahos, Kiowas, and Comanches. Throughout its life the post was the southwestern hub of army supply services, with a military and civilian population which at times reached three thousand persons. It functioned as a source of incoming news by mail and telegraph, as a trading post, and finally as a social center.

These latter years were not without their sophisticated amenities. In 1882 the Young Men's Club held social hops. In 1883 the *Las Vegas Optic* hailed the Dramatic Club, filling a two-day engagement there, as a "First Class organization" with talent "entitled to a place on the legitimate stage." And a Grand Leap Year Party by the ladies of the post caused one reporter to admit that he "had no idea that such delicate dishes could be prepared at Fort Union." A Comedy Company was active in 1884. In 1885 the Twenty-third Infantry Band was giving three "very enjoyable open air concerts" each week, lawn tennis had become popular, and new books appeared regularly in the post library.

As a guardian of the frontier, Fort Union had obviously outlived its usefulness. In 1891 the War Department agreed and ordered its abandonment. Its crumbling ruins became a national monument in 1956.

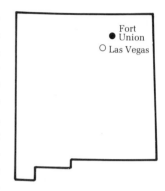

Fort Union, as depicted in W. W. H. Davis's 1857 book El Gringo. *This military post, the largest on the Southwest frontier in the nineteenth century, was situated on Coyote Creek, near the junction of the Mountain Route and the Cimarron Cutoff of the Santa Fe Trail, some twenty-five miles northeast of Las Vegas.*

Jim Arga

Fort Union National Monument preserves impressive rock and adobe ruins dating from the 1860's, when the original (1851) log fortress was rebuilt. Massive and distinctive, their flat roofs rimmed by heavy coping of red brick, these buildings set the pattern for the "Territorial" style that characterizes modern architecture throughout New Mexico.

Jim Arga

166

Lincoln New Mexico

La Placita del Río Bonito ("Little Town by the Pretty River") seems an unlikely setting for one of the frontier West's most famous feuds. Certainly nothing in its early years hinted at the climactic violence of the Lincoln County War of 1878. A typical Spanish village (fifty-eight miles west of Roswell), it was settled in the early 1850's by families who drifted in from the older Río Grande settlements to the west. They irrigated their fields, tended their small herds, opened a few stores, and, as a watchtower refuge from Indians, erected a three-story, circular rock *torreón*. The establishment of Fort Stanton (ten miles to the west) in 1855 brought no important changes, nor did the Civil War. Then in the late 1860's, as the advancing cattleman's frontier engulfed it from the east, La Placita moved on stage.

In 1869, Lincoln County was formed (for a time it later included all of the Territory's southeastern corner), and the village, as its seat, became Lincoln. The area's vast ranges soon supported some 300,000 cattle (John Chisum alone ran 80,000 head), with near-by Indian reservations and military posts providing ready markets. But as Lincoln's importance grew—and it became more Anglicized—so did its problems. Like cowtowns throughout the West, it attracted cowboys, badmen, gun fighters, rustlers, soldiers, and famous lawmen and acquired vexing disputes over water, government beef contracts, and grazing rights. A fierce commercial and political feud finally triggered the explosion in 1878.

On February 18, John H. Tunstall, English associate of Alexander McSween, was shot to death by a posse sent to serve him with a writ of attachment brought by L. G. Murphy, McSween's mercantile rival. Tunstall's cowboys (including William H. "Billy the Kid" Bonney) subsequently killed two members of the posse and ambushed and killed Sheriff William Brady. The population was soon divided into two armed camps—the Murphy forces and the Tunstall-McSween followers—and spasmodic fighting continued for five months, culminating in a three-day fight on Lincoln's main street that ended July 19 with the burning out of the McSween forces.

Lincoln today, once again a sleepy adobe village (it lost the county seat in 1913), is best known for its violent past. But it is also a remarkably unspoiled example of the frontier cowtown, with most of its 1878 buildings surviving almost untouched by time. Still to be seen are the old Tunstall store and the impressive two-story "Big Store" of L. B. Murphy & Company (built in 1874), which became Lincoln County Courthouse in 1880. Restored, it is now a museum.

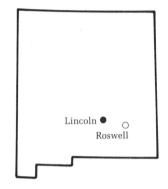

Lincoln in 1886. At the rear of the courthouse (largest building) stood the jail (now demolished). The ladder to the second-story rear window provided the only access to the Masonic meeting room.

Courtesy Mrs. Henry Fritz and the Old Lincoln County Memorial Commission

Built in 1874 as the "Big Store" of L. G. Murphy & Company, this two-story adobe-brick building was headquarters for the Murphy-Dolan forces in the Lincoln County War. It served as Lincoln County Courthouse from 1880 to 1913. Now restored, it is preserved as Lincoln State Monument by the Museum of New Mexico.

Courtesy Museum of New Mexico

Mesilla   New Mexico

Mesilla, its century-old adobes and dusty plaza dozing quietly on the Río Grande's east bank near Las Cruces, is one of New Mexico's most historic territorial towns. The village was founded in 1852, just after the Mexican War, by a group of New Mexicans who preferred to remain under Mexican rule. These settlers received land under the Mesilla (Little Tableland) Colony Grant in 1853, the same year the Gadsden Purchase put the area back under United States jurisdiction. On July 4, 1854, there was a gala flag-raising ceremony at the bandstand in the center of the plaza. Gov. David Meriwether was down from Santa Fe for the occasion, and troops from near-by Fort Fillmore helped swell the large crowd of local citizens.

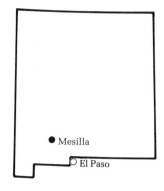

The plaza was soon to witness more exciting—and bloodier—events. Mesilla was an important stop on both the El Paso–Fort Yuma stage line (1857) and the Butterfield Overland Mail route (1858–61), and coaches occasionally made unscheduled stops at San Albino Church to disgorge victims of Indian raids before pulling up at the regular station, a large adobe with high-walled corral located on the plaza just south of Col. A. J. Fountain's new store. (Mid-point on Butterfield's Missouri-to-California route, Mesilla wagered heavily in 1858 on which coach—from the East or the West—would first reach the town. The one from the West won.) In July 1861, Lt. Col. John R. Baylor captured Fort Fillmore for the Confederates and established his headquarters in Mesilla. In August 1862 the California Volunteers arrived (after the Texas invaders had fled), and Brig. Gen. James H. Carleton made Mesilla headquarters of the Military District of Arizona. In post–Civil War days, territorial politics at times flared into violence, and one pitched battle on the plaza between Democrats and Republicans resulted in the killing of nine men.

Mesilla was long associated, too, with the range-cattle industry. Here at various times came such New Mexico figures as Pat Garrett, Billy the Kid, Albert B. Fall, Eugene Manlove Rhodes, Oliver Lee, and others. And before there was a town, the area witnessed the passage of Spanish soldiers, priests, and colonizers. On *El Camino Real* between Chihuahua and Santa Fe, it was perhaps first visited by the Chamuscado-Rodríguez expedition of 1581–82. Juan de Oñate arrived in 1598 on his way north to establish (June 11) the first Spanish capital in New Mexico at the Tewa village of Yugeuingge.

A state monument, the plaza is being preserved—and in part restored—as a charmingly sleepy reminder of Mesilla's past greatness.

Painting by Albert J. Fountain showing the plaza at Mesilla in 1854 as the United States takes formal possession of the Gadsden Purchase.

Courtesy Mrs. Elizabeth Fountain Armendariz and the Gadsden Museum

Newly restored plaza at Mesilla with San Albino Church in the background.

Courtesy New Mexico Tourism

Pembina North Dakota

Pembina—where the Pembina River joins the Red River of the North—is the cradle of white settlement in North Dakota. At this site in 1797, Charles Chaboillez established the state's first trading post. Shortlived, it was replaced in 1801 by another North West post under Alexander Henry, Jr. With rival Hudson's Bay and X Y posts near by, Pembina was soon the scene of vicious competition and unscrupulous trading. One of Henry's journal entries reads: "Feb. 9, 1806. Men and women have been drinking a match for three days and nights, during which it has been drink, fight—drink, fight—drink, and fight again—guns, axes, and knives their weapons—very disagreeable."

Colonization of the Red River Valley was started in 1812 by the Earl of Selkirk. At Fort Daer, a fortified cluster of cabins and storehouses, the ill-fated Selkirkers, mostly Scotch and Irish peasants, had a hard time of it. They did, however, establish a church—and North Dakota's first school, with some sixty children, white, and halfblood. ("Half-breeds" to the disapproving English, *métis* to the more indulgent French, these colorful mixed bloods tended to congregate in the valley, where they lived primarily by trapping and buffalo hunting.) Then in 1822, four years after the area became United States territory, Fort Daer was dismantled and the Selkirkers were ordered to Winnipeg. The 350 who chose to remain continued "Pembina" as the valley's first American settlement.

Two events in 1823 strengthened their decision. In May, the *Virginia* steamed into Mendota (*q.v.*) to open navigation on the Upper Mississippi. Two months later, Stephen H. Long's expedition arrived in Pembina to erect a row of oak posts along the international boundary, but the distinctive Red River cart had already made them unnecessary. "Men now go for buffalo meat with small, low carts," Henry noted in 1801, "the wheels of which are of one solid piece sawed from the ends of trees whose diameter is three feet." Cheap, durable, and perfectly adaptable to the flatlands, they revolutionized buffalo hunting, fur trading, and life in the Northwest in general. The first six-cart train blazed the Red River Trail to St. Paul in 1844. By 1860 as many as six thousand carts—improved to carry eight hundred pounds of buffalo robes, pemmican (from 1820 to 1870 the colorful spring and fall buffalo hunts were a unique feature of the Pembina scene), grain, and trade goods—were sent south annually from the Red River settlements.

Agriculture developed apace. In 1851, Minnesota's visiting territorial governor, Alexander Ramsey, was surprised to find a community of 1,134, largely métis, cultivating more than 2,000 acres and owning hundreds of horses and cattle.

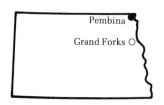

Pembina in 1822, from a water color by Peter Rindisbacher. The view is to the west across the Red River.

Courtesy Public Archives of Canada

A cut-down section of one of these four officers' buildings at Fort Pembina (1870–1895) stood until recently, the last structure on a site related to the fur trade from as early as 1797.

Courtesy North Dakota Historical Society

An old Red River ox cart now preserved in the Minnesota Historical Society Museum at St. Paul. These cheap, durable carts revolutionized life in the Northwest at the beginning of the nineteenth century.

Courtesy Minnesota Historical Society

Fort Mandan North Dakota

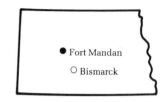

Alexander Henry, Jr., of the North West Company visited the Mandan Indians about 1800, shortly after they had moved to a site near the mouth of Knife River (below present-day Stanton, North Dakota) from their former villages some sixty miles down the Missouri (*see* Fort Abraham Lincoln). "The whole view was agreeable," he said of their earthen lodges and farmlands, "and had more the appearance of a country inhabited by a set of savages." Previously the friendly and generous Mandans had been visited by David Thompson (1797), James McKay (1787), and possibly Pierre Gaultier de Varennes, Sieur de La Vérendrye (1738). It was logical, then, that the Lewis and Clark expedition, being well received by the Mandans, should decide to spend the winter of 1804–1805 with them.

William Clark describes the establishment of the fort: "This Morning [November 2] at Daylight I . . . proceeded down the river three miles & found a place well Supld. with wood. . . . [November 3] we commence building our Cabins . . . the men were indulged with a Dram, this evening. . . . [November 4] we continued to cut down trees and raise our houses, a Mr. Chaubonie . . . Came to See us . . . this man wished to hire as an interpiter. . . . [November 6] Continue to build the huts, out of Cotton-[wood] Timber, &c. this being the only timber we have. . . . [November 10] continued to build our fort. . . . [November 16] a verry white frost . . . all the men move into the huts which is not finished."

Four days later, however, the fort was completed, and a well-nigh impregnable structure it was, according to François Antoine Larocque, the North West Company trader. "Arrived at Fort Mandan," he wrote on December 16, "which is Constructed in a triangular form Ranges of houses Making two Sides, & a Range of amazing large Pickets; the front; The whole is made so Strong as to be almost, Cannon Ball proof."

On April 7, 1805, the expedition set out up the river in two pirogues and six canoes. On August 17, 1806, on their return to St. Louis, Clark landed "to view the old works" and discovered "the houses except one in the rear bastion was burnt by accident, some pickets were standing in front next to the river."

Although the fort was gone, the expedition itself had been an eminent success, with at least part of the credit due "interpiter" Touissant Charbonneau (Clark's "Mr. Chaubonie") and his wife, Sacagawea (*see* Fort Manuel). The Snake (Shoshone) girl, then perhaps only sixteen, had been captured by the Minnetarees near Three Forks (*q.v.*) and brought to the fort, where the French trader had bought and married her. Here, six weeks after Christmas, "Jene Baptiest" (*see* Pompeys Pillar) was born.

The Interior of the Hut of a Mandan Chief, *by Karl Bodmer (1833). Lewis and Clark located Fort Mandan on the left (north) bank of the Missouri River near one of the friendly Mandans' fortified villages. The Missouri has removed all traces of the fort.*

Courtesy Library of Congress

Mandan earth-lodge village on the Missouri at the time of the bull dance, from a painting by George Catlin (1832).

Courtesy U.S. National Museum

174

Fort Union North Dakota

On August 4, 1867, the crew of the steamboat *Miner* broke up the old kitchen at Fort Union for fuel. General demolition of the trading post began August 7, and thus disappeared one of the West's most historic structures. Established in 1828 by Kenneth McKenzie of the American Fur Company as Fort Floyd (on the north bank of the Missouri about three miles above the mouth of the Yellowstone) and renamed Fort Union in 1830, it was a formidable structure physically, a popular rendezvous for travelers socially, and one of the most important fur trading houses in the United States commercially. It played a dominant role in the development of the Upper Missouri Basin for forty years.

McKenzie ruled Fort Union in regal splendor, his pomp and ceremony earning him the title "King of the Missouri." And Union's guest register over the years reads like a *Who's Who in the Frontier West*. George Catlin stopped to paint the fort in 1832, as did Karl Bodmer in 1833. With Bodmer was Prince Maximilian, who saw "the handsome American flag, gilded by the last rays of the evening, floating in the azure sky, while a herd of horses grazing animated a peaceful scene."

Nathaniel J. Wyeth visited the fort in 1833, too. (It was he who reported McKenzie's still to government officials at Fort Leavenworth.) Other notables include Auguste Chouteau and Fr. Pierre Jean De Smet (1840), John James Audubon (1843), Jim Bridger (1844), the Pacific Railway Exploring Expedition with Isaac I. Stevens and the artist John Mix Stanley (1853), and the fantastic hunting expedition of Sir George Gore (1856).

June 17, 1832, was an important day in the life of Fort Union, marking the arrival of the first steamboat, the *Yellowstone*. Five years later, on June 24, the *St. Peter's* docked, a memorable day, too, for aboard it was smallpox (*see* Fort Clark). The resulting plague ran well into 1838 and ravaged the various Indian tribes for hundreds of miles around.

Audubon, whose 1843 visit found the post in its heyday, left a detailed description of the 200-foot-square structure. He mentions the 20-foot pickets "of large hewn cottonwood, and founded upon stone," the two stone bastions "over 30 feet high," the 3-foot-thick whitewashed wall, the two 25-foot flagstaffs "on which wave the proud Eagle of America," the bourgeois' weatherboarded home, "painted white, and with green window-shutters," the icehouse, and the substantial powder magazine.

By August 1864, however, when Gen. Alfred H. Sully moved a company of infantry into the fort, it was "an old dilapidated affair, almost falling to pieces." The star of Fort Union—and the fur trade—had set.

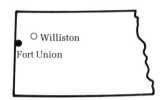

Fort Union in 1853, from a lithograph by John Mix Stanley. Goods are being distributed to the Assiniboins. The fur trade had long since reached its peak, and when near-by Fort Buford was established in 1866, the post was abandoned to the Indians.

Courtesy University of Oklahoma Library

This flagstaff is the first stage of the reconstruction now underway at the Fort Union Trading Post National Historic Site.

Courtesy National Park Service

Fort Clark   North Dakota

John James Audubon came up the Missouri River in 1843, found Fort Clark "a poor miniature representation of Fort Pierre" (*q.v.*). The similarity was logical, since both were important American Fur Company posts. With Fort Union (*q.v.*), they buttressed the company's long-time trade monopoly in this region. James Kipp started construction in the fall of 1830, and palisades were erected the following spring. (The post was not abandoned until the early 1860's.) Only archaelogical remains mark the site today.

To Fort Clark as factor, in 1834, came Francis A. Chardon, best known for the revealing journal he kept until May 1839. From it, says National Park Service historian Ray H. Mattison, we get "a very illuminating picture of the sordid life at that outpost as well as the methods of the American Fur Company in its relations with the Indians." (Chardon apparently had a penchant for taking Indian wives—he had three of them—and killing rats. He kept close count of the latter. In the summary of his first fourteen months at the post he notes that he has killed "1056 House Rats and have Made a Fine Boy who I have named Andrew Jackson in Honour of the Old Gentleman." The late Bernard DeVoto is perhaps justified in seeing "a clear symbolism" in the inventory.)

Chardon's journal is particularly valuable because it chronicles the devastating smallpox epidemic of 1837. The pestilence was carried up the Missouri that summer aboard the steamboat *St. Peter's,* which stopped at Fort Clark on June 19. On July 14 the first Mandan died and by August 11 they were dying so fast that Chardon could no longer keep an accurate count. On September 19 he guessed at least 800 Mandans had died. By the end of the year their population, an estimated 1,600 in June, had dropped to about 100. (As the epidemic pushed up the Missouri to other tribes, an estimated 15,000 Indians died.)

> In my young days there were no white men, and we knew no wants. . . . The white people came, they brought with them some good, but they brought smallpox, and they brought evil liquors; the Indians since diminish and they are no longer happy.

Thus, briefly and poignantly, did one Indian chief evaluate the white man's influence. Certainly liquor and smallpox were twin scourges, particularly along the Missouri. And the fur trade bears a heavy responsibility for introducing them both—the first deliberately, as an accepted merchandising technique, the second admittedly by chance. Fort Clark, then (although, unlike Fort Union, it never operated its own still), serves as something of a symbol for both evils and for their tragic consequences.

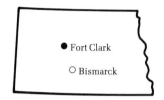

Mandans on the Frozen Missouri, *by Karl Bodmer. Fort Clark is in the background. Maximilian, who accompanied Bodmer (they spent the winter of 1833–34 here), described the post: "The front and back of the square are forty-four paces in length, the sides, forty-nine paces [132x147 feet]. The northern and southern corners have block-houses; the buildings are of one story, and they are just erecting a new one, with a couple of rooms, having good glass windows."*

Courtesy North Dakota State Historical Society

Entrance to the site of Fort Clark, now Fort Clark State Historic Site, on the west bank of the Missouri River nine miles below Stanton, North Dakota. One can still trace the outline of the stockade and find evidence of the Mandan earth lodges that once surrounded it.
Courtesy North Dakota State Historical Society

178

Fort Berthold North Dakota

On September 4, 1868, Gen. Philippe Regis de Trobriand recorded that

this morning seven Sioux, believing themselves sufficiently protected by the river, came to the bank opposite Berthold, more through bravado than anything else, and fired some shots at those of our Indians who were on the bank on this side. Immediately the warriors of the Gros Ventres, Rees, and Mandans ran for their horses and crossing in bullboats over the Missouri, gave chase to the imprudent seven. They caught up with one of them . . . killed, scalped, and mutilated him. . . . There will be dances and rejoicing at Berthold for a week.

Skirmishes between the Sioux and the Fort Berthold Indians (the so-called Three Affiliated Tribes) were more than routine for Like-a-Fishhook Village. They were, in fact, its *raison d'être* and that of the complex of trading posts, military forts, Indian agencies, and missions which subsequently developed along this stretch of the Missouri River northwest of Bismarck.

Long the separate masters of the Dakotas, the three tribes were greatly reduced in numbers by the smallpox epidemic in 1837 (*see* Fort Clark). Thus weakened, they were soon forced by mounting pressure from Sioux and whites to seek a new home and, eventually, to unite for common protection. The Gros Ventres were the first to move, establishing Like-a-Fishhook Village in 1845. Adjacent to it the American Fur Company promptly built stockaded Fort Berthold. The Mandans moved to this area a few years later, the Arikaras around 1860.

Meanwhile, in 1859, Fort Atkinson had been established, a rival trading post some 200 yards south of Berthold. When the AFC bought out its competitor in 1862, it moved into Atkinson, renaming it Fort Berthold. This second post, 120 feet square, perched on the lower end of a high bluff midway between the village and the river. Here, in 1864, Gen. Alfred H. Sully left a company of infantry. Troops remained at Fort Berthold until the summer of 1867, when they were transferred to newly established Fort Stevenson some 18 miles downstream. (In addition to protecting the Three Affiliated Tribes, Stevenson was a vital communications center at the crossroads of the river route to Fort Benton, Montana, and the overland route from St. Paul, Minnesota.)

The Fort Berthold Agency was established in 1868, the first Fort Berthold Mission in 1876. As for Fort Berthold itself, much of the old post was destroyed by fire in October 1874. Like-a-Fishhook Village, beginning to decline soon afterward, had ceased to exist by the end of the century.

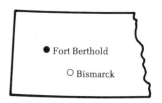

Fort Berthold, as painted by Gen. Philippe Regis de Trobriand, who commanded near-by Fort Stevenson from 1867 to 1869. A French aristocrat by birth, he was equally skilled as a writer and as an artist.

Courtesy North Dakota State Historical Society

Standing figures mark the outside perimeter of the Fort Berthold trading post. The Smithsonian Institution excavated the site before it was flooded by the waters of Garrison Reservoir.

Courtesy National Park Service

Fort Abercrombie North Dakota

George Catlin had written the epitaph:

Dakota is that part of the Great Plains which is and ever must be useless.

And for a time following the Sioux uprising on August 18, 1862, few at Fort Abercrombie would have quibbled with him. In 48 hours some 2,000 white settlers had been killed and more than 300 women and children taken captive. In a territory 200 miles long by 50 miles wide, stretching from south-central Minnesota into the Dakotas, more than $3,000,000 worth of property had been destroyed. Fort Abercrombie itself had been under siege (lifted September 23 with the arrival of 350 infantrymen from Fort Snelling), the area around it devastated. By 1863, hardly a cabin or human being remained in the Red River Valley from Abercrombie north to Pembina (*q.v.*).

The fort was established on the west bank of the Red River on March 3, 1857 (troops arrived August 28, 1858), and named for its builder, Lt. Col. John J. Abercrombie. The first federal post in what is now North Dakota and the most westerly outpost of the settlers' advance during the following decade, it became the logical gateway to the largely unexplored plains of the Northwest.

The paddle-wheeler *Anson Northrup*, negotiating the tortuous 417 river miles between Abercrombie and Fort Garry (Winnipeg) in 1859, gave the fort one of its more dramatic developments. (The ship had been dismantled in Mississippi River headwaters, carted and sledded overland to the Red for reassembling.) But for all the high hopes of its promoters, steamboating on the Red was short lived. More important by far, to both Fort Abercrombie and Dakota Territory, were overland supply and communication routes, the most significant being Fort Totten Trail.

From Fort Snelling (St. Paul), military headquarters for the Department of Dakota in the post-Civil War years, Fort Totten Trail ran west through Forts Abercrombie, Totten, Stevenson, and Buford to Fort Benton (*q.v.*). Hostile Sioux vied with blizzards to harry mail carriers along the way. Although a contract was once issued for a pony express between Abercrombie and Fort Benton, men on snowshoes—and dog teams—were used the winter of 1867–68 to maintain communications. The fort was also on two of the three trails used by the creaking cart trains on the Red River Trail between Pembina and St. Paul.

Fort Abercrombie in 1870 was the scene of the treaty between the Chippewas and the Sioux that freed eastern Dakota Territory of most Indian troubles. Soon settlers in covered wagons were rolling westward, and the fort was no longer needed. It was abandoned in 1877.

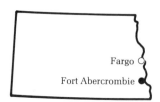

Fort Abercrombie in 1863, showing the stockade added after the Sioux attack of the preceding fall. Defenders fought off that five-week siege with a breastwork of cordwood eight feet high.

Courtesy Minnesota Historical Society

Fort Abercrombie State Historic Site, showing the reconstructed palisades and blockhouse. The site also includes a small museum.

Courtesy North Dakota Travel Division

182

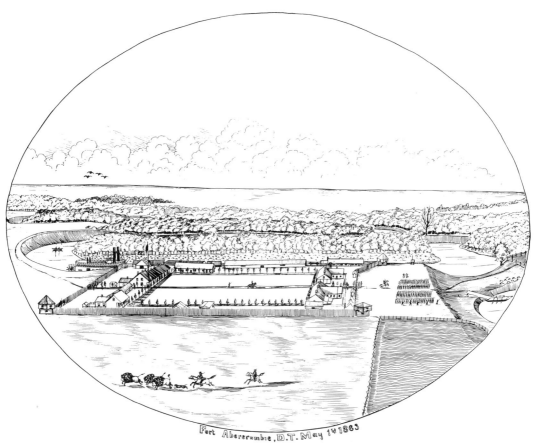

Fort Abercrombie, D.T. May 1st 1863

Fort Rice North Dakota

Gen. Philippe Regis de Trobriand, visiting the important Upper Missouri post of Fort Rice (forty-four miles below modern Bismarck) in 1867, was not impressed:

On a raised point on the right bank of the river stands a square enclosure of palisades with block-houses projecting from two of its corners. This is Fort Rice. Outside are built several traders' cabins; inside, four companies of the Twenty-second, commanded by Lieutenant Colonel Otis, have their quarters, cramped. . . . The officers' quarters are cabins of squared logs, chinked with clay; one-storied, whitewashed inside, and of very poor appearance.

The fort, established July 7, 1846, by Gen. Alfred H. Sully as a base for his First Northwest Expedition against the Sioux, had more serious worries. From October 1864 to May 1865, eighty-one men had died—only eight killed by Indians, but thirty-seven by scurvy. (Not until 1873, when the daily vegetable allowance was raised to sixteen ounces, was the disease curbed.)

In 1868, however, the original dirt-roofed log buildings were replaced by more substantial ones of frame or sawed logs, some lined with adobe and sporting shingled roofs. An active post throughout its fourteen-year existence (abandonment came November 25, 1878), its garrison averaged 235 men. Although Indians occasionally raided the horse and cattle herds, the fort was never assaulted.

The most significant event in the history of Fort Rice was the great peace council with the Sioux in July 1868. Fr. Pierre Jean De Smet had assisted the War Department and the Indian Bureau in getting the various bands together, even going to Powder River to make a special appeal to Sitting Bull (the "Black Robe" gave him a brass-and-wood crucifix, which he prized highly the rest of his life, although he never professed Catholicism), but the Sioux leader would not attend the council. Instead he sent his chief lieutenant, Gall, whom he instructed to say: "Move out the soldiers, and stop the steamboats and we shall have peace."

The result of the council—despite Sitting Bull's absence and his subsequent refusal to sign the agreement—was the historic Treaty of 1868. In it the government guaranteed the Sioux their freedom in the territory between the North Platte and the Missouri and Yellowstone rivers. But the discovery of gold in the Black Hills in 1874 (*see* Gordon Stockade) led to violation of the treaty and precipitated the hostilities which ended on the Little Big Horn in June 1876.

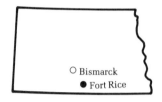

Fort Rice, as painted by Seth Eastman in the early 1870's.

Courtesy The Capitol, Washington, D.C.

Vandals have only recently burned these two reconstructed blockhouses at Fort Rice State Historic Site. Re-reconstruction plans are still incomplete.

Courtesy Margaret Rose

184

Fort Abraham Lincoln North Dakota

Elizabeth B. Custer records the poignant drama of two days in the life of "Custer's Post":

[May 17, 1876] When our band struck up "The Girl I Left Behind Me," the most despairing hour seemed to have come. All the sad-faced wives of the officers who had forced themselves to their doors to try to wave a courageous farewell and smile bravely . . . gave up the struggle at the sound of the music. The first notes made them disappear to fight out alone their trouble and seek to place their hands in that of their Heavenly Father, who, at such supreme hours, was their never failing solace.

[July 5, 1876] The sun rose on a beautiful world, but with its earliest beams came the first knell of disaster. A steamer came down the river bearing the wounded from the battle of the Little Big Horn, of Sunday, June 25. This battle wrecked the lives of twenty-six women at Fort Lincoln, and orphaned children of officers and soldiers joined the cry to that of their bereaved mothers. From that time the life went out of the hearts of the "women who weep," and God asked them to walk on alone and in the shadow.

On May 17 her colorful husband led his Seventh Cavalry, flags flying, band playing, out of the fort. On July 5, after making the 710-mile trip down the Yellowstone and the Missouri in 54 hours, Capt. Grant Marsh and the *Far West* arrived with the wounded of Maj. Marcus A. Reno's command (*see* Custer Battlefield) and news of the Little Big Horn disaster.

Established June 14, 1872, as Fort McKeen—a typical infantry post protected by blockhouses and palisades—and renamed November 19, 1872, Fort Abraham Lincoln (on the west bank of the river four miles south of Bismarck) became a cavalry post when Custer and the Seventh arrived in the fall of 1873 and was expanded the following year to accommodate six companies of cavalry, three of infantry. A few of the buildings were built of logs, but most were frame structures and, in later years, painted dark blue. The post declined rapidly after 1880, and abandonment came July 22, 1891.

Lewis and Clark visited this strategic site at the mouth of the Heart River on the "20th of October Saturday 1804," according to Clark. "After brackfast," he continues, "I walked out on the L. Side to See remains of a village . . . on the Side of a hill . . . the Chief with Too né tells me that nation lived in a [number of] villages I on each Side of the river and the Troublesom Seaux caused them to move to the place they now live [*see* Fort Mandan]."

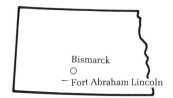

Bismarck
O
— Fort Abraham Lincoln

Fort Abraham Lincoln in the 1870's was not entirely lacking in the amenities: Mrs. Custer staged balls and musicales. Social life was considered "a credit to any city," and for those who preferred less-rarified activities, there was the Point, a little settlement of dance halls and saloons on the opposite bank of the Missouri.

Courtesy Minnesota Historical Society

Reconstructed blockhouse and Mandan earth lodge at Fort Abraham Lincoln State Park.

Photos by Kevin Jeffrey Courtesy North Dakota Tourism

Chateau de Mores North Dakota

What guide California Joe (with the W. P. Jenney exploratory expedition of 1875) foresaw for western Dakota Territory also held true for much of the Great Plains:

There's gold from the grass roots down, but there's more gold from the grass roots up. No matter how rich the gold placers in the Black Hills may prove to be, the great business in this region in the future will be stockraising.

In the 1870's and 1880's the cattleman was king across the vast, unfenced grasslands of America's mid-section. From West Texas to Montana, stock raising became big business as giant cattle companies carved sprawling empires out of the "Great American Desert."

The Medora area, on the Little Missouri River in the Badlands, was in the center of one of the last great natural pastures to be opened to cattlemen. Here in 1883 came two colorful, high-spirited young men.

The Marquis de Mores, French born and educated, came west with money, a desire for adventure, and a basically sound idea: to slaughter cattle on the range, thus eliminating the expense of shipping live animals to eastern packing plants. He bought land, founded Medora, formed the Northern Pacific Refrigerator Car Company, and built a packing plant. Operations began in October 1883, employing at their peak 150 cowboys on the range and another 150 men in the plant. In 1880 more than 6,000 tons of ice were cut from the Little Missouri and stored in icehouses.

For a number of reasons—cut-rate competition from eastern packers, public preference for grain-fed beef, his own inexperience and personal unpopularity—the Marquis' experiment failed (last slaughter: November 1886), as did his attempt to establish a Medora-Deadwood stage line. The chimney of the packing plant and the lavishly furnished Chateau de Mores remain as dramatic symbols of his dream.

Theodore Roosevelt, then twenty-five, was Medora's second noteworthy citizen. Arriving in 1883 to hunt buffalo, he bought the Maltese Cross cattle and brand within three weeks and established his Elkhorn Ranch on the Little Missouri the following summer. Like the Marquis, he added spirit and color to the scene while suffering sharp financial setbacks. The disastrous winter of 1886–87 (the "big die-up" that wiped out many cattle outfits—the Hash-Knife alone lost sixty-five thousand head—and ended the cattle empire's boom days) cost him perhaps three-fourths of his herd, yet he wrote later: "I never would have been President if it had not been for my experience in North Dakota." His ranches (sold in 1897) are now included in Theodore Roosevelt National Park.

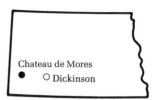

Chateau de Mores
● ○ Dickinson

Chateau de Mores in the 1880's, a striking symbol of cattle-empire opulence. Built by the Marquis for his beautiful wife, Medora, the French-appointed mansion had twenty-six rooms.

Courtesy North Dakota State Historical Society

The lavishly furnished Chateau de Mores is now a state monument. It and the chimney of the Marquis' packing plant are all that remain of his dream of an integrated cattle empire in North Dakota.

Courtesy North Dakota State Historical Society

188

Fort Gibson Oklahoma

On the east bank of the Grand, just above Three Forks—where the Grand, Verdigris, and Arkansas rivers join—Fort Gibson was established April 21, 1824, by Col. Matthew Arbuckle. Founded originally to check the Osages, the post had an important civilizing influence on the entire Southwest and was a frequent conference site, outfitting point for military and exploratory expeditions, and rendezvous for army officers, government commissioners, writers, artists, missionaries, traders, and adventurers. Until the coming of the railroad in 1872, a score of steamboats piled its landing with supplies destined for transshipment south and west in Texas Road freight wagons.

If Fort Gibson's location was strategically ideal (Lt. James B. Wilkinson recommended the site in 1806), so was it undeniably beautiful. George Catlin saw the fort, in 1834, "in the midst of an extensive and lovely prairie," with tall grass "waving in the breeze and sparkling with daisies, buttercups, roses." Ironically, it was also unhealthful.

To December 1853, a total of 9 officers and 561 privates had died at the post; Gibson was becoming "the graveyard of the army." Crudely built, its green logs decayed rapidly, necessitating constant repairs. The arrival in 1832 of the Mounted Rangers (part of the First U.S. Dragoons in 1834) led to additional construction, but no pattern was followed and in 1844 Inspector General George Croghan was complaining of "buildings scattered about amidst weeds, gardens, patches of corn, old hay stacks, etc." He recommended relocation of the post to a hill on the east and a "well-matured plan not to be deviated from." Work began on permanent stone buildings in 1845, but only one was finished when the fort was abandoned to the Cherokees in September 1857. (Reconstruction was completed during the Civil War when Union forces reoccupied the post. Final abandonment came in 1890.)

Fort Gibson was long a travelers' mecca. Sam Houston arrived in late 1829, between Tennessee and Texas adventures, to run a trading post and marry a Cherokee girl. Visitors in 1832 were Washington Irving and Englishman Charles J. Latrobe, who found "strange scenes and sights daily passing before our eyes" and hunting to "make an English sportsman's mouth water." In 1843, Nathan Boone (son of famed Daniel) left Gibson for his trip to the Great Salt Plains.

The post's most colorful event came in June 1834. Before a great gathering of Cherokees, Osages, and Choctaws, the Seventh Infantry and the First U.S. Dragoons were reviewed by Gen. Henry H. Leavenworth. James Hildreth called it a "novel and thrilling scene," with each company of dragoons strikingly mounted on horses of different colors.

Fort Gibson in 1868, from a water color by Vincent Colyer. Post commanders were resourceful in combating drunkenness. One offender was made to stand on the head of a barrel with an empty bottle in each hand, a board around his neck reading "Whiskey Seller."

Courtesy Edward Eberstadt & Sons, New York

At Fort Gibson, now reconstructed and owned by the Oklahoma Historical Society, the Seminoles on March 28, 1833, signed a treaty in which they agreed to move in with the Creeks of Indian Territory.

Courtesy Jim Argo

Fort Towson   Oklahoma

The observer (1837): Presbyterian missionary Cyrus Kingsbury. The object of his fulsome praise: Fort Towson, established by Col. Matthew Arbuckle in May 1824 on Gates Creek, about seven miles from the Red River (a mile northeast of the present town of Fort Towson).

I have never seen a place where there was a more decided religious influence. Those who have never witnessed the dissipation and almost total disregard of morality and religion among soldiers at our frontier posts can have but a faint conception of the happy change that has been made here.

Others were impressed with Towson's remarkable behavior. In 1834, Gen. Henry H. Leavenworth complimented Lt. Col. J. H. Vose, the commanding officer, on the "highly moral condition of the troops." And ten years later, Methodist missionary W. M. Goode noted: "The establishment is altogether superior to any other I have visited on this frontier in point of neatness and permanence of improvements, comfort and good order, and especially the moral and religious influences among the soldiers." He went on to say that large numbers of "pious" soldiers attended the Sunday services, that the temperance society was flourishing, that two prayer meetings were held each week. (The high moral tone is perhaps all the more remarkable in the light of an 1844 official report on sleeping conditions: "The men, to avoid the bed bugs, which are in countless numbers, sleep either upon the galleries or the floor of their quarters.")

Intended as a stabilizing center of government influence among the recently removed Choctaws—as Fort Gibson (q.v.) was among the Cherokees and Creeks—the first Cantonment Towson consisted of wooden shacks and tents, which were abandoned in June 1829. When it was designated a permanent fort in November 1830, it was substantially constructed. Though unpalisaded, it was long considered the best-built and best-kept military post in the West. When Mary Marcy arrived in 1849 (Capt. Randolph B. Marcy was then the commandant), she found Towson a "beautiful" place, with a large parade and "great walks running in every direction. There are also many trees within the enclosure, which add much to the beauty of the place."

During the Mexican War, Fort Towson was a busy post. Then, as the frontier moved westward, it lost its military importance and was abandoned on June 8, 1854. During the Civil War, however, Confederate troops used the fort. Gen. S. B. Maxey made it his headquarters in 1864. And here, in June 1865, two months after Appomattox, Gen. Stand Watie surrendered his Indian troops, said to have been the last organized Confederate force to do so. The fort fell into ruins soon afterward.

Fort Towson, second in age (by a few months) and importance only to Fort Gibson among early-day military posts in Oklahoma, as re-created by Vinson Lackey. Shown here as it looked about 1845, it was once considered the prettiest post on the southwestern frontier.

Courtesy The Thomas Gilcrease Institute of American History and Art, Tulsa, Oklahoma

Only excavated ruins mark the site of Fort Towson, second oldest military post in Oklahoma. It is now an Oklahoma Historical Society property.

Courtesy Jim Argo

192

Park Hill Oklahoma

Park Hill (four miles south of Tahlequah) was, in the years before the Civil War, an impressive symbol of Indian courage and vision. Here at the tragic end of the Trail of Tears, Cherokee leaders proceeded to re-establish the good life from which they had been uprooted by the white man in the southeastern states. And, ironically enough, the prime mover was a dedicated white missionary, Rev. Samuel Austin Worcester.

Worcester came to Dwight Mission (first among the Cherokees in the West, established in 1830 about twenty miles south of Park Hill) in May 1835. With him was Indian Territory's first printing press. Later that year he moved some fifty miles to the northwest to reopen Union Mission (organized in 1820 for the Osages, closed when they were moved away). At Union Mission, still in 1835, appeared the first book published in Oklahoma, *The Child's Book*. In late 1836, Worcester moved again, founding Park Hill Mission. Set on a pleasantly wooded elevation above the Illinois River, the settlement became almost at once the center of life in this part of the Cherokee Nation.

Worcester built homes for the missionaries and teachers, a boardinghall, and a gristmill and established (July 1837) the Park Hill Press. Here he began publishing parts of the Bible (which he translated, using the Cherokee alphabet devised by Sequoyah in the early 1800's), countless tracts, the *Cherokee Almanac*, and many schoolbooks. (On September 26, 1844, from a Cherokee-owned press in Tahlequah, appeared Oklahoma's first newspaper, the *Cherokee Advocate*, a continuation of the *Cherokee Phoenix*, which had been published in Georgia.)

In November 1846 the Cherokee National Council (the Cherokees' constitution, the first for any tribe, had been adopted at Tahlequah, the Cherokee capital, on September 6, 1839) authorized creation of two seminaries, or high schools. The Female Seminary was built at Park Hill, the Male Seminary a little closer to Tahlequah. Both were three-story brick structures; both opened their doors on May 7, 1851. Before long, Cherokees were studying Greek and Latin, while many of the whites in Indian Territory could not sign their own names.

Tragically, it was another white conflict, the Civil War, that destroyed Park Hill as a cultural center. With their roots in the South, the Cherokees raised troops for the Confederacy. Four years of raiding and pillaging damaged the town so severely that it never fully recovered its former importance. The handsome Murrell House (built in 1844, now a state historical monument) and several old cemeteries (one of which contains the graves of Samuel and Ann Worcester) are about all that remains today of the Cherokee town.

Cherokee Female Seminary in 1852, a year after it was opened. (It is believed that the Cherokees learned brickmaking from a party of Utah-bound Mormons.) Reopened after the Civil War, the school continued to serve the Cherokees until it was destroyed by fire in 1887. Only the brick columns remain standing today.

Courtesy Muriel H. Wright

The Murrell home, built in 1845, is almost the last vestige of the grandeur of the Park Hill community when it was "The Athens of Indian Territory." Now owned by the state, it is open to the public.

Courtesy Jim Argo

194

Boggy Depot   Oklahoma

Old Boggy Depot (fifteen miles southwest of Atoka) was an important Choctaw-Chickasaw town that grew from a log cabin—built in 1837 by Cyrus Harris, who later became governor of the Chickasaw Nation—to a flourishing trade and transportation center and Civil War army post. The name of the town comes from that of Clear Boggy Creek, about one mile west.

The Clear Boggy, Muddy Boggy, and North Boggy streams seem to have been given their names by early French traders, working into this area from Louisiana, who called them *Vazzures* (*vasseuse,* French for "miry" or "boggy"). Americans probably adopted the translation about the time of the exploratory expedition made in 1805 by Dr. John Sibley, who wrote in his report: "We arrived at the mouth of the *Vazzures,* or Boggy River." The "Depot" was added after the Choctaw-Chickasaw treaty of 1837, when the Chickasaws emigrated from the East and were paid annuities at "the Depot on Boggy." The Post Office Department officially named the town in 1849. A boundary treaty in 1855 placed it in the Choctaw Nation.

With the establishment of Fort Washita (*q.v.*) in 1842, the Fort Smith–Boggy Depot Road became increasingly important. The north-south Texas Road also passed through Boggy Depot, and by the 1850's the settlement was thriving. Several large two-story residences were built. The town's church, erected in 1840 by Rev. Cyrus Kingsbury (the "Father of the Choctaw Missions," who came from Mississippi with the tribe in the 1830's), served as the Choctaw capitol in 1858 when Chief Basil LeFlore ordered the National Council to meet there temporarily during a factional dispute. The third week in September of 1858 saw the arrival of the first coach of the famed Butterfield Overland Mail Company. Boggy Depot was then the largest and most important settlement between Fort Smith and Sherman, Texas.

The Confederates made Boggy Depot a military post during the Civil War and the Stars and Bars floated from a flagpole in the center of the town for four years. (There is a long row of Confederate graves in the cemetery.) Incongruously, the Indian troops fighting for the South liked to gallop at full speed around the flag, whooping and yelling and singing the Choctaw war song. Boggy Depot remained important after the war, but when the Missouri-Kansas-Texas Railroad, building through Indian Territory in 1872, bypassed the town, it declined sharply. Traces of the main streets, along with tree-choked foundations, abandoned wells, and cement cisterns, are still visible, but the town's last important landmark, the home of Chief Allen Wright, was destroyed by fire in 1952.

Boggy Depot was the home of Chief Allen Wright, who suggested the name Oklahoma *(Choctaw for "red people") for the proposed Indian Territory. His house, shown here as it looked in 1940, was built in 1860, burned to the ground in 1952.*

Courtesy Muriel H. Wright

The cemetery—containing the graves of Chief Allen Wright, Rev. Cyrus Kingsbury, and other prominent pioneers—is all that remains of once-important Boggy Depot. The site is now a state recreation area, and markers have been erected to locate the various points of historical interest.

Courtesy Jim Argo

Fort Washita Oklahoma

Fort Washita was established April 23, 1842, on the Washita River near its confluence with the Red (now on the east bank of Lake Texoma fourteen miles northwest of Durant) by "Old Rough and Ready" Zachary Taylor, then commander of this district. Construction fulfilled treaty obligations to protect the Choctaws and Chickasaws, recently removed to Indian Territory, from the Comanches and other troublesome Plains Indians farther to the west. The post was never attacked, however, and its period of greatest importance came with the discovery of gold in California. On the main road from Fort Smith to El Paso, it served as a rendezvous for emigrant parties preparing for the dreaded trip across the Texas "desert."

Though planned as a permanent post, Fort Washita was comparatively crude at first. In June 1844 the Inspector General found "temporary huts of round logs, placed without regard to order." However, he considered the men's quarters "convenient and comfortable." Built of oak logs hewn on the inside "with no eye to permanency, they will nevertheless answer every purpose [until] the erection of barracks of a better and more durable description." And the mess was better than that at most posts, with the gardens furnishing "a variety and abundance of fine vegetables."

The setting was pleasant, too. The countryside was "very pretty," Mary Marcy wrote in 1850. (She found little else to praise. Her husband, Capt. Randolph B. Marcy, who combined exploring and writing with soldiering, was in and out—mostly out—of the fort for many years, leaving here on April 22, 1852, to begin his important exploration of Upper Red River.) Assistant Surgeon Rodney Glisan appreciated the "lonely, undulated prairies, covered with nature's carpet of green grass and wild flowers in profusion." He thought it a "magnificent country . . . a future home of thousands of agriculturists." And Capt. George B. McClellan, with Marcy's 1852 expedition, wrote: "Washita is a very beautiful place. It is built in a clump of trees on a knoll in the prairies—good quarters and nobody near it."

By this time it had been vastly improved. The surge of California-bound gold seekers had prompted construction of massive stone buildings. The gold rush was nearly over, however, before they could be completed. In the 1850's, Washita watched the flow of settlers into Texas. Then, as new forts marked the westward movement of the frontier, its importance dwindled. And on May 1, 1861, when Confederate forces appeared at the gates, the garrison—four troops of cavalry—surrendered the post and rode away. The South used it until 1865. Fort Washita was never again occupied by U.S. troops.

Fort Washita, established in 1842, as pictured behind its stone wall in Harper's Weekly, March 16, 1861. Near here in 1834, Gen. Henry H. Leavenworth was fatally injured in a buffalo hunt. Col. Henry Dodge assumed command of the Dragoon Expedition (which included Lt. Jefferson Davis and George Catlin) and west on to Devil's Canyon and a peace conference with the Plains Indians.

Courtesy University of Oklahoma Library

Ruins of Fort Washita's imposing stone barracks, constructed about 1850 of shell limestone quarried nearby. The remains of several dozen buildings dot the 115-acre site, now owned by the Oklahoma Historical Society. A reconstructed barracks serves as visitors' center and museum.

Courtesy Jim Argo

Camp Supply Oklahoma

Camp Supply, located where Wolf and Beaver Creeks join to form the North Canadian River, was just that: an advanced base of operations for Gen. Philip H. Sheridan's 1868 campaign against the Cheyennes and Arapahos. Gen. Alfred H. Sully established it in November with five companies of the Third Infantry under Capt. John H. Page, who supervised the construction. A supply train of 450 wagons was sent down from Fort Dodge (q.v.) with building materials. Accompanying the expedition was Lt. Col. George A. Custer, recently reinstated from a disciplinary suspension, with eleven troops of the Seventh Cavalry. Impatient, as ever, Custer promptly left the site, pushed on southward in a snowstorm to overwhelm Black Kettle's sleeping Cheyenne camp in the so-called Battle of the Washita on November 27.

Gen. Sheridan was on hand a day or two later when Custer marched gaily into Camp Supply, with the band playing *Garry Owen* and long lines of silent Indian women and children. Many more women and children were killed, with the men, along the Washita. Scout California Joe was asked if it was much of a fight. "You may call it fightin' but I calls it wipin' out the varmints." The massacre helps to explain the ferocity of the Cheyennes who joined the Sioux on the Little Big Horn eight years later.)

Although not abandoned until 1893, Camp Supply was never considered a permanent post, hence it never received another name. Its temporary nature was reflected by its buildings. "This place is quite as dreadful as it has been represented to us," wrote Frances M. Rae, an officer's wife, in 1872. Her house had a pole-and-dirt roof. The dining room floor was sand, "and almost every night little white toadstools grow up all along the base of the log walls." The walls themselves sheltered an "army of bugs that hide underneath the bark during the day and march upon us at night."

For all its crudity, the post managed for its first Thanksgiving (1868) a dinner one trooper described as "worthy of all praise as an exhibition of the culinary art." Meats included wild turkey, buffalo hump and tongue, antelope, red and "common" deer, rabbit, quail, and "Pinnatted Grouse." Desserts included rice pudding, pies, and tarts. From soup (wild turkey) to wines and liquors (champagne, "Pinetop Whiskey," ale), it was a remarkable banquet. But then the fort was located in a "red man's paradise." Game was so plentiful that "every one soon became surfeited, and returned to salt meat with an evident relish."

Near Camp Supply ran the famed Western Trail, over which, from 1874 to 1893, an estimated seven million cattle and horses were driven northward from Texas to railheads in Kansas (*see* Fort Dodge).

Camp Supply, as sketched by A. R. Waud for Harper's Weekly, February 27, 1869. Described as "one of the most defensible works of its kind on the plains," it was constructed of heavy timber (cut near by) and surrounded by stockade ten feet high.

Courtesy University of Oklahoma Library

Abandoned in 1893, Fort Supply was turned over to Oklahoma Territory and became Western State Hospital in 1903. Early-day buildings still standing include the original guardhouse, a teamster's cabin (below), and "Custer House."

Courtesy Jim Argo

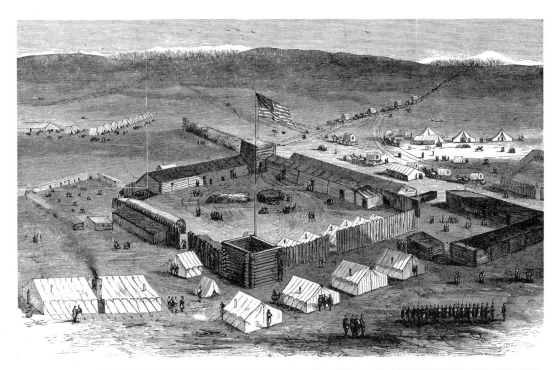

Fort Sill Oklahoma

"In my humble judgment," Capt. Randolph B. Marcy wrote July 19, 1852, "a military post established in the vicinity of these mountains, and garrisoned by a force of sufficient strength to command the respect of the Indians would add [greatly] to the efficiency of the army . . . in western Texas." His judgment was sound, although it was not until January 8, 1869, that Gen. Philip H. Sheridan staked out Camp Wichita (for an abandoned Wichita Indian village) along Medicine Bluff Creek. As Fort Sill (which it became on July 2, honoring Gen. Joshua W. Sill), it played a long and important role in the pacification of the nomadic Southern Plains tribes.

Ironically, the Indians lost, along with their land, the "good medicine" of near-by Medicine Bluff, a 300-foot-high granite and porphyry ridge that was for young braves a semisacred retreat for fasting and meditation. Soon its low stone altar would give way, as a symbol of the area, to the post guardhouse, where in bitter defeat were housed such famed Kiowa warriors as Satanta, Satank, and Big Tree and the Apaches' Geronimo.

Gen. Benjamin H. Grierson directed construction of the fort. With the nearest railroad three hundred miles away and mail from Washington often requiring two weeks, he depended primarily on his own resources. A sawmill, quarry, and limekilns were established, and soldiers performed most of the chores. Work began early in 1870. (First structure completed: the still preserved corral, loopholed for defense.) By October 1 the post boasted storehouses, commissary, post headquarters, one barrack—and the Fort Sill Jockey Club. By mid-spring of 1871 the other buildings were completed and occupied. Together they formed a prepossessing, if bleak, limestone square. By the 1880's, however, the post had become something of a stone village of lawns, gardens, and picket fences.

Although Fort Sill was never attacked, the Southern Plains Indians on and off the reservation were long restless and hostile. In 1873–74 alone sixty persons were reported killed in the region. Their strongest effort against the whites came in June 1874 with the disastrously unsuccessful assault on a camp of buffalo hunters at Adobe Walls in the Texas Panhandle. That summer a strong column of troops under Lt. Col. John W. Davidson used Fort Sill as a base of operations against the hostiles. The last important resistance was that of the famed Quanah Parker and the Quahada Comanches. They surrendered in June 1875, the last of the southern tribes to yield to the inevitable.

In 1905, with the frontier vanished, Fort Sill was extensively rebuilt and expanded as an artillery center. Today, with most of its old buildings still preserved, it is an important guided-missile center.

Barracks at southeast corner of the Old Post quadrangle shortly after completion. Although built as a defensive bulwark against the Plains Indians, Fort Sill had little of the conventional fortress about it. There was no moat, no parapet, no cannon-mounted embattlement, and the stone buildings were not connected to form a stockade.

Courtesy U.S. Army Artillery and Missile Center Museum, Fort Sill

Sprawling over 100,000 acres beyond the northern city limits of Lawton, modern Fort Sill is the nation's Artillery and Guided Missile Center. Many of its early buildings remain, including the stone corral and the old guardhouse (below), both a part of the post's extensive museum. Preserved, too, is the small, ivy-covered Old Chapel, built in 1870.

Courtesy Jim Argo

Darlington Agency

Darlington Agency (on the north bank of the North Canadian River about six miles northwest of El Reno) for the Cheyennes and Arapahos was established in 1870 by Brinton Darlington, the Quaker whom President U.S. Grant appointed Indian agent. Fort Reno (one and a half miles to the southwest on the opposite bank of the river) came into being as a result of the Indian uprising of 1874. Together the two establishments played an important role in preserving the peace and directing the orderly transition of this part of Oklahoma from Indian reservations to white farms and ranches.

Fort Reno was declared a military reservation on July 17, 1874, with the troops quartered temporarily at Darlington. The following July, Agent John D. Miles (who replaced Darlington in 1872, stayed on until 1885) and Capt. T. Wint selected the site for the permanent post. The first regular commandant, Maj. John K. Mizner of the Fourth Cavalry, took charge in 1876. But the frontier was already beginning to change. Troops accompanied the Indians on their annual buffalo hunt that fall, when about 7,000 animals were taken. The 1877 hunt, however, was a failure, with only 219 robes prepared for sale. By 1879 the buffalo, once numbered in the millions, were all gone and the Indians were living on government-issue beef.

Darlington, meanwhile, was developing into an important little settlement and a regular stop on the Chisholm Trail. The agency acquired a post office in 1873. John H. Seger was superintendent of the Indian school and the Mennonites started mission work among the Arapahos a mile to the east in 1881. By this time mail and stage service extended north to Caldwell, Kansas, south to Fort Sill (q.v.), and west to Fort Elliot—and the *Cheyenne Transporter* had become (in 1880) the first newspaper in the western half of Oklahoma.

The area's most dramatic event began with the arrival (on August 5, 1877) of 937 Northern Cheyennes from Montana, rounded up after the Battle of the Little Big Horn. Homesick and ill, they broke away the next year and headed north, led by Little Wolf and Dull Knife. In a remarkable show of courage and military skill—George Bird Grinnell says there were only 60 or 70 fighting men; the rest were old men, women, and children—they eluded the army to reach their old hunting grounds.

Fort Reno soldiers fired the shots (April 22, 1889) that started the "run" of settlers into Oklahoma Territory. On April 19, 1892, the Cheyenne and Arapaho reservation was opened: the frontier had vanished. On February 24, 1908, Fort Reno was abandoned as a military post, and Darlington Agency was moved to near-by Concho in 1909.

An Indian encampment near Darlington Agency. The clarity and dramatic composition of this picture makes it one of the classics of Indian photography.

Courtesy Bethel College Historical Library

Early-day Darlington. The agency, established in 1870, played an important role until well after the opening of the Cheyenne and Arapaho Indian reservation to settlement in 1892.

Courtesy University of Oklahoma Library

Darlington today is a state game farm. When abandoned as a military post in 1908, near-by Fort Reno became Fort Reno Remount Station. This was closed in 1949, and the military reservation has now been returned to the Cheyennes and Arapahos. The commissary and warehouse building shown here was built on the west side of the parade in 1884.

Courtesy Jim Argo

Fort Clatsop Oregon

On December 7, 1805, William Clark recorded that "after brack-fast I delayed about half an hour before York Came up, then pro-ceeded around this Bay which I call . . . Meriwethers Bay the Christian name of Capt. Lewis. . . . This is certainly the most eligable Situation for our purposes of any in its neighbourhood."

From the north shore of the Columbia River (*see* Baker Bay) the expedition was moving to the south shore (two miles from the river, three from the ocean, on what is now the Lewis and Clark River). Here "in a thick groth of pine . . . on a rise about 30 feet higher than the high tides leavel" the party set to work building a log stockade. And Clark was happy to escape the "re-peeted roling thunder" of the roaring seas. (He called it "the Great Western Ocian, I cant say the Pasific as since I have seen it, it has been the reverse.")

Christmas was a special day:

at day light this morning we we[re] awoke by the discharge of the fire arm[s] of all our party & a Selute, Shouts and a Song which the whole party joined in under our windows. . . . we would have Spent this day the nativity of Christ in feasting, had we any thing either to raise our Sperits or even gratify our appetites, our Diner concisted of pore Elk, so much Spoiled that we eate it thro' mear necessity.

Otherwise, the days were filled with household chores (on De-cember 27 Willard and Wiser were dispatched to carry "the Kit-tles &c. to the Ocian" to make salt) and minor inconveniences (fleas so "troublesom that I have slept but little for 2 night[s] past"). The weather was uniformly bad, but the Indians, fortu-nately, were not unfriendly. (On January 27, Lewis notes: "Goodrich has recovered from the Louis Veneri which he con-tracted from an amorous contact with a Chinnook damsel, I cured him . . . by the use of mercury.") Gradually the party set-tled into a monotonous, watchful routine. Then on March 23, 1806, Clark made a final entry:

loaded our canoes & at 1 P. M. left Fort Clatsop on our homeward bound journey, at this place we had wintered and remained from the 7th of Decr. 1805 to this day and have lived as well as we had any right to ex-pect, and we can say that we were never one day without 3 meals of some kind a day . . . notwithstanding the repeated fall of rain.

William Clark's plan of Fort Clatsop. Completed January 1, 1806, the fort was a log stockade fifty feet square. Three rooms on one side faced four on the other across a twenty-foot court.

Courtesy Oregon Historical Society

The reconstructed fort in Fort Clatsop National Memorial, located just off US 101 some eight miles southwest of Astoria, Ore-gon.

Courtesy Oregon Depart-ment of Transportation

Astoria Oregon

Astoria

○ Portland

"This River in my opinion wou'd be a fine place for to set up a *Factory*," wrote John Boit, an officer with Capt. Robert Gray (*see* Baker Bay), in 1792. "The Indians are very numerous, and appear'd very civil (not even offering to steal)." In 1810, John Jacob Astor agreed, organizing the Pacific Fur Company and sending the *Tonquin* around Cape Horn to establish it. The ship arrived in March 1811 and Astor partners Duncan McDougal and David Stuart promptly selected "a handsome and commanding situation, called Point George" (as Ross Cox saw it in 1812). A clearing was made, a log residence, storehouse, and powder magazine erected, and a vegetable garden planted. The post was named Astoria.

(Duncan McDougal, a colorful man, married a daughter of friendly one-eyed Chinook Chief Comcomly. Described as possessing "one of the flattest and most aristocratical heads in the tribe," she appeared for the wedding painted with red clay and annointed with fish oil. But "by dint . . . of copious ablutions, she was freed from all adventitious tint and fragrance, and entered into the nuptial state, the cleanest princess that had ever been known." A resourceful factor, McDougal once saved the besieged fort by threatening to uncork a small bottle. The resulting fear-inspired peace earned him the Indian name "The Great Smallpox Chief.")

In early 1812, Wilson P. Hunt, heading the overland party of Astorians, "swept round an intervening cape, and came in sight of the infant settlement . . . with its magazines, habitations, and picketed bulwarks." When Ross Cox arrived aboard the supply ship *Beaver* in May, the post had "5 proprietors, 9 clerks, and 90 artisans and canoe-men, or . . . *voyageurs*. We brought an addition of 36 . . . so that our muster-roll, including officers, etc. amounted to 140 men."

The War of 1812 brought changes. The North West Company bought the post in 1813 and renamed it Fort George. In 1821 that English fur outfit merged with the Hudson's Bay Company, which moved its headquarters to Fort Vancouver (*q.v.*) in 1824. Astoria became a minor trading post, but by 1841 it had virtually disappeared.

Events, however, proved the prophetic truth of Thomas Jefferson's 1813 tribute to the founder of the post. "I view it [Astoria] as the germ of a great, free, independent empire. . . . It must be still more gratifying to yourself to foresee that your name will be handed down with that of Columbus and Raleigh as the founder of such a empire." In 1846 all of the Northwest below the forty-ninth parallel became American.

The North West Company bought the Pacific Fur Company's post at Astoria in 1813 and renamed it Fort George. It is shown here in a drawing from Franchère's Narrative of a Voyage to the Northwest Coast of America.

Courtesy Oregon Historical Society

John Jacob Astor's trading post of 1811 has blossomed into the bustling port city of Astoria, Oregon. Ships from most of the world's major ports cross the bar at the mouth of the Columbia River, seen in the background.

Courtesy Oregon State Highway Department

Champoeg   Oregon

On July 5, 1843, at the little Willamette River settlement of Champoeg, a group of Oregon pioneers laid the groundwork for American civil government beyond the Rockies:

We, The people of Oregon Territory For purposes of mutual protection, and to secure peace and prosperity among ourselves, Agree to adopt the following Laws & regulations until such time as the U S A extend their jurisdiction over us

This informal declaration, with the detailed organic law that followed, was authorized by an earlier meeting—held, with complete irony, in a corner of the Hudson's Bay Company warehouse and attended by a number of loyal HBC employees. Another so-called Wolf Meeting, it passed over the more prosaic matter of livestock predators to "take into consideration the propriety of taking measures for civil and military protection of this colony." A preliminary resolution to that effect was voted down, but many of those loyal to England then left, and after considerable confusion (there are several versions of the meeting), a second—and favorable—vote was taken, preparing the way for the July 5 declaration.

Champoeg (originally *Cham-poo-ick,* Indian for the edible plant growing there) appears to have been an Indian village, and the Astorians may have started the "Willamette Post" three miles up the river, although evidence is scant and somewhat contradictory. By January 1814, however, Alexander Henry, Jr., found the North West Company's post flourishing at that site and control of the area passed to the Hudson's Bay Company in 1821. Dr. John McLoughlin expanded operations and started raising grain to make the post more self-sufficient. Retired HBC trappers began to settle here with their Indian wives, and American immigrants soon followed. Buildings sprang up along Boulevard Napoleon and Champoeg became one of the Willamette Valley's chief settlements.

After July 5, 1843, the political scene shifted to Oregon City (*q.v.*), but river traffic maintained Champoeg's economic importance. Nationalism remained strong. The July 4 celebration of 1854 saw a gala procession march through the town, then listen attentively as Dr. Edward Shiel read the Declaration of Independence. Later, according to the Salem *Statesman,* "the celebrants enjoyed a sumptuous dinner . . . given beneath the roof where the first celebration took place in Oregon, and where the first laws . . . were enacted. After dinner the guests proceeded on a pleasure excursion . . . on board the steamer *Fenix.*"

Two serious fires and a major flood (December 1861) took their toll. The lower (original) town was finally destroyed by the flood of 1892.

George Gibbs made this pencil sketch of "Champoeg and the prairies beyond" in April 1857.

Courtesy Peabody Museum, Harvard University

The visitor's center at Champoeg State Park architecturally complements the many historic buildings in the Champoeg area.

Courtesy Oregon Department of Transportation

Oregon City Oregon

The 1818 agreement providing for joint occupancy of Oregon Territory by the Americans and the British forced the Hudson's Bay Company to modify its preoccupation with the fur trade. "It becomes an important object to acquire as ample an occupation of the Country and Trade as possible," company officials noted in 1828, "on the South as well as on the North side of the Columbia River." Dr. John McLoughlin, chief factor at Fort Vancouver (*q.v.*), was therefore ordered to set up a sawmill at "the falls of the Wilhamet [south of the Columbia] where the same Establishment of people can attend to the Mill, watch the Fur & Salmon Trade, and take care of a Stock of Cattle."

Several log houses were built on the site (the Willamette River drops forty-two feet here from a basaltic ledge with a crest more than three thousand feet wide) in the winter of 1829–30. By 1832, McLoughlin had blasted out a millrace and constructed a flour mill and sawmill—the first use of water power in Oregon. He ordered the town platted in 1842. As Oregon City, it soon became the chief town of the Oregon country. Here in 1838, Jason Lee founded the Oregon Temperance Society, first of its kind in the region. In 1842 the pioneer Multnomah Circulating Library was organized—with three hundred dollars. The following year saw the cultural scene enriched by the Oregon Lyceum and the Falls Debating Society, which frequently devoted itself to such questions as "Resolved, That it is expedient for the settlers on this coast to establish an independent government."

In June 1844 the first provisional legislature (*see* Champoeg) met here. By 1846, Oregon City had seventy houses and some five hundred inhabitants. That same year, the *Oregon Spectator* began publication and the first Masonic lodge west of the Missouri River was organized. From February to September 1849 the Oregon Exchange Company produced $58,000 in five- and ten-dollar gold pieces, called "beaver money" because each was stamped with a likeness of the animal on which the territory had first developed.

In 1846, Dr. McLoughlin moved his family to the city he had founded almost twenty years before. Having resigned as Hudson's Bay Company factor, he became an American citizen in 1851 and spent the rest of his life operating his store and mills. Although a nationalist minority element embittered his last days with legal battles that took from him much of his original Oregon City land claim, the "Father of Oregon" was vindicated after his death (September 3, 1857). His restored home is now a National Historic Site.

Oregon City in 1845, from a Henry James Warre painting. Chosen as capital of the provisional government in 1843, Oregon City became territorial capital in 1848, remained so until 1852, when the seat of government was moved to Salem.

Courtesy Oregon Historical Society

McLoughlin House National Historic Site preserves the home of the "Father of Oregon," Dr. John McLoughlin, who championed the cause of Oregon and did much to save it for the Union.

Courtesy Oregon State Highway Department

Dr. McLoughlin's home is furnished with period items. This dining-room furniture is said to have seen service at Fort Vancouver, where Dr. McLoughlin was factor for the Hudson's Bay Company.

Courtesy Oregon State Highway Department

Methodist Mission Oregon

Jason Lee was the first missionary to respond to the "Macedonian Call" (*see* Lapwai) of the Nez Percés and Flatheads. With his nephew Daniel and three other men, he came west in 1834, arriving on September 15 at Fort Vancouver, where they "had the pleasure of sleeping again within the walls of a house after a long and fatiguing journey replete with menaces, deprivations, toil and adversity." Dr. John McLoughlin's courtesies did not end with bed and board (a dinner "as good and served in as good style as in any gentleman's house in the east"). After persuading Lee that the Willamette Valley south of Vancouver promised a more fertile field than the Flathead country, he provided a Hudson's Bay Company boat and crew to transport the missionary party to the newly selected site some seventy-five miles up river.

By October 6 work had begun on the mission. Additional workers, arriving in 1837 (thirteen in May, four more in September), found a good farm, well stocked with cattle (McLoughlin had lent Lee eight oxen, the same number of cows and calves, and a bull), and a three-room log house that served for preaching and schooling. McLoughlin and his men sent along a gift of $130, with the hope that "our heavenly father, without whose assistance we can do nothing . . . will vouchsafe to bless and prosper your pious endeavors."

Converts were few, however. The near-by French-Canadian trappers-turned-farmers, who (like McLoughlin) were Catholics, found little appeal in Methodism, and disease wiped out many of the area's Indians, but the mission witnessed two significant developments of a more secular nature. Here on February 17 and 18, 1841, mass meetings (attended by nearly every white male south of the Columbia) were held to appoint a judge to probate the estate of the wealthy Ewing Young, who had died without a will—predators attacking his free-roaming cattle led eventually to the so-called Wolf Meetings (*see* Champoeg)—the first positive step toward self-government in Oregon. Here, too, on February 1, 1842, a called public meeting was held to consider the education of the children of the missionaries. From it emerged Oregon Institute, a "literary and Religious Institution of learning." As Salem's Willamette University, it is the oldest institution of higher learning west of the Rockies.

In the spring of 1841, Methodist Mission was moved up river to Chemeketa (now Salem), where new buildings were erected; the town was platted in 1846. In 1850, with a population of 252—including 7 merchants, 7 blacksmiths, 5 doctors, 4 lawyers, 3 tailors, and 19 carpenters—it was named territorial capital. Salem became state capital in 1859.

Salem in 1858, a year before it was designated capital of the state. Jason Lee moved Methodist Mission here from Mission Bottom in 1842.

Courtesy Oregon State Highway Department

This statue of Jason Lee, at the east end of Oregon State Capitol in Salem, looks south toward Willamette University, directly behind the capitol building.

Courtesy Oregon State Highway Department

REV. JASON LEE
1803 – 1845

FIRST MISSIONARY
IN OREGON
COLONIZER
1834 – 1843

The Dalles Oregon

The Dalles—named by *voyageurs* who saw in the great flat rocks of the Columbia River below the present city of The Dalles a resemblance to French flagstones, *les dalles*—was an important settlement site to Indians for thousands of years. Lewis and Clark called it "the great mart of all this country," stopping (October 1805) "to treat these people verry friendly & ingratiate our Selves with them, to insure us a kind & friendly reception on our return." (Nathaniel J. Wyeth, in 1832, hired about fifty of them "for a quid of tobacco each to carry our boats about 1 mile round the falls.") Astorian Robert Stuart called near-by Celilo Falls "one of the first rate Salmon fisheries on the river. . . . I say that an experienced hand would by assuidity catch at least 500 daily."

Establishment of fur posts on the Lower Columbia made The Dalles a rendezvous for traders and Indians, but the first white settlement was the Methodist mission started by Daniel Lee (*see* Methodist Mission) and H. K. W. Perkins in 1838. (A Catholic mission was begun three years later; according to one observer, the "two missions spent much more time striving against each other instead of striving to save the Indians' souls.") Below Pulpit Rock, a natural formation (Twelfth and Court streets) from which the missionaries first preached, Lee found "a valuable spring of water, some rich land, and a good supply of timber, oak, and pine." Here the mission buildings were erected. "The Indians assisted in cutting the timber, and bringing it upon the spot."

The Whitman Massacre in 1847 (*see* Waiilatpu) led to the abandonment of the mission. Fort Dalles (later called Fort Lee) was promptly established to protect Oregon Trail travel, and by 1852 a town had grown up around the military post. At The Dalles travelers were forced to abandon their trains and take to the Columbia on rafts (*see* Cascades of the Columbia) or, after 1846, take the Barlow Toll Road south around Mount Hood to the Willamette Valley. By this time many of the emigrants were near the end of their resources:

We left our wagon on the Umatilla. . . . We packed our bedding on Old Nig, the last ox left us, and started on afoot. . . . My father sold him [Old Nig] at The Dalles for $20 to buy food. . . . Father found an old stove and rigged up a table out of some old endgates and sideboards of an abandoned wagon and ran a lunch counter for the soldiers and civilians who were building the military post there.

The Dalles, with Mount Hood and Indians drying salmon, as seen by John Mix Stanley in 1853.

Courtesy University of Oklahoma Library

The surgeon's quarters, built in 1858, is all that remains of Fort Dalles, established after the Whitman Massacre in 1847 to protect the increasing flow of travelers on the Oregon Trail. It serves as a museum.

Courtesy Oregon State Highway Department

Fort Dalles in 1867, as photographed by Carleton E. Watkins from across the Columbia River.

Courtesy Oregon Historical Society

Cascades of the Columbia Oregon

A pioneer recalls the rigors of the Barlow Toll Road, blazed in 1846 (*see* The Dalles) to avoid the hazards of the Cascades of the Columbia River:

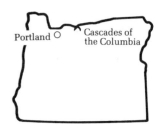
Portland ○   Cascades of the Columbia

Some men's hearts died within them and some of our women sat down by the roadside—and cried, saying they had abandoned all hope of ever reaching the promised land. I saw women with babies but a week old, toiling up the mountains in the burning sun, on foot, because our jaded teams were not able to haul them. We went down mountains so steep that we had to let our wagons down with ropes. My wife and I carried our children up muddy mountains in the Cascades, half a mile high and then carried the loading of our wagons upon our backs by piecemeal, as our cattle were so reduced that they were hardly able to haul up our empty wagons.

Both the road and the rapids were stubborn challenges to the courage and ingenuity of Oregon-bound emigrants. Here in the gorge the river dropped almost forty feet in a churning cataract (now submerged behind Bonneville Dam) formed by great masses of rock and earth from Table Mountain. Occasionally, during spring freshets, skilled Indian paddlers and adventuresome French-Canadian boatment were able to shoot the Cascades rapids, but usually even the most daring disembarked here and portaged their cargoes. Wagons had to be dismembered and loaded on rafts that were guided through the dangerous white water by shore lines.

There were other dangers, too. Writing of Robert Stuart's portage in 1812, Washington Irving noted that "the greatest precautions were taken to guard against lurking treachery or open attack." Lewis and Clark had previously discovered "the Wahclellahs . . . to be great thieves . . . so arrogant and instrusive have they become that nothing but our numbers saves us from attack." (Having learned that they had carried off Lewis' dog, Clark reports that "Three men, well armed, were instantly dispatched . . . with orders to fire if there were the slightest resistance or hesitation." They returned with the dog!)

In 1856 a portage wagon road was constructed on the Oregon side of the river; it was a twisting affair that climbed 425 feet above the Cascades. (Present US 30 has evolved from a narrow, crooked road authorized by the Oregon legislature in 1872.) Increased travel on the Columbia brought construction (in late 1858 or early 1859) of a wooden-railed portage tramway. (A similar railroad was built along the north shore, in Washington, in 1851.) As profits mounted, steel rails replaced the wooden ones and on May 10, 1862, the tramway's mules were retired in favor of the San Francisco-built *Oregon Pony*, the first locomotive to operate in the area north of California.

Cascades of the Columbia—which Washington Irving called "the piratical pass of the river"—as seen in 1853 by John Mix Stanley. The treacherous cataract is now submerged by the waters behind Bonneville Dam.

Courtesy University of Oklahoma Library

The Oregon Pony, *with David Hewes (foreground), who presented the gold spike at Promontory (q.v.). The 1862 locomotive is now on public display at Portland's Union Station.*

Courtesy Southern Pacific Historical Collection

Columbia River Gorge today. The building at right is Vista House, which overlooks the river from the Oregon side.

Courtesy Oregon Department of Transportation

218

Verendrye Hill   South Dakota

Scratched in French on one side of a small lead plate (6½ x 8½ x ³⁄₁₆ inches), the following announcement is firm evidence of the first visit of white men to a gumbo knoll overlooking the Missouri River near present-day Fort Pierre, South Dakota:

Placed by the Chevalier de la Vérendrye
Lo [Louis] Jost [Joseph Vérendrye]
Louis La Londette
 A Miotte
  The 30th March 1743

On the opposite side is a more formal Latin inscription prepared two years before:

In the 26th year of the reign of Louis XV the most illustrious Lord, the Lord Marquis of Beauharnois being viceroy, 1741, Peter de La Vérendrye placed this.

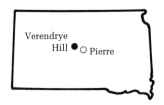

Photograph of the back side of the original Vérendrye plate, now on permanent display at the state museum in Pierre, South Dakota.

Courtesy South Dakota Department of Highways

Marker on Verendrye Hill, overlooking Fort Pierre, and the Missouri River, where the Vérendryes buried a lead plate on March 30, 1743, to claim this region for France.

Courtesy South Dakota Department of Highways

Obviously, few of the details of this important event can be stated categorically, but this much seems certain. Canadian-born (1685) Pierre Gaultier de Varennes, Sieur de La Vérendrye, entered the fur trade early in his life and by 1729 had conceived the idea of a waterway to the Pacific. Two years later he and his three sons—Pierre, Louis, and François—established Fort St. Charles on the Lake of the Woods. By 1738 they had pushed on beyond present-day Winnipeg to build Fort La Reine at Portage la Prairie. That year and again in 1740 various members of the family sought unsuccessfully the westward-leading waterway.

On April 29, 1742, sons Louis and François, with two other men, left Fort La Reine on the third expedition. And on July 2, 1743, after more than a year of wandering about in the Upper Missouri River Valley (never, it is now strongly believed, penetrating beyond the boundaries of what are now North and South Dakota), they returned home, "to the great joy of my father . . . and to our great satisfaction."

Of the burying of the plate, the Vérendrye journal says: "I placed on an eminence near the fort [they stayed here fourteen days] a tablet of lead, with the arms and inscriptions of the King and a pyramid of stones for Monsieur le General; I said to the savages, who did not know of the tablet of lead I had placed in the earth; that I was placing these stones as a memorial of those who had come to their country."

The plate was uncovered, by accident, on February 16, 1913. Today, its authenticity unquestioned, it is on display in the state museum at Pierre, across the Missouri from the hill.

Fort Manuel   South Dakota

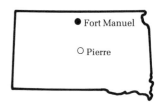

Manuel Lisa (1772–1820) was a prominent Upper Missouri fur trader and a leading spirit in the organization of the St. Louis Missouri Fur Company in 1809 and its successor, the Missouri Fur Company, in 1812. His name is attached to such widely separated posts as Fort Lisa (near Omaha), Lisa's Fort (among the Mandan villages in North Dakota), and Fort Manuel (at the mouth of the Rosebud).

Fort Manuel (this one in South Dakota, on the Missouri's west bank, eight miles below the North Dakota line) was established in 1812, abandoned in 1813. The post is notable for at least two mysteries that surround it. One concerns Lisa's role in the War of 1812. It is believed by many that his dealings with the Sioux helped to undermine their alliance with the British and contributed to the final outcome of the war and the retention of American sovereignty in the area.

The second mystery concerns Sacagawea ("Boat Pusher" in Shoshoni; also spelled *Tsakakawia,* Hidatsa for "Bird Woman"), the young Indian woman who helped guide the Lewis and Clark party. On the strength of a December 20, 1812 entry in the journal of John C. Luttig, a Lisa employee—"This Evening the Wife of Charbonneau a Snake Squaw, died of a putrid fever she was a good and the best Women[*sic*] in the fort, aged abt 25 years she left a fine infant girl"—the "Dakota" school of thought places her grave near Fort Manuel. (Supporting this claim is a recently discovered notebook in which Clark had written, about 1830, the word "dead" after Sacagawea's name.) The "Wyoming" school holds that she died and was buried at Fort Washakie in 1884.

Luttig's journal also shows the day-to-day progress in the building of the fort. The 88-man party arrived at the site August 9 and started work the next day. Luttig reports: "[September 7] . . . moved into the new house. . . . [September 18] . . . raised the Mens house. . . .[October 3] . . . all hands employed to cut Picketts. . . . [October 6] . . . raised the right wing of the out houses and Kept our horses housed. . . . [October 11] . . . this Day finished our new Provision Store and go on with the other houses. . . . [October 22] . . . commenced the Stockade of the fort."

Then on November 19 he records the great day: "At four o'clock in the after noon hung the great Door of the Entrance of the fort, which ceremony was saluted by 7 Guns and 3 rounds of Musquetry, made the Tour—around the Fort and Baptised the same MANUEL in the Evening a good Supper and a cheerful glass of Whiskey was given to the Men, and a Dance at which all the ladies then in the fort attended, concluded the Day."

Fort Manuel in 1812, from a drawing by W. A. Bassford. Evidence indicates the post was burned in March 1813 by British-inspired Sioux.

Courtesy South Dakota State Historical Society

Little remains today of this reconstruction of Fort Manuel, built in the 1930's by the Bureau of Indian Affairs. The archaeological evidence is visible only when the waters of the Oahe Reservoir are lower than maximum levels.

Courtesy National Park Service

Fort Manuel ~ 1812.

Fort Pierre South Dakota

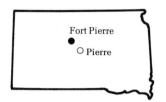

Fort Pierre (three miles north of the present-day town of Fort Pierre) was, after Fort Union (*q.v.*), the most important and best-equipped American Fur Company trading post on the Upper Missouri. It replaced near-by Fort Tecumseh, one of several posts established around this important junction of the Bad River (Lewis and Clark's Teton River) and the Missouri. Work on Fort Pierre began in 1831. The following June, with Pierre Chouteau, Jr., present, it was christened in his honor.

Strategically located and dependably hospitable, the new post had many visitors. Artist George Catlin arrived in 1832 aboard the *Yellowstone* (which had reached this point the year before to become the first steamboat on the Upper Missouri). Prince Maximilian (with artist Karl Bodmer) was an 1833 visitor. He found the fort "in excellent condition," the surrounding plain "covered with scattered tents of the Sioux.") As for factor William Laidlaw's house, it "consisted of one story only, but was very conveniently arranged, with large rooms, fire-places, and glass windows." Buffalo were scarce, however, as were Indian dogs: "Twelve dollars were paid for the dog destined for our repast today." Nevertheless, the table offered "new wheaten bread . . . potatoes, cabbages, carrots, several kinds of preserves and pickles, as well as coffee, sugar, tea, &c."

Edward Harris, who visited Fort Pierre in 1843 with naturalist John J. Audubon, noted the "strong pickets planted close together to the depth of 4½ feet and 22 feet high above the ground. The enclosure is 265 feet square, occupying therefore more than an acre of ground, within are all of their buildings—dwellings, warehouses, stabling for their horses and cattle." Francis A. Chardon in 1847, when Andrew Drips was factor, commented appreciatively on the post's amenities. Coming opposite the fort, his party fired some shots as a signal, "on which they sent boats to take us and our horses across; and we were by no means sorry to find ourselves comfortably installed in time for breakfast."

By this time however, the fur trade was all but wiped out. The silk hat had replaced the beaver hat as a mark of distinction, and the 1837 smallpox epidemic had greatly reduced the Indian population. The outbreak of hostilities with the Sioux in 1854 and Gen. William S. Harney's punitive expedition of 1855 gave Fort Pierre another brief flurry of activity. Sold by the fur company to the government in April 1855 for $45,000, it served as a military base (albeit a rather unsatisfactory one) until 1857, when troops and all movable stores were taken to Fort Randall (*q.v.*). It was dismantled in 1859. Today only a plaque on an upright stone marks the old post. The site is closed to the public until further archaeological investigation can be made.

Fort Pierre, as painted by Karl Bodmer in 1833, two years after it was established. Sale of the American Fur Company trading post to the government in 1855 inaugurated a thirty-eight-year period of military occupation of the Missouri River waterway.

Courtesy Joslyn Art Museum

The mighty Oahe Dam (shown here under construction), a few miles up river from the site of Fort Pierre, is now the area's dominant tourist attraction, as was the old American Fur Company post a century and a half ago.

Courtesy South Dakota Department of Highways

Fort Randall   South Dakota

Fort Randall, established in June 1856 by Gen. William S. Harney (on the Missouri opposite Pickstown, South Dakota), played an important third-act role on the western frontier, figuring in the Indian wars that followed the Minnesota Sioux uprising of the early 1860's and in the Black Hills gold rush of the 1870's and the ensuing Dakota land boom. Handy's Point, however, the bluff at the river bend just above the old fort (and serving it as a beacon), was important to the white man long before that time.

"Cut more wood at 6 a.m., some miles below Handy's," the log of the steamboat *Omega* states on May 22, 1843. ("It is necessary to take wood wherever one can find it.") Then, while the *Omega* was passing the point itself, "a party of savages fired a volley at us, two shots of which passed through the men's cabin." Fortunately, no one was hit. "It is probably those rascally Santees," the writer of the log concludes. "No one else would be capable of such an attack." Already disappeared from the scene, presumably, since the log makes no mention of it, was Handy's Trading Post, of which little is known today.

Fort Randall was described by Dr. Elias J. Marsh in June 1859 as "no fort at all, only barracks, log cabins occupied by the soldiers, and better ones by the officers, all facing an open square, in the center of which is a dial and flagstaff, with a stand for the musicians." This original post was, for the most part, torn down and a new one (only the ruined church of which stands today) built during 1870–72 a bit farther from the river and slightly downstream from the first post. An important station on the Missouri waterway, Fort Randall played host to such noted Indian fighters as Generals Sheridan, Sherman, Custer, Sully, and Terry; to Fr. Pierre Jean De Smet; and to the warriors Spotted Tail and Sitting Bull. The latter was held prisoner here in 1883 following his arrest in Canada.

The detention of the famed Sioux chief, victor over Custer in the Battle of the Little Big Horn, is perhaps an apt symbol of the white man's conquest of the West: the frontier had passed. Fort Randall, "a major base of operations which helped to wean Dakota Territory," in the words of historian Merrill J. Mattes, was only a skeleton post after July 22, 1884, and was officially abandoned in 1892. Today, most of the historic sites along the Missouri, from the old fort up river to Big Bend, lie under the waters of the Lake Francis Case.

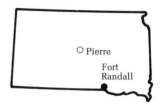

A battalion of the Twenty-fifth U.S. Infantry, with band (left), at Fort Randall in 1880.

Courtesy National Archives

Unstabilized ruins of the Fort Randall church, built in 1876, all that remains of the old post. The Missouri River site is now overshadowed by the giant Fort Randall Dam.

Courtesy National Park Service South Dakota Department of Highways

Fort Sully South Dakota

Fort Sully, its abandoned foundations and cellar pits now lying much of the time below the surface of Oahe Reservoir, was named for Gen. Alfred H. Sully, who established the original post by that name. This first Fort Sully (on the east bank of the Missouri about four miles below the city of Pierre) was used as a base of supplies in 1863 following Sully's punitive operations against the Sioux. By 1866, however, the fort—its temporary buildings dilapidated, timber and grass scarce, and steamers forced to dock three miles away—needed a new site.

The second Fort Sully (still on the east bank, but thirty-two river miles farther up the Missouri) was located July 25, 1866; construction began in August. Progress was slow, however, which explains the unfavorable report made by Gen. Philippe Regis de Trobriand, who visited the new post on August 13, 1867. "Arrived at the landing . . . toward ten o'clock in the morning," he records in his journal. "Needless to say, the landing consists only of half-a-dozen posts planted in the prairie, alongside which the steamboats moor. The post is a mile or two away on a point of bluff where not a shrub grows. . . . There is absolutely no justification for calling it a fort, for the location is not even protected by a moat or a palisade."

Construction was completed in 1868, and the following year, in July, photographer Stanley J. Morrow found Sully quite impressive:

The fort consists of an enclosure 1400 feet long and 800 feet in width. . . . The buildings are well and substantially built . . . principally of pine. The outer sides of the barracks form nearly half of the enclosure. At the southeastern exposure of the stockade are three bastions, one at each corner, and one in the center, containing guns of different calibre and commanding a wide range of country, including the river.

By 1872, Fort Sully was considered the finest and best built post on the Missouri. It accommodated four companies of infantry and the regimental band. Average garrison strength, up to the time it was officially abandoned on October 31, 1894, was 192 men.

More active than most of the Missouri River military posts, Fort Sully stood guard over the Cheyenne River Sioux, aided in various campaigns (culminating in the Battle of the Little Big Horn), supplied two companies of the escort for the survey of the proposed line of the Northern Pacific Railroad, attempted to prevent whites from moving into western Dakota following the discovery of gold in the Black Hills in 1874, and helped neighboring Fort Bennett, eight miles up the Missouri, to suppress the "Ghost Dance Rebellion" (*see* Wounded Knee Battlefield) in 1890 and 1891.

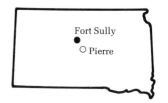

Fort Sully as it appeared about the time of its abandonment in 1894. The first Fort Sully was established in 1863 about thirty-five miles down the Missouri.

Courtesy National Archives

In this 1952 photo, stone marks the site of the first Fort Sully, built on the east bank of the Missouri River about four miles below Pierre, South Dakota. The site is now often flooded by the waters of Lake Oahe.

Courtesy South Dakota State Historical Society

Gordon Stockade South Dakota

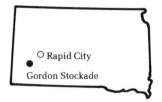

Gordon Stockade (three miles east of Custer) represents the first successful penetration of the Black Hills gold fields. It was also the first fruit of Gen. George A. Custer's deliberate violation of the 1868 treaty (*see* Fort Rice) which guaranteed to the Sioux possession of their sacred *Paha Sapa*. Here on French Creek, on August 2, 1874, William T. McKay and Horatio N. Ross—civilian prospectors accompanying Custer's "exploratory" expedition—had "struck color." McKay, an early account relates, "held up his pan in the evening sun and found the rim lined with nearly a hundred little particles of gold. These he carried to General Custer, whose head was almost turned at the sight." As news spread of gold "from the grass roots down," the nation's head was turned, too. By October 6, the Gordon party had left Sioux City.

The group (twenty-six men, Mrs. Annie D. Tallent, the Hills' first white woman, and ten-year-old Bird Tallent) reached "Custer's Park" on December 23. The story of its experiences there, until April 10, 1875, when U.S. cavalry escorted it to Fort Laramie, is well told in the letters and journals of its members.

"We proceeded at once to erect a stockade," J. Newton Warren reported, "eighty feet square, of logs one foot in thickness, which projected ten feet above the ground. Within this was erected six comfortable log cabins." Safe from Indians and the weather, "we commenced prospecting."

"Gold we find in every pan," R. R. Whitney wrote his wife on January 31, 1875, "and it is my opinion that it is as rich here as it ever was in far-famed California."

The cold drove the frost down from one to three feet, which hampered prospecting. But the gold seekers dug an eight-foot hole in a corner of the stockade (for dirt with which to cover their charcoal pit), and there, John Gordon reported, they found "better prospects than at any previous place they had struck."

"There is gold here as plenty as is needed," wrote T. H. Russell (one of the expedition's promoters) on February 3. "All we want is lumber and the necessary tools to work it." On February 15 he wrote: "We are finding gold everywhere we prospect."

"I have set my pile at $150,000 before I leave the Black Hills," Whitney noted on February 16, enough "to pay me for what I suffered to get into this country."

After April 10, the Black Hills area was free of white men again—but not for long (*see* Deadwood): federal troops were soon withdrawn. The town of Custer was staked out in 1875 and had a population of five thousand by April 1876. The Sioux had lost the *Paha Sapa* for good.

Lt. Col. George A. Custer with a bear killed on his 1874 expedition to the Black Hills. The Indian at left is Bloody Knife, one of Custer's scouts. The gold discovered by two prospectors accompanying the expedition helped bring on the Battle of the Little Big Horn two years later.

Courtesy South Dakota Department of Highways

Gordon Stockade in the summer of 1875. The photograph was taken a few months after the army had escorted the gold seekers from the Black Hills.

Courtesy South Dakota State Historical Society

The replica of Gordon Stockade in Custer State Park offers living history presentations.

Courtesy South Dakota Division of Tourism

Deadwood South Dakota

On a flat piece of limestone found by Louis and Ivan Thoen in 1887 at the foot of Lookout Mountain near Spearfish, South Dakota, was discovered news of the first Black Hills gold strike:

Came to these hills in 1833, seven of us
DeLacompt   Ezra Kind   G W Wood   T Brown
R Kent   Wm King   Indian Crow   All ded
but me Ezra Kind   Killed by Indians beyond
the high hill got our gold June 1834

On the back of this so-called Thoen Stone was this ironic post-script:

Got all gold we could carry   Our ponys
all got by Indians   I have lost my gun
and nothing to eat and Indians hunting me

Proof of the Hills' long-rumored gold, however, had come a dozen years too late. Deadwood, some fifteen miles to the southeast, was already the possessor of one of history's richest gold mines—and of a reputation as one of the West's wickedest, least-inhibited mining camps.

The Sioux had long resisted white penetration of the *Paha Sapa,* and when the break finally came (*see* Gordon Stockade), it first enveloped the southern Hills. Then in the late fall of 1875, John B. Pearson discovered rich placer diggings in Deadwood Gulch.

Deep snows held up news of the strike until the following March, but by the summer of 1876 an estimated seven thousand miners, including most of those from Custer, were swarming over Deadwood, Whitewood, and related gulches. (Some fifty mines were discovered in the near-by Lead area alone in 1876, one of them the famed Homestake. Still active, and the greatest producer in the Western Hemisphere, it has yielded more than $500,000,000 in gold.) A substantial and impressive city soon crowded Deadwood Gulch. Despite a devastating fire (1879), an equally destructive flood (1883), and the inevitable decline in small-mine operations, enough of Deadwood's early buildings survive to create the appearance—and atmosphere—of an old mining town.

One of Deadwood's most widely known events, still recalled regularly in summer for the benefit of visitors, was, appropriately enough, a shooting. A routine notice announced the outcome:

Died in Deadwood, Black Hills, August 2, 1876, from the effects of a pistol shot, J. B. Hickok (Wild Bill) formerly of Cheyenne, Wyo. Funeral Services will be held at Charlie Utter's camp, this afternoon, Aug. 3, at 3 p.m. All are respectfully invited to attend.

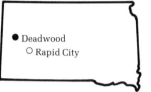

Deadwood in 1876, its first year. By 1881, according to Harper's New Monthly Magazine, *the newly incorporated seat of Lawrence County "supports three national banks . . . two daily and two weekly newspapers . . . four imposing church edifices." It also boasted a telephone exchange "employing 136 men and using 400 miles of wire."*

Courtesy Chicago, Burlington & Quincy Railroad

Grave of James B. "Wild Bill" Hickok in Mt. Moriah Cemetery on a hill overlooking Deadwood. The famed gunman was shot by Jack McCall in the Number Ten Saloon on August 2, 1876, while holding the "Dead Man's Hand" of aces and eights.

Courtesy South Dakota Department of Highways

Wounded Knee Battlefield

The Battle of Wounded Knee ("battle" to an embarrassed U.S. Army, "massacre" to the embittered Indians—a tragic confrontation for which neither side was completely blameless) was fought near the Pine Ridge Agency of the Sioux in South Dakota on December 29, 1890. Its seed was planted the year before in Nevada, where a quiet, unwarlike Paiute named Wovoka had a vision. With a curious mixture of Christian and Indian thought, his vision evolved into a magnetic message of hope: "The good days of the plentiful buffalo herds are coming back again. The son of God has come to earth again, and this time he has come to the Indian alone. The white people will all be destroyed because long ago they killed him!"

The "Messiah Craze" swept across the West like a prairie fire. The Indians believed because they wanted to believe, and the Sioux, their desperation sharpened by hunger, were among the fiercest converts, characteristically introducing a new dogma of their own. To the ritual of the Ghost Dance (so called because it supposedly enabled participants to go into a hypnotic trance and see the spirits of the dead), they added the sacred ghost shirt, which they believed could turn away bullets. Women donned the shirt, with the warriors, and the dances began. The stage for Wounded Knee was set.

Sitting Bull supported the new religion and the first Ghost Dance at his camp was held October 9, 1890. The longer the Indians danced, the more frightened the whites became. Finally, Agent James McLaughlin received his order: "Arrest Sitting Bull." When the Sioux chief hesitated, a shot was fired into his cabin. The fight lasted only a few minutes, took the life of Sitting Bull, his son, and six other Sioux. That was December 15.

Two weeks later the fugitives under Big Foot surrendered unconditionally to the Seventh Cavalry and were herded into a camp on Wounded Knee Creek. There, under a white flag of truce and guarded by 470 men and four Hotchkiss guns, they were ordered to turn in their weapons. The Indians were resentful, the troops inexperienced. There was a quick gesture of defiance, then a shot from an Indian's concealed gun, and the killing began. When it was over, some 300 of the Sioux were dead, two-thirds of them women and children. Thirty-one soldiers died, many by their comrades' crossfire. Eighteen others received the coveted Medal of Honor—"for distinguished conduct."

The Sioux were finally crushed, and the Seventh Cavalry had at last avenged its humiliating defeat at the Little Big Horn. As Senator Karl Mundt has said, with wry understatement: "It can hardly be classed as the white man's proudest hour."

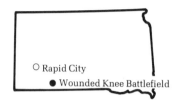

Pine Ridge Indian Camp on January 17, 1891, virtually deserted, like other camps in the area, following the tragedy at Wounded Knee.

Courtesy Historical Society of Montana

Big Foot Massacre Monument marks Wounded Knee Battlefield, sixteen miles northeast of Pine Ridge, South Dakota. Here some three hundred Sioux died in this last important conflict between Indian and white man.

Courtesy South Dakota Department of Highways

234

El Paso   Texas

The historic mountain gateway between Mexico and the Upper Río Grande, *El Paso del Norte* had been an important avenue of trade and culture for more than four centuries. Álvar Núñez Cabeza de Vaca may possibly have traversed the vicinity of modern El Paso (where Mexico corners with both Texas and New Mexico) in 1536. Fr. Agustín Rodríguez came by here in 1581, as did Capt. Antonio de Espejo in 1582, but the name "The Pass of the North," and the formal possession claim for King Philip II of Spain came from Juan de Oñate in 1598. On the Río Grande below the pass on Holy Thursday, he halted his New Mexico-bound expedition for an impressive religious service.

"Don Juan ordered a large chapel built," wrote Don Gaspar Pérez de Villagrá. "That night was one of prayer and penance for all. The women and children came barefoot to pray. . . . The soldiers, with cruel scourges, beat their [own] backs unmercifully until the camp ran crimson with their blood. . . . Don Juan, unknown to anyone except me, went to a secluded spot where he cruelly scourged himself, mingling bitter tears with the blood which flowed from his many wounds."

Descendants of these first colonists were among the harassed refugees who retreated to the pass in 1680 following the bloody Pueblo Revolt. With still-loyal Tigua Indians, they established the mission of Isleta del Sur (then on the Mexican side of the Río Grande, since the early 1800's on the Texas side near present-day Ysleta). By 1731 several missions had been established along the river, and civilization centered about their heavily buttressed walls (none of the original structures remain) and the presidios built to protect them. "For hospitality, generosity, docility, and sobriety," wrote Zebulon M. Pike (*see* Pike's Stockade) in 1807, "the people of New Spain exceed any nation perhaps on the globe."

Modern El Paso, first settled in 1827, is more American than Spanish. (Called Franklin for many years—Ciudad Juárez, across the Río Grande in Mexico, was long known as El Paso—it was not incorporated until 1873, with a population of 173.) The 1848 Treaty of Guadalupe Hidalgo gave this area to the United States, and Fort Bliss was established the following year to maintain American authority. Known then as Post of El Paso (at Smith's Ranch, now downtown El Paso), it was moved to the near-by trading post of Magoffinsville (Magoffin and Octavia streets) in 1854 and renamed for Col. W. W. S. Bliss. "The fort is pleasantly situated," Edward F. Beale noted in 1857, "overlooking the river and meadow land lying on either side." Two more moves—to Concordia in 1868, to Hart's Mill in 1879—and present Fort Bliss (U.S. Army Air Defense Center) was finally built on the northeast edge of El Paso in 1893.

Post of El Paso, the original Fort Bliss, as painted by H. C. Pratt in 1853. The site, at Smith's Ranch in what is now downtown El Paso, was the first of five occupied by the fort following its establishment in 1849.

Courtesy Col. M. H. Thomlinson and Texas Memorial Museum, Austin

Present-day Fort Bliss, on the northeast edge of El Paso, combines the old and the new. A replica of the second fort (on the Magoffinsville site) stands near the forts' missile test-firing facilities.

Courtesy El Paso Chamber of Commerce

236

San Antonio Texas

The valley of the San Antonio River, the "Cradle of Texas Liberty" in the nineteenth century, was, in the eighteenth, an important center of Spanish colonialism. In 1716, Franciscan Fr. Antonio de San Buenaventura Olivares established San Antonio de Padua Mission on the river's west bank. In 1718 it was moved to the east bank (a "more convenient site, about two gun-shots distant from the original site") and renamed San Antonio de Valero in honor of the Spanish viceroy. When a guard of soldiers was left behind, the Villa de Bejar (later spelled *Bexar*) came into being. Within the next thirteen years, in a seven-mile stretch of the valley, four more missions were founded: Concepción, San Juan, Espada, and San José (*q.v.*).

The missions flourished for a time. The convent and weaving room at San Antonio were completed in 1744, the cornerstone of the church laid. By 1761, seven stone houses and the church tower were finished and an acequía dug to bring water from the river. Then followed a period of gradual decline. Secularized in 1793, the mission joined with the near-by settlements to become San Antonio de Bexar, the capital of the province. The mission building itself, known by then as "The Alamo," was a dilapidated ruins in December 1835 when Gen. Martín Perfecto de Cos and his Mexican forces surrendered it to Texas revolutionaries under Ben Milam. The stage was set for Texas independence.

Col. William B. Travis took over the walled mission grounds, had time only to make a few defensive repairs before another Mexican army, commanded by Gen. Antonio López de Santa Anna, arrived. Travis refused the order to surrender. The siege began February 23, 1836, and ended at dawn on March 6. Travis, James Bonham, David Crockett, James Bowie, and 183 other men—including 32 reinforcements who had arrived from Gonzales on March 1—were dead. But the heroic stand had given the cause of Texas independence a rallying point and, in "Remember the Alamo," an effective war cry.

The mission-fort was occupied briefly by the U.S. Army after the Mexican War. Of the original structures, all that remain today are the low gray chapel and some crumbling, ivy-covered walls. The renovated chapel is maintained as an historic shrine.

The Alamo, from a water color painted by Seth Eastman in November 1848. He found San Antonio "a wretched place, full of desperate characters," but concluded that is was "rapidly becoming yankeeized." The "Alemo," then in ruins, he considered "well built and much ornamented."

Courtesy Peabody Museum, Harvard University

The Alamo today. The present building is the old mission chapel of San Antonio de Valero.

Courtesy San Antonio Convention and Visitors' Bureau

San José Mission Texas

Of the five missions established along the San Antonio River from 1716 to 1731 (*see* San Antonio), San José y San Miguel de Aguayo was, in many ways, the most remarkable. Five miles to the south of the original San Antonio de Padua Mission, San José was founded in 1720 by the Franciscans. It developed steadily and by 1749 had acquired most of its permanent buildings, with the exception of the church, which was started in 1768. By 1778, at the height of its power and influence, Fr. Juan Antonio Morfi was able to write:

> It is, in truth, the first mission in America, not in point of time, but in point of beauty, plan and strength, so that there is not a presidio along the entire frontier line that can compare with it. The living quarters and public offices form a square 216 varas on each side [actually about 500x600 feet]. There are four identical gates on the four corners, over the top of each of which a bastion has been built to defend them, and on the sides of the hollow of each gate, loopholes have been made through the walls of the adjoining rooms, where the most trusted Indians lived, that they may fire safely upon the enemy should the gates be stormed.

Fr. Morfi praised the new church, still under construction, for "its size, good taste, and beauty," adding that "no one could have imagined there were such good artists in so desolate a place." He also described in detail the granary (oldest building in the mission group, remarkable for its flying stone buttresses and vaulted roof), the convent, and other features of the mission, including the extensive farming operations. (Irrigation water was brought to the gristmill, where it turned the turbine in a lower chamber before flowing through a deep ditch into the adjacent fields). Mission Indians, members of various Coahuiltecan tribes, numbered approximately 350 men.

In 1813, however, came secularization, and the mission buildings, used for many different purposes, were allowed to deteriorate. Not until the 1930's did serious restoration work begin. Since 1941 the remarkably complete mission complex has been preserved as a National Historic Site. Outstanding are the church's façade, ornamented in a rich Renaissance style, and the so-called Rose Window, carved with great skill and artistry by one of Fr. Morfi's "good artists," Pedro Huizar.

San José Mission in 1848, as painted by Seth Eastman. Founded in 1720, it was described (in 1778) by Fr. Juan Antonio Morfi as "the first mission in America, not in point of time, but in point of beauty."

Courtesy Witte Museum, San Antonio

Just south of San Antonio, San José Mission is today a National Historic Site. Administered with it are the near-by Missions La Purésima, Concepción de Acuña, San Francisco de Espada, and San Juan Capistrano.

Courtesy San Antonio Chamber of Commerce

San Felipe de Austin Texas

San Felipe de Austin, at the old Atascosito Crossing on the Brazos River (forty-five miles west of modern Houston), was the cradle of Anglo-American settlement in Texas. Here, in the then Mexican state of Coahuila, Stephen F. Austin brought his first band of settlers (in July 1823) and maintained for a dozen years an unofficial capital of the colony. (In 1820, St. Louis banker Moses Austin had secured Spanish authority to settle 300 families in Texas but died before he could do so. His son assumed the colonizing task in 1821, the year Mexico freed herself from Spain, and by 1831 had brought in 5,600 settlers.)

Life at San Felipe was hard. The twenty log cabins erected by 1828 were bare, some windowless. Calico sold for fifty cents a yard, flour for twenty-five dollars a barrel. (A housewife originated the familiar expression "Texas is a heaven for men and dogs, but hell for women and oxen.") Initially, however, it was law abiding. Austin insisted that each colonist have a "perfectly unblemished" character and show proof "that he is a moral and industrious man, and absolutely free from the vice of intoxication." In 1829 he wrote: "You will be astonished to see all our houses with no other fastening than a wooden pin or door latch." (It was later that "G. T. T."—"Gone To Texas"—became synonymous for flight to escape justice.)

Opposition to Mexican rule soon developed, despite Austin's early attempts to reduce the symptoms of conflict. The glowing accounts of early Texas travelers ("[A] most delightful champaign country," wrote a U.S. senator in 1829, "dry, pure, elastic air, springs of sweet waters.") brought more and more settlers, and increased tensions created mounting pressures for independence. A convention held in San Felipe in October 1832 sought greater liberties under Mexican law, and another in 1833 adopted a state constitution which Austin carried to Mexico for approval. His imprisonment further strained relations and the 1835 consultation in San Felipe led to the open break that gave Texas its independence in 1836.

Ironically, the provisional capital had made its last notable contribution to Texas history. In April 1836, San Felipe was burned. It was partially rebuilt the following year, but on August 11, 1843, visitor William Bollaert wrote its epitaph:

Ferried over the Brazos. . . . On the western side stands the remains of San Felipe de Austin; it is now a "deserted village." One or two families reside here only; weeds and bushes have grown up in the streets and unoccupied lots, so that one has a difficulty in tracing his way to the main road.

San Felipe de Austin ● ○ Houston

Ferry at San Felipe, on the Río de los Brazos de Dios (River of the Arms of God), where Anglo-American settlement in Texas began in 1823.

Courtesy Texas State Parks Board

Replica of the Austin cabin in Stephen F. Austin State Park at San Felipe. Here Texas got its first Sunday school, its first newspaper, and one of its first English-speaking schools.

Courtesy Texas Parks and Wildlife Department

Fort Belknap <small>Texas</small>

Fort Belknap, key link in a chain of military posts designed to protect the expanding frontier in northern and western Texas, was established in June 1851 by Gen. William G. Belknap. He selected the site (on the Brazos River just south of present Newcastle), curiously enough, because he considered it "the most western point that a post can be established [beyond which], on account of the scarcity of timber and water, it is not probable that white settlements will be made for a century to come, if ever."

Belknap undersold the pioneers. Following the annexation of Texas and the Mexican War, settlers had pushed into this region. To protect them from the Kiowas and Comanches, an inner ring of posts was established—Fort Graham in 1848, Forts Worth, Gates, Croghan, and Mason in 1849—which the advancing frontier engulfed even before it could be completed. Anchored by Fort Belknap, an outer ring was authorized: Phantom Hill in 1851, Forts Chadbourne, McKavett, and Clark in 1852. After the Civil War, during which Belknap was occupied by Confederate troops, even this fortification chain was bypassed by the swiftly moving frontier. Discontinued as a permanent post in 1867 because of its unreliable water supply (a problem that had necessitated a two-mile move in November 1851), Fort Belknap was finally abandoned in 1876.

Aside from its role in protecting the settlers from Indians, Belknap was an important communications center and base for military operations. From the post in 1852, Capt. Randolph B. Marcy and Lt George B. McClellan conducted their exploration of the Upper Red River, and on September 22, 1858, the first (westbound) stagecoach of John Butterfield's Overland Mail Company (running between St. Louis and San Francisco) stopped at the fort for breakfast—and to change its horses for mules. (Butterfield continued operations until 1861, spurring development of the area. Within a year the adjacent town of Belknap was reported as having five general stores, three hotels, a blacksmith shop, two wagon yards, and several comfortable homes.) On September 15, 1858, Maj. Earl Van Dorn set out on his expedition against the Comanches in Indian Territory.

The first buildings at Fort Belknap were *jacales,* crude Spanish-type houses made of pickets filled in with a screen of wood, mud, or adobe. These were soon replaced by stone structures, one of which remains on the site today: the arsenal, built in 1852 (part of the old four-foot-high stone wall also survives). Six of the former buildings have been carefully restored on the original foundations, including barracks, kitchen, and the commissary (the "corn house"), containing a pioneer museum.

An old map of Fort Belknap in the National Archives is the only known representation of this important outpost on the Texas frontier.

Private Papers of Fort Belknap in Ben G. Oneal Collection

Restored buildings at Fort Belknap. The site is now a county park.

Courtesy *Wichita Daily Times,* Wichita Falls

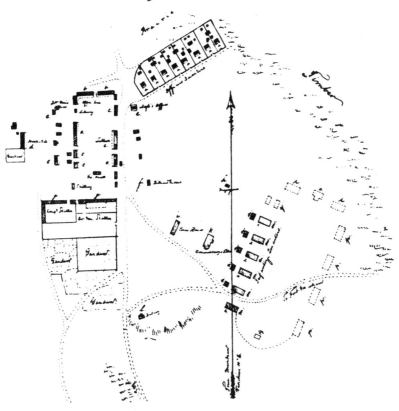

Sketch of Fort Belknap, Texas

Fort Davis Texas

Army doctor (later a general) Albert J. Myer probably wasn't thinking of Apaches and Comanches when he said, in February 1855, "The climate of this [southwestern] part of Texas is probably the finest in the world." Myer—later to become one of the country's leading authorities on climate and an organizer of the U.S. Weather Bureau—wrote his report from Fort Davis, a military outpost established October 7, 1854, by Lt Col. Washington Seawell to protect transportation and communication lines in this area from Indian raids. (Myer served three years at the fort, where he studied Apache and Comanche signal techniques. His recommendations led to the organization of the U.S. Army Signal Corps, of which he was the first officer.)

Antonio de Espejo and his party, returning to Mexico from New Mexico the summer of 1583, were probably the first white men to see the Davis Mountains. On August 13 they stopped under the cottonwoods along Limpia Creek, where the Fort Davis pump house was later built. Almost three centuries later the spot became a campground for California-bound gold seekers on the fine natural road between San Antonio and El Paso, and it was primarily to protect them from the Mescalero Apaches that Secretary of War Jefferson Davis ordered the post built. Notable visitor in 1857: the short-lived Camel Corps (*see* Fort Tejón), on its way from Galveston to California.

Outbreak of the Civil War caused the temporary abandonment of the fort in 1861. When U.S. troops returned in 1867, the old establishment, some sixty-five sawed-pine and cottonwood-slab structures, had been virtually destroyed by Indians. A new and more elaborate fort of rock and adobe materials was built. Until 1880, it served as a base of operations against the Comanches and played a prominent role in the wars against Victorio and the Warm Springs and Mescalero Apaches. Afterward, with the Indian menace removed, cattlemen began to establish ranches in the area. Its usefulness outlived, the fort was abandoned July 31, 1891.

Today the remains of Fort Davis (thanks to the permanent nature of its construction) are probably more extensive and impressive than those of any other frontier post in the West. The walls of nine sets of adobe officers' quarters are still standing. Seven other sets, of slab limestone, are in excellent condition, complete with roofs. The adobe commissary and barrack-like shop, the ruins of a large stone tank used as a reservoir for water drawn from Limpia Creek, and the remains of a number of other buildings dot the 400-acre reservation, established by Congress as a National Historic Site under the National Park Service.

Fort Davis in 1885. The location—site of a primitive settlement called Painted Comanche Camp—was chosen "because of the salubrious climate and pure water," according to War Department records.

Courtesy Estate of David A. Simmons

Officers' Row at Fort Davis. In a columned curve of red rock cliffs in the Davis Mountains of southwestern Texas, the ruins are as extensive and impressive as any in the West. The officers' quarters, commissary, and kitchen are restored and open to visitors in the summer. A former barracks serves as visitors' center.

Courtesy National Park Service

Goodnight Ranch Texas

Palo Duro Canyon, a colorful, twisting gash in the flat Staked Plains of the Texas Panhandle (some twenty-five miles southeast of Amarillo), is thought by some to be the "arroyo flowing between some barrancas [cliffs] in which there were good meadows" visited by Francisco Vásquez de Coronado in late May of 1541. Certainly Pedro de Casteñeda's description of the Llano Estacado is still apt: "The country is like a bowl, so that when a man sits down, the horizon surrounds him all around at the distance of a musket shot." Almost three centuries later, in 1832, Albert Pike was equally impressed: "Its sublimity arises from its unbounded extent, its barren monotony and desolation, its still, unmoved, calm, stern, almost self-confident grandeur." And as late as 1875 the *Texas Rural Register and Immigrants' Handbook* doubted it could "ever be adapted to the wants of man."

But the vastness of the land was matched by the vision of pioneer rancher Charles Goodnight (1836–1929). Palo Duro, nearly a thousand feet in depth and varying in width from a few hundred yards to several miles, had the water, wood, and grass to provide an unexcelled winter range for cattle, and here, in late 1876, Goodnight ran his herd down a 700-foot rockslide to the grassy bottom of the canyon. The dismantled chuck wagon and a supply of provisions were packed down and the "Old Home Ranch"—first in the Texas Panhandle—was established: a few corrals and picket houses built with near-by timber. (As the JA, so called for partner John G. Adair, Irish nobleman and financier, it was to become one of the West's greatest ranches, with 40,000 head of cattle grazing 700,000 acres of grasslands.)

James T. Hughes, a Goodnight rider that first winter, attests to the rigors of pioneer life on the plains. Two blizzards caught them before they had a house built, "and doing everything, especially getting out of bed, in a snow storm is 'bracing' to say the least." On December 15, "we finished the first room. . . . On the 23d and 24th it snowed. We all shaved and 'greased up' with bear oil for Christmas—the only thing we could think of doing, as we had run out of all grub except flour; but then flour, bear, buffalo and turkey is pretty good living."

Goodnight dominates the history of the cattle frontier in Texas. He rode bareback from Illinois to Texas when he was nine, launched his cattle business at twenty, blazed the famed Goodnight Trail (cattle) to Wyoming at thirty, established the Old Home Ranch at forty, and became, at sixty, one of the West's greatest scientific breeders of ranch cattle. Still active at ninety, he was an internationally recognized authority in that highly specialized field.

Original Goodnight Ranch headquarters in Palo Duro Canyon, established in 1876. This sketch by Harold D. Bugbee is based on information obtained from four former ranch hands who had lived in the original house.

Courtesy Harold D. Bugbee

Palo Duro Canyon, long thought by many to be the "arroyo flowing between some barrancas" visited by Coronado in late May of 1541. In the nineteenth century it was the heart of the range of the Comanches and Kiowas and the scene of the final Comanche defeat in 1875. Twelve miles east of the city of Canyon, it is now a state park.

Courtesy Texas State Parks Board

"old Lone Ranch"
from photo in collection
of Frank Mitchell

Miles Goodyear Farm   Utah

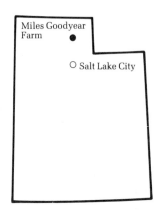

Miles Goodyear Farm

○ Salt Lake City

Fate, in awarding history's leading players, is not always just. In Utah, Miles Goodyear's name is not borne by a single hill, creek, town, park, or school, yet he was the state's first bona fide citizen, builder of its first structure, raiser of its first crops, and first resident on the site of its second largest city.

A New England orphan, Goodyear came west with Dr. Marcus Whitman's party in 1836 while still in his teens. He came into camp, William H. Gray reports, "having on an old torn straw hat, an old ragged fustian coat, scarcely half a shirt, with buckskin pants, badly worn, but one moccasin, a powder horn with no powder in it, and an old rifle." They hired him on, outfitted him, and he "made an excellent hand," helping Dr. Whitman make history by driving a wagon over the trail as far as Fort Hall (*q.v.*).

Goodyear dropped out of the party here, staying at Fort Hall for a number of years and learning the Indian-trading business. In 1845 he struck out for the south and located a farm on the Weber River just above its confluence with the Ogden River in what is now the city of Ogden. Here he built a cabin of cottonwood logs and planted a garden. The following year, he erected a stockade, a corral for his growing herds, and several additional buildings. With these amenities, the farm was called Fort Buenaventura.

The establishment caught the eye of John Brown on August 9, 1847, a few weeks after he had reached Great Salt Lake Valley with Brigham Young's first group of Mormon pioneers. "At Weber River we found the fort of Mr. Goodyear which consisted of some log buildings and corrals stockaded in with pickets. He had a small garden of vegetables, also a few stalks of corn . . . which proved to us that with proper cultivation corn would do well." On November 25 of that year, for the sum of $1,950, Goodyear sold out to the Mormons, turning over the land and improvements, 75 cattle, 75 goats, 12 sheep, 6 horses—and a cat. He kept his furs, skins, traps, and most of his horses and set out for California.

The farm produced one hundred bushels of wheat in 1848. In 1851 the fort was incorporated and renamed for Peter Skene Ogden, who trapped Ogden's Hole (to the east) for the Hudson's Bay Company as early as 1825. Here on the site of Ogden was held the summer rendezvous of 1826, highlighted by the arrival of Gen. William H. Ashley's one hundred pack animals. "The unpacking of the *medicine water*," Jim Beckwourth recalled, "contributed not a little to the heightening of our festivities."

Miles Goodyear's cabin, built of cottonwood logs in 1845 as the first non-Indian dwelling in present Utah, was moved to Tabernacle Park in Ogden in 1928 by the Daughters of the Utah Pioneers. It is now preserved under a canopy adjoining Pioneer Hall Museum.

Courtesy Ogden Chamber of Commerce

The Miles Goodyear log cabin, as carefully re-created on the original site near Ogden, Utah, is a feature of Fort Buenaventura State Historical Monument.

Courtesy Golden Spike Empire

Salt Lake City Utah

"Brannan," Brigham Young is supposed to have said to one of his followers, "if there is a place on this earth that nobody else wants, that's the place I am hunting for." In Great Salt Lake Valley many thought he had found it. Mountain men, entering the valley from the north in the 1820's, didn't think much of it, and some of the Saints themselves were skeptical. One thought it "a vast desert whose dry and parched soil seemed to bid defiance to the husbandman."

Young apparently knew his followers better than they knew themselves. The vanguard of the pioneers (143 men, 3 women, and 2 children in all) began to plow the desert on July 23, 1847, building an irrigation dam the same afternoon. The following day (Saturday), Brigham Young arrived with the remainder of the company. Sunday, Orson Pratt preached the first sermon.

On Monday, Young called a meeting of the Council of the Twelve Apostles. Walking to what is now Temple Square, he punched his cane into the ground and said, "Here will be the Temple of our God." The following Sunday, ten days after their arrival, the first Bowery for religious services was built on Temple Square. The next day, Pratt laid out around the square a city of 135 10-acre blocks flanked by 132-foot-wide streets and 20-foot sidewalks. One of the blocks (present Pioneer Park) was selected for a stockaded fort of log and adobe cabins where the pioneers could live until permanent structures were erected.

Spiritual matters were not forgotten. Ground-breaking ceremonies in 1853 launched construction of the Temple, and ox teams were soon hauling great granite blocks from Little Cottonwood Canyon, some twenty miles away (its highest spire 210 feet, it was not completed until 1892). By 1855 a fifteen-foot adobe and sandstone wall surrounded the square. In 1862 work began on the oval-domed Tabernacle, still today an architectural and engineering marvel. It was finished in 1867, and its magnificent organ (27 pedals, 2,638 pipes, 35 stops) was installed in 1870.

In March 1849—after having memorialized Congress for the creation of a territorial government—the Mormons adopted a constitution: "WE, THE PEOPLE, grateful to the SUPREME BEING for the blessings hitherto enjoyed, and feeling our dependence on Him for a continuation of those blessings, DO ORDAIN AND ESTABLISH A FREE AND INDEPENDENT GOVERNMENT by the name of the STATE OF DESERET." Primarily because of a conflict growing out of the Mormon practice of polygamy, statehood was delayed until January 4, 1896, when Utah became the forty-fifth state.

Great Salt Lake City in 1853. In 1847 a crude shelter of brush and boughs served as the first Bowery, and a near-by creek was dammed to form a pool in which many of the newly arrived Saints were rebaptized.

Courtesy Library of Congress

Temple Square, with most of its buildings and monuments essentially unchanged from the time they were completed, is a dramatic symbol of Mormon achievement in building a prosperous new Zion on the Utah desert. At left is the Tabernacle; center, the Temple.

Courtesy Utah Tourist & Publicity Council

Fort Utah Utah

Historically, few groups of whites managed to establish and maintain as generally harmonious relations with their Indian neighbors as did the Latter-day Saints. Fort Utah (present-day Provo, the state's third largest city) was one of the first Mormon settlements to profit from Brigham Young's enlightened (for his day) views on Indian-white affairs. ("Whenever the citizens of this Territory travel the roads," he wrote in 1857, "they are in the habit of giving the Indians food, tobacco and a few other presents." He added: "I have proven that it is far cheaper to feed and clothe the Indians than to fight them.") So warmly did Sowiette, principal war chief of the Utes, regard his Mormon friends that in the early 1850's, when Chief Walker planned to attack Fort Utah, he moved his own warriors inside the stockade and prepared to help in its defense. Walker and his braves circled the fort all night, finally withdrew without attacking. Sowiette Park (Fifth West and Fifth North streets, on the site of the fort) now honors this gallant Ute.

Settlement of the south bank of the Provo River near its mouth in Lake Utah was begun in March 1849 when John S. Higbee, at the head of thirty families, left Salt Lake City (forty-five miles to the north) with wagons, horses and cattle, seed, farming implements, and household furnishings. Within a few weeks the colonists had built a simple Fort Utah, plowed 225 acres, and planted rye, wheat, and corn. That same year, Samuel Clark established a tannery and John Blackburn erected the first sawmill. Before long a gristmill was built and two large canals dug to divert irrigation water from the river. By 1851 a carding mill was in operation. The Fort Utah area was beginning to fulfill the promise envisioned for it by its earliest boosters.

Probably the first white men to see Utah Lake were two Spanish priests, Fr. Francisco Silvestre Vílez de Escalante and Fr. Francisco Antanasio Domínguez. In September 1776 they "ascended a low hill and beheld the lake and extended valley of Nuestra Señora de la Merced de los Timpanogotz . . . surrounded by the peaks of the Sierra." Provo River, Fr. Escalante recorded, "runs through large plains of good land for planting . . . plenty . . . if irrigated, for two and even three large villages."

The Mormons agreed. Orson Pratt scouted the valley on July 27, 1847, just three days after the main body of Mormons reached Great Salt Lake Valley. The same day, L. B. Myers reported "plenty of timber" east of "Eutaw Lake," and in early August, Jesse C. Little noted "that the land there was well adapted for cultivation."

The city and river are named for Étienne Provost, a young French-Canadian who explored the valley with a party of trappers in 1825.

Fort Utah in the valley of the Great Salt Lake. This Ackerman lithograph is from Howard Stansbury's Exploration and Survey of the Valley of the Great Salt Lake of Utah (1852).

Courtesy Library of Congress

Pioneer Museum in Sowiette Park, Provo. The park, named for Ute Chief Sowiette, stands on the site of Fort Utah.

Courtesy Provo Chamber of Commerce

Mount Timpanogos and Utah Valley, with the village of Alpine in foreground. Cascade Mountain is at right.

Courtesy Utah Tourist & Publicity Council

254

St. George Utah

A Dixie poet sang of the weather in southwestern Utah:

> The wind like fury here does blow
> That when we plant or sow, sir,
> We place one foot upon the seed
> And hold it till it grows, sir.

"I believe we were close to hell," Orson Huntsman said following a visit in 1870, "for Dixie is the hottest place I ever was in." However, mild winters gave Dixie crops denied the northern Mormon settlements. And the more products raised, or mined, or manufactured, the greater the Saints' self-sufficiency, the better their chance of attaining economic and political independence.

The "iron mission" to Parowan and Cedar City in 1850 had been the first great Mormon colonizing expedition. A few years later Brigham Young sent settlers farther south into the Santa Clara and Virgin basins to start the "cotton mission." (In 1868 silkworms were imported from France and soon Dixie streets were lined with mulberry trees.) Cotton gave the planters "a sad experience picking the seed out," one pioneer recalled; it "made our fingers sore." But the results encouraged Young to order a large-scale colonization of St. George. In October 1861, 309 families were "called," instructed "to supply the territory with cotton, sugar, grapes, tobacco, figs, almonds, olive oil, and such other useful articles as the Lord has given us."

By December 1861 more than two hundred wagons were on the site, two long rows of wagons facing each other across a ditch. St. George was incorporated before the first house had been erected. Cotton was planted on June 1 and the 1862 crop yielded fifty tons of seed. (Tobacco, eschewed by the faithful, was never grown extensively in Dixie, but grapes did become an important crop—some 544 acres yielded 1,700 tons in 1875—and high-quality wines and brandies were produced until around 1900, when the temptation to local consumption led Church authorities to order the vines pulled up.)

St. George's origins were humble enough. Logs were hard to come by, so inexpensive adobe was used extensively—leading to the complaint of one old-timer whose house "riz right up outa the mud she stood on, 'n' when it rained, oozed right back down again." But near-by vermilion-hued sandstone was soon being used for more substantial structures. The Tabernacle was completed in 1871, the gleaming white stucco Temple in 1877. Brigham Young built a home here (which still stands) in 1869, and St. George in the 1870's was the informal "winter capital" of Utah.

Mormon Temple in St. George under construction. Work began in 1861, was completed in 1877.

Courtesy Utah State Historical Society

St. George's snowy white Temple today. Since it was built on swampy ground, its foundations consist of hundreds of tons of volcanic rock, all of it beaten down by a horse-powered pile driver made of an old cannon.

Courtesy Office of the Historian, The Church of Jesus Christ of Latter-day Saints

Cove Fort Utah

The social amenities came early to Cove Fort. Pioneer photographer William Henry Jackson camped near by, with his party, shortly after the fort was built. His diary contains this curious entry for June 10, 1867:

Made a short drive of some 6 or 7 miles to Cove Creek, arriving there quite early in the p.m. Had a general barbering & scrape. Dan cut Jim's & my hair, Jim cut Sam's hair, & Sam cut John's, giving him a regular Dead Rabbit cut. I then shaved Sam, & all the others, myself included, shaved themselves. Took a good shampooing all around also.

Cove Creek Fort was built by the Mormons (at a cost of $25,000) in 1867, during the Black Hawk Indian War, to protect the Church's newly completed Deseret Telegraph line. One of its twelve original rooms served as the telegraph station. Typical of the low-walled forts common in the Territory in early days—and well preserved today—it was constructed of volcanic rock, its eighteen-foot-high walls forming an enclosure one hundred feet square. A deep well in the center of the square provided the Saints with water; a bell hanging near by was a tocsin for Indian attacks. Now privately owned, Cove Fort served for many years as a Church-operated communications center, way place, supply station, and cattle ranch.

Part of the Church's over-all plan for self-sufficiency, and a dramatic example of the zeal and tireless effort with which the Saints tackled all such co-operative enterprises, the construction of the telegraph was ordered by Brigham Young on the day the first transcontinental telegraph was completed in 1861. The Civil War, however, prevented the Mormons from getting the necessary equipment until 1866. In the meantime, during the winter of 1865–66, a Church school of telegraphy was opened in Salt Lake City. Under Church supervision, the line—to run from Logan (in Cache Valley) on the north to St. George in the southwest—was surveyed, poles cut, funds were collected, and construction was begun. By the middle of February 1867 the entire 500-mile line was in operation. The cost was $56,000 in cash for wire and equipment, plus $24,000 in tithing credit for labor, a total of $80,000, or $160 per mile.

John C. Clowes, a Western Union official granted a leave to supervise the work for the Mormons, has left this testimonial to their organizational efficiency: "Not a man on this line ever worked a telegraph line before, the line was strung and put into operation in the middle of the winter. . . . I think the working of the same almost a miracle."

Cove Fort, some 185 miles south of Salt Lake City, was built in 1867 by the Mormon Church as a travelers' way station and a refuge from the Indians.

Courtesy David E. Miller

Typical of early-day forts in Utah Territory, Cove Fort is remarkably well preserved. It is now privately owned.

Courtesy Utah Tourist & Publicity Council

Promontory Utah

The event was to be one of the most significant in American history—the completion of the nation's first transcontinental railroad—and the waiting crowd was happily representative. On hand were excursionists from California and Salt Lake City; Irish and Chinese laborers, teamsters, cooks, and engineers; train crews and high railroad officials; distinguished guests; and a scattering of saloonkeepers, gamblers, and strumpets. On hand, too, were the symbolic stars of the drama, the Central Pacific's *Jupiter* and the Union Pacific's *No. 119,* plus a bewildering assortment of ceremonial ties, spikes, and hammers. Clicking out the story to a breathless nation was an anonymous telegrapher.

About noon, May 10, 1869, the program began with a long prayer. Then followed almost an hour of speech-making while ceremonial spikes were exchanged. Finally the climactic moment arrived. The traditional "golden spike" from California (attached to a telegraph wire) was placed in the predrilled hole in a polished tie of California laurel. The silver hammer (also attached to a telegraph wire) was handed to Gov. Leland Stanford. He took a mighty swing—and missed. The alert telegrapher saved the day, however; he touched his key and the resulting click set off a wild tumult in cities all across the country. Toasts were exchanged, and the majestic message went out over the wire: "The last rail is laid. The last spike is driven. The Pacific railroad is finished."

The feat was worthy of the celebration. First only the dream of visionaries, the idea of a transcontinental railroad became a vital necessity with the acquisition of California in 1847 and the discovery of gold the following year. In July 1862, Congress authorized the "42nd Parallel route" and provided the necessary subsidies. Soon the Union Pacific, with Grenville M. Dodge, Oaks and Oliver Ames, Thomas C. Durant, and thousands of Irish immigrants, was pushing west from Omaha. Eastward from Sacramento came the Central Pacific (now the Southern Pacific), with the "Big Four" of Mark Hopkins, Collis P. Huntington, Charles Crocker, and Leland Stanford and several thousand Chinese coolies.

The town of Promontory was short lived. The official rail junction was soon moved to Ogden, and completion of the Lucin Cutoff across Great Salt Lake in 1903 doomed this section of track to oblivion. But the Promontory "meet" itself had already insured the continental development of the United States and—in the words of the National Park Service, which now preserves the site—given "added reality to the decision of the Civil War that the Union was indissoluble."

Railroading's most celebrated "meet." The Central Pacific's wood-burning Jupiter (left) *and the Union Pacific's coal-consuming* No. 119 *touch cowcatchers at Promontory, Utah, on May 10, 1869, to give the nation its first transcontinental railroad.*

Courtesy Union Pacific Railroad

These are exact replicas of the Central Pacific's Jupiter *and the Union Pacific's* 119, *which met at Promontory Summit on May 10, 1869. They are used daily during the summer as part of the interpretive programs at Golden Spike National Historic Site.*

Courtesy National Park Service

Hole-in-the-Rock Utah

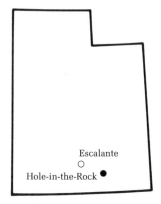

Escalante

Hole-in-the-Rock

Platte D. Lyman, chief chronicler for the Hole-in-the-Rock Expedition of the San Juan Mission, squeezes much of the drama from the trek's greatest single feat. His journal reads: "Jan. 26, 1880. Today we worked all the wagons in this camp down the Hole and ferried 26 of them across the river. The boat is worked by 1 pair of oars and does very well."

Eilzabeth Morris Decker is less matter-of-fact. Crossing the river, she wrote her parents, "was the easiest part of our journey. Coming down the hole in the rock to get to the river was ten times as bad. . . . It nearly scared me to death. The first wagon I saw go down they put the brake on and rough locked the hind wheels and had a big rope fastened to the wagon and about ten men holding back on it and then they went down like they would smash everything. I'll never forget that day. When we was walking down Willie looked back and cried and asked me how we would get back home."

The group—approximately 250 men, women, and children in some 80 wagons with more than 1,000 head of cattle, several hundred horses, and uncounted chickens—had no intention of returning to the Mormon settlements of southwestern Utah. In answer to a "call" from their church, these dedicated families were setting out across what is still one of the wildest, least-known regions in American to establish a new home in the San Juan Valley of southeastern Utah. A survey party had recommended the 200-mile, roadless "short cut" from Escalante east to the site of present Bluff. With supplies for a six-week trip and courage born of the supreme confidence that they were doing the Lord's will, the pioneers got under way the middle of October 1879.

Christmas found them still at the "Hole" (atop the west wall of the Colorado's Glen Canyon about six miles above the mouth of the San Juan River), hard at work on three road projects: widening and deepening the Hole itself to permit passage of a wagon, constructing just below it a pole-buttressed shelf road, and cutting a solid-rock dugway out of the gorge to the east. Not until the end of January were the pioneers safely across the river (no wagon or horse was lost). It was the first week of April before they reached their new home, with three babies born en route. The expedition, says historian David E. Miller, is "an excellent case-study of the highest type of pioneer endeavor that broke the wilderness and brought civilization to the West."

Hole-in-the-Rock, where the Christmas of 1879 was celebrated with races, a rifle shoot, wrestling matches, and a dance. The "road" was abandoned in 1881, but for almost a year, as the major link between the Utah settlements and San Juan County, it accommodated considerable traffic—both ways.

Courtesy Stan Rasmussen, Bureau of Reclamation

Platte D. Lyman's "cleft in the solid rock wall" (center foreground), looking east across the Colorado toward the San Juan. The "Hole" has not been flooded by Lake Powell, created by Glen Canyon Dam.

Courtesy Utah Tourist & Publicity Council

Baker Bay Washington

William Clark recorded the achievement—by Meriwether Lewis on November 16, by Clark himself two days later—of one of the expedition's primary objectives:

Nov. 17, 1805 At half past 10 Clock Capt. Lewis returned haveing traversed Haley Bay [now Baker Bay] to Cape Disapointment and the *Sea* coast to the North for Some distance. . . . I directed all the men who wished to see more of the main *Ocian* to prepare themselves to Set out with me early on tomorrow morning.

Nov. 18, 1805 this appears to be a very good harber for large Ships. here I found Capt. Lewis name on a tree. I also engraved my name, & by land the day of the month and year, as also Several of the men. . . . I crossed the neck of Land low and ½ of a mile wide to the main Ocian. . . . men appear much Satisfied with the trip beholding with estonishment the high waves dashing against the rocks & this emence Ocian

In eighteen months they had pushed halfway across the continent to trace the Columbia River to its mouth in the Pacific Ocean. In doing so they had strengthened the American claim to Oregon Territory made fourteen years before by Capt. Robert Gray, the first (so far as records show) to discover the river's mouth from the sea.

On May 11, 1792, Gray had steered his ship *Columbia Rediviva* past Cape Disappointment (which the English Capt. John Meares had named in 1788 after failing to recognize the mouth of the river) and anchored off the north bank of the river. He went ashore on May 19, traditionally raising the flag of the United States as a symbol of possession and naming the river for his ship.

The site (now marked by a flagpole and tablet just southeast of the village of Chinook) was that used by Lewis and Clark for their last camp. On November 15, Clark wrote: "the emence swells from the Main Ocian . . . raised to such a hite that I concluded to form a camp . . . and proceed no further by water." They walked to the Pacific, then, and because game was scarce, they crossed the river to establish Fort Clatsop (*q.v.*).

The mouth of the Columbia was of tremendous strategic importance, but not until 1862 did Congress appropriate money for permanent defense works. Fort Canby (originally Fort Cape Disappointment) was established April 5, 1864. Fort Columbia, on Chinook Point near Gray's landing site and the Lewis and Clark camp, was established July 15, 1896. Both have now been abandoned. The latter is a state park.

O Aberdeen

● Baker Bay

Capt. Robert Gray's ship Columbia Rediviva *anchored in the mouth of the Columbia River in 1792. The Chinook Indians came to trade—and to marvel at the great winged vessel.*

Courtesy Washington State Historical Society

Commanding officer's house at Fort Columbia, established in 1896 near the site of Gray's landing. Abandoned in 1950, it is now preserved as Fort Columbia Historical State Park.

Courtesy Washington State Historical Society

Spokane House Washington

Alexander Ross extolled the amenities at Spokane House (about 1817) when it was North West Company headquarters in the Columbia territory:

At Spokane House . . . there were handsome buildings. There was a ball room and no females in the land so fair to look upon as the nymphs of Spokane. No damsels could dance so gracefully as they; none were so attractive. But Spokane House was not celebrated for fine women only, there were fine horses also. The race ground was admired, and the pleasure of the race. Altogether, Spokane House was a delightful place.

Then on March 21, 1826, the post journal rang down the final curtain:

The blacksmith and cook, the only two men we have now here, employed collecting all the iron from the place, stripping the hinges off the doors.

For sixteen years Spokane House had bartered for the furs of the Great Oregon Wilderness. At the junction of the Spokane and Little Spokane rivers, the post was established in 1810 by David Thompson, the famed English geographer-explorer. Competition arrived in 1812. John Clarke, chief trader of Pacific Fur Company, built near-by Fort Spokane. Its grand opening—attended by Indians, traders, and trappers and including speeches, the displaying of merchandise, and dancing to fiddle music—was perhaps the first big social event of the Spokane country. Briefly the Astorians and Nor'Westers traded side by side.

It was a "most unsuitable place" for a trading post, Ross admitted. Men and supplies had to be carried two hundred miles north by water, then almost as far south again by land. But there "the Bourgeois who presided over the Company's affairs resided, and that made Spokane House the centre of attraction." There, too, the wintering parties were outfitted. "It was the great starting place."

In the spring of 1823 the Spokane factor sent an expedition into the dangerous Snake country under the veteran Finan McDonald, who wrote of his experiences:

We had Saviral Battils with the nasion on the other side of the Mountins Poore Meshel Bordoe was kild with 5 more of the Band there dath was revenge as well as we Could revenge it for no less than 68 of them that remane in the Planes as Pray for the wolves and those fue that askape our Shotes they had not Britch Clout to Cover them selves.

With Spokane House dismantled, the Hudson's Bay Company (which absorbed the North West Company in 1821) moved operations to Fort Colville, at Kettle Falls on the Columbia.

Spokane House, as recreated in a mural by Bertha Ballou. Alexander Ross described its location as a "most unsuitable place" for a trading post.

Courtesy Lincoln First Federal Savings & Loan Association, Spokane

Spokane House interpretive marker. Logs in background mark the site where the stockade and buildings stood. Signs describe points of interest on the grounds.

Courtesy Albert H. Culverwell, Washington State Parks and Recreation Commission

SPOKANE HOUSE

IN 1810 THE NORTH WEST COMPANY
A CANADIAN CONCERN, BUILT SPOKANE
HOUSE NEAR THIS SITE THE AREA WAS
A FAVORITE CAMPING GROUND OF THE
SPOKANE INDIANS AND THEIR NEIGHBORS
IN 1812 THE PACIFIC FUR COMPANY,
AN AMERICAN FIRM FOUNDED BY JOHN
JACOB ASTOR, ESTABLISHED A COMPETING
POST KNOWN AS FORT SPOKANE ON THE
SPOT WHICH IS MARKED WITH LOGS. AFTER
THE WAR OF 1812, THE 'NORTHWESTERS'
MOVED INTO THIS POST, CHANGING ITS
NAME TO SPOKANE HOUSE. IN 1821
THE NORTH WEST COMPANY MERGED WITH
THE HUDSON'S BAY COMPANY UNDER THE
LATTER'S NAME.
THE BUSINESS WAS MOVED IN 1826
TO FORT COLVILLE NEAR KETTLE FALLS

Fort Okanogan   Washington

Fort Okanogan, located beside the Okanogan River on a narrow spit of land between that river and the Columbia (four miles east of present Brewster, Washington), was established by the Astorians in 1811. David Stuart and a small party that included clerk Alexander Ross left Astoria (*q.v.*) on July 23. On September 2, some 540 river miles up the Columbia, they started work on a crude 16x20-foot trading post built of driftwood. If Ross's account is to be trusted, that first winter's trade, which he says he conducted with no more company that a dog, must have been fantastically successful. He "procured 1,550 beavers, besides other peltries, worth in the Canton market £2,250 sterling, and which stood the concern . . . in round numbers, £35!" (Here the American flag first flew over a settlement in the present state of Washington.)

The War of 1812 resulted in the transfer of Fort Okanogan, first to the North West Company, and then, following the merger of the two great British fur outfits in 1821, to the Hudson's Bay Company. Joseph McGillivray, a North West partner, was put in charge of the post in 1813. In a letter dated February 1814 he wrote: "This is a horribly dull place." And he soon set about improving it. Logs were floated down the Columbia. By September 1816, Ross Cox wrote, "we had erected a new dwelling house for the person in charge, containing four excellent rooms and a large dining-hall, two good houses for the men, and a spacious store for the furs and merchandise, to which was attached a shop for trading with the natives. The whole was surrounded by strong palisades fifteen feet high, and flanked by two bastions."

This improvement in defenses and living conditions, however, led to another problem. In 1824 aristocratic George Simpson became governor of Hudson's Bay Company. One inspection tour convinced this crusty martinet that the traders spend undue time worrying about the faithfulness of their Indian wives and were "not satisified unless they have a posse of Clerks Guides Interpreters and Supernumeraries at their disposal." He wanted them to farm, and when they complained that this was not a part of the fur trade, he replied, with canny Scot logic: "Every pursuit tending to leighten the Expence of the Trade is a branch thereof."

In the 1830's the HBC moved Fort Okanogan to the bank of the Columbia River about a mile away. Abandonment of the post, begun after the Treaty of 1846, was finally completed about 1860. Few traces of either fort can now be found, but the near-by Fort Okanogan Historical Museum re-creates their history.

Fort Okanogan about 1853, as drawn by John Mix Stanley. The Hudson's Bay Company started abandoning this important trading post after the Treaty of 1846 established the present United States–Canada boundary.

Courtesy University of Oklahoma Library

Fort Okanogan Historical Museum, built and maintained by the Washington State Parks commission, interprets the history of this important area from the days of the Indians' Caribou Trail down to the present.

Courtesy Albert H. Culverwell, Washington State Parks and Recreation Commission

Fort Nez Percés   Washington

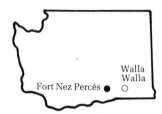

The decision of the North West Fur Company to establish Fort Nez Percés was made at Fort George (*see* Astoria) on June 5, 1818. Needed, says Alexander Ross, was a site "more central for the general business of the interior than that of Spokane House. . . . And I was appointed to take charge of that important depot." On July 11, Donald "McKenzie, myself, and ninety-five effective men encamped on the site [on the Columbia] about half a mile from the mouth of the little river Walla Walla."

A dozen years before, on April 29, 1806, the returning Lewis and Clark expedition had camped here, finding the "Wallahwallah River . . . a handsom Stream," the Indians of that name "honest friendly people." Ross found the site "commanding," with "a spacious view of our noble stream in all its grandeur," but he found the Indians hostile. At one time, not knowing "how affairs might terminate, all work was suspended" and they stood guard "for five long summer days."

The finished post was an imposing affair, one hundred feet square, surrounded by an outer wall of whipsawed planks thirty inches wide, six inches thick, and twenty feet high. A four-foot balustrade provided loopholes, an inside gallery enabled guards to patrol the wall. Ross summarized the weapons of defense— four pieces of ordnance, ten wall pieces or swivels, sixty stands of muskets and bayonets, twenty boarding pikes, a box of hand grenades—and concluded that it was "at once the strongest and most complete fort west of the Rocky Mountains and might be called the Gibralter of the Columbia."

Nathaniel J. Wyeth was not so impressed. Spending five days at the fort in October 1833, he described it as being "of no strength merely sufficient to frighten Indians." Capt. B. L. E. Bonneville, another American visitor (1834), also minimized its strength, but he admitted that it was "handsomely built" and that he received "a polite reception" from Pierre C. Pambrun, who had assumed control (for the then Hudson's Bay Company) in 1832. The Marcus Whitmans (*see* Waiilatpu) also appreciated Pambrun's hospitality. Arriving September 1, 1836, they were offered a private room—with bedstead—and at mealtime were surprised to see cabbage, turnips, potatoes, beets, melons, tea, and bread and butter.

The Oregon Treaty of 1846, however, placed this area under American control. The Hudson's Bay Company abandoned Fort Walla Walla (as Fort Nez Percés came to be known) in the late 1850's and it was burned by Indians. The near-by town of Wallula was platted in 1862 as the western terminus of the Mullan Road from Fort Benton (*q.v.*). Until the coming of the railroad in 1882, it was an important stage and freighting center.

Fort Nez Percés about 1840. In 1833, Nathaniel J. Wyeth saw "a bull and cow & calf, hen & cock, punkins, potatoes, corn, all of which looked strange and unnatural."

Courtesy Public Archives of Canada

*The site of Fort Nez Percés (*left, beyond island*) is today covered by the waters of the Columbia, backed up by McNary Dam.*

Courtesy Eastern Washington State Historical Society

Fort Vancouver Washington

Fort Vancouver (on the Washington side of the Columbia one hundred miles above its mouth) was headquarters and depot for all Hudson's Bay Company activities in the Northwest from 1824, when the company moved here from Fort George (*see* Astoria), to 1846, when the forty-ninth parallel became the international boundary between the United States and Canada. By this time the Oregon Trail was bringing more and more Americans into the region, and the trading post—an economic, political, social, and cultural center for a vast, largely uninhabited wilderness—had become an important part of the heritage of the two countries.

The fort itself was prepossessing, a 325x732-foot log stockade guarded by a single bastion. To the west was "the village," some thirty to fifty wooden dwellings of the lesser employees. Dominating the two dozen major buildings inside the stockade was the impressive residence of chief factor (1824–46) John McLoughlin, the "Father of Oregon" (*see* Oregon City). Here, thousands of miles from sophisticated courts and salons, he maintained a splendid symbol of urbane propriety amid rough trappers and Indian wives dressed in the finest of Chinese silks, French lace, and London busks. Friend and foe alike shared his hospitality. Dining was a ceremony. A Highland piper was stationed behind his chair at the head of a banquet table that gleamed with linen and silver. Toasts were drunk in English port. And bagpipes were prominent on all state occasions.

Few travelers to the Northwest bypassed the fort. David Douglas (for whom the Douglas fir is named) arrived in 1825 to study the region's vegetation. Nathaniel J. Wyeth was one of the first American visitors, in 1832. With him was John Ball, who opened the first school in present-day Washington. "I feel I have come to a father's house indeed," wrote Narcissa Whitman (1836). She stayed long enough to teach the children *Rock of Ages* and other hymns. John C. Frémont and his party arrived in 1843.

But McLoughlin saw to the company's business, too. The fort shipped supplies to trappers as far inland as Utah and Montana and to coastal points from California to Alaska. Furs from all stations were gathered here for shipment to England. McLoughlin also supervised nearly two thousand acres of farmlands. He built up beef-cattle herds, planted the Northwest's first orchards, and established sawmills, shipyards, salt works, and fisheries.

Hudson's Bay Company influence declined rapidly, however, after the Treaty of 1846. The United States established Vancouver Barracks in 1848 (it was not abandoned until 1947) and the company gave up all operations in 1860. Fire destroyed the stockade six years later.

Fort Vancouver about 1845, when it was still the hub of all Hudson's Bay Company activities in the Northwest. This view is by Henry James Warre.

Courtesy Public Archives of Canada

Reconstructed stockade and blockhouse at Fort Vancouver. The visitors' center at the National Historic Site has an exhibit room that interprets the role of the Hudson's Bay Company and the participants in the fur trade in the development of the Pacific Northwest.

Courtesy National Park Service

Fort Nisqually Washington

Fort Nisqually (spelled *Nesqually* until 1843, when it was re-built) was established on Puget Sound about seventeen miles south of what is now Tacoma in 1833 by Archibald McDonald of the Hudson's Bay Company as an important ploy in the contest for the Oregon country. Since 1819, Great Britain and the United States had jointly occupied the territory, and the original 15x20-foot trading house of hand-hewn logs (the stockade was added later) was an attempt to strengthen England's hand. Factor John McLoughlin of Fort Vancouver (*q.v.*) put it this way: "It is formed in consequence of the American Coasters of later years frequently visiting the Strait of Juan De Fuca which obliged us to keep a party constantly in Puget Sound, and if by being station-ary it can also attend a farm so much the better."

The fort controlled 160,000 acres of fine land, and its first seven cows were unloaded from the brig *Llama* in 1834. So well did they do that long-horned Spanish cattle were soon being driven up from California. Sheep were introduced in 1838, and in 1839 the Puget Sound Agricultural Company was formed as a subsidiary of the Hudson's Bay Company, which saw in it an opportunity to provide for its retired trappers, populate Oregon with English-minded settlers, and produce needed food and grain. In December 1840 the Puget Sound Company took over Fort Nisqually but left the post's fur trade in HBC hands.

With the arrival in 1836 of the steamship *Beaver*—first of its kind on the North Pacific—Nisqually's commercial importance grew rapidly. In April 1839, David Leslie and Dr. William Holden Willson established a Methodist mission a short distance north-east of the fort. American influence was reinforced in 1841 when Capt. Charles Wilkes anchored his two ships, the *Vincennes* and the *Porpoise,* at the mouth of the Nisqually River. Dr. John P. Richmond of the mission delivered a patriotic address to the crews in one of the West's first offical Fourth of July celebrations.

Dr. William Frazier Tolmie became a factor in 1843; he moved Fort Nisqually to a new site about two miles to the northeast. Three years later, however, the international boundary was established at the forty-ninth parallel, putting the new post in American territory. The Puget Sound Company moved its head-quarters to Victoria in 1859, but relations between it and Amer-ican settlers worsened steadily and in 1867 the U.S. government purchased the company's holdings for $650,000. By 1934 only portions of the granary and the factor's house remained. These were moved to Point Defiance Park in Tacoma, where a careful reconstruction of the important post now stands.

Fort Nisqually, as sketched by James Alden in 1857. Although estab-lished as a fur post in 1833, the fort served as headquarters of the Puget Sound Agricultural Com-pany, a Hudson's Bay Company subsidiary, from 1839 until 1867, when its holdings were purchased by the U.S. government.

Courtesy Washington State Historical Society

Restored Fort Nisqually in Point Defiance Park at Tacoma. Two of the orig-inal buildings were moved from the first site, some seventeen miles to the south.

Courtesy Steve Ander-son, Point Defiance Park

Waiilatpu Washington

It was on December 10, 1836, that Narcissa Whitman moved into her new cottonwood-log home, "a house reared & the lean too enclosed, a good chimney & fire place & the flour laid. No windows or door except blankets. My heart truly leaped for joy as I alighted from my horse and entered and seated myself before a pleasant fire." Hers was the universal response of the young bride. Though crude, and surrounded by hostile Indians, it was her own. Their first child, expected in a few months, would be born at Waiilatpu.

Narcissa and Marcus had been married in the East on February 18. With the Henry Spaldings (*see* Lapwai) they had come over the Oregon Trail that summer, arriving at Fort Vancouver (*q.v.*) September 12. While the men located mission sites, the women bought food, clothing, and household goods. On November 3 they set out, first up the Columbia, then the Walla Walla, to the mouth of Mill Creek. Here at Waiilatpu, the "Place of Rye Grass," Whitman had built their first—and last—home.

Alice Clarissa arrived March 14, 1837 (the first American white child born west of the Continental Divide). Soon Narcissa was teaching again. If the Cayuse Indians were indifferent to religious worship and schooling, they loved to hear her sing. (Her clear soprano was "as sweet and musical as the chime of bells.") Whitman was wisely supplementing his theology with agricultural and industrial instruction. Myron F. Eells reported in 1838: "There are a number of wheat, corn and potato fields about the house, besides a garden of melons and all kinds of vegetables." In time a gristmill and blacksmith shop were added. Results were disappointing, but the Whitmans worked with boundless energy and self-sacrificing devotion. As more American settlers poured into the Northwest, their hospitality made Waiilatpu a popular haven to Oregon Trail travelers.

By late 1847 the mission community totaled seventy-four persons, excluding Indians. Increasing immigration was making the Cayuses uneasy, and an epidemic of measles aggravated the situation. Although Dr. Whitman's medicine kept most of the white children alive, it had little effect on the Indian children, who possessed virtually no natural immunity to the white man's diseases. Rumor spread that the missionaries were poisoning the Indians.

On November 29 the Cayuses struck. Whitman, Narcissa, and twelve others (all men) were killed and the mission buildings, orchards, and other developments destroyed. Fifty-one captives, mostly women and children, were ransomed by Peter Skene Ogden of the Hudson's Bay Company. Two young girls died in captivity. The massacre brought an abrupt end to mission work among the Oregon Indians.

The Whitman mission, sketched from a picture by H. B. Nichols. Converts were few—one Cayuse and twenty-one Nez Percés—but its influence was significant in the development of Oregon Territory.

Courtesy Washington State Historical Society

Great Grave at Whitman National Monument, six miles west of Walla Walla, Washington. Great Grave was built in 1897, the fiftieth anniversary of the Waiilatpu Massacre, on the same site as the earlier graves.

Courtesy National Park Service

THE WHITMAN MISSION

Green River Rendezvous Wyoming

Alfred Jacob Miller, accompanying Sir William Drummond Stewart on his trip to the Far West in 1837, spent a month at the trappers' rendezvous, held that year on the Green River a few miles below present-day Daniel, Wyoming:

At certain specified times during the year, the American Fur Company appoint a "Rendezvous" . . . for the purpose of trading with Indians and Trappers. . . . The first day is devoted to "High Jinks," a species of Saturnalia, in which feasting, drinking, and gambling form prominent parts. . . . The following days exhibit the strongest contrast to this. The Fur Company's great tent is raised;—the Indians erect their picturesque white lodges;—The accumulated furs of the hunting season are brought forth, and the Company's tent is a besieged and busy place.

A colorful mixture of business and fun, these annual get-togethers (initiated by William H. Ashley in 1824 and held at various spots in this general region until 1840) were exciting affairs. Miller was the first and perhaps the best artist to put them on canvas.

Trappers trekked in singly, in pairs, and in groups to swap their year's catch for ammunition, traps, whiskey, tobacco, and other supplies. In addition to these staples, Indians bartered furs for vermilion, beads, mirrors, and bright cloth. Trading went on briskly at fixed hours. Then came the target shooting, wrestling, horse racing, singing, cursing, brawling, courting (of not unwilling Indian maidens), and story telling.

Ashley revolutionized fur trading. He mounted his men, employing only good riders and expert shots. For established forts and trading posts, he substituted the rendezvous—and he made the system pay. More importantly, he helped American interests, following an essential policy of free trade, to out-hustle and out-compete the more tradition-bound British companies. The latter (the Hudson's Bay Company alone after 1821) did not react fast enough, or strongly enough: traders switched to the Americans because they paid more. And the prize, to a great extent, was Oregon.

Rendezvous were also held beside the Green in 1833, 1835, 1836, 1839, and 1840. The 1835 rendezvous was memorable for the presence of Dr. Marcus Whitman (*see* Waiilatpu) and Rev. Samuel Parker, who added sermons to the regular program of gambling and horse racing, and Dr. Whitman was able to relieve Jim Bridger of the arrowhead he had carried in his back for three years (*see* Three Forks). The following year, the rendezvous was softened even more by the attendance of Narcissa Whitman and Eliza Spalding, the first white women to cross Wyoming.

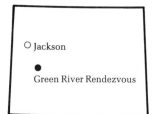

Rendezvous (1837), by Alfred Jacob Miller. In this typical scene of relaxation and fun (note Indians bathing in the river) the memorable feature is "Capt. Bridger in a full suit of steel armor . . . imported from England and presented to Capt. B. by our commander." Needless to say, it "created a sensation when worn by him on stated occasions."

Courtesy Walters Art Gallery

The historic rendezvous of the fur trappers in the 1820s and 1830s is relived each year in Wyoming's Green River country.

Courtesy Wyoming Travel Commission

278

Fort Laramie   Wyoming

From the winter of 1812–13, when returning Astorian Robert Stuart commented on the site, to March 2, 1890, when the Seventh Infantry marched away, the junction of the Laramie and North Platte rivers in southeastern Wyoming was an important area in Old West history. Trappers and fur traders reached the region as early as 1821, when Jacques La Ramée, as tradition has it, was killed by Indians near the stream now bearing his name. Explorers, adventurers, missionaries, homeseekers, Mormons, Argonauts, and soldiers soon followed.

The first Fort Laramie (officially Fort William) was built in 1834 by William Sublette and Robert Campbell. Jim Bridger, Thomas Fitzpatrick, and Milton Sublette bought the post in 1835, the year Dr. Marcus Whitman and Rev. Samuel Parker paused briefly on their way to Oregon.

The American Fur Company took over in 1836. Alfred Jacob Miller arrived in 1837 to paint the only known pictures of the first fort, where, he said, the Indians "camped 3 or 4 times a year, bringing peltries to be exchanged for dry goods, tobacco, beads, and alcohol." Two years later Dr. Frederick A. Wislizenus, the German adventurer, noted that the center court had "a tall tree in it, on which the flag is raised on occasions of state." Fr. Pierre Jean De Smet stopped at "Fort La Ramée" in 1840.

By the time the second Fort Laramie was built (as Fort John) in 1841 the fur trade was declining and the first party of covered-wagon emigrants (John Bidwell and Joseph Williams) had passed. In 1843 came Dr. Whitman's "Cow Column," the first important Oregon migration, with nearly one thousand people. The number swelled to three thousand in 1845, the year Col. Stephen Watts Kearny stopped with the First U.S. Dragoons. The initial Mormon emigration to Utah appeared in 1847. (Diaries of the Saints confirmed the findings, the spring before, of Francis Parkman: "Prices are more extortionate: sugar, two dollars a cup; five-cent tobacco at a dollar and a half; bullets at seventy-five cents a pound.")

In 1849 the fort became a military post, and the frontier gradually receded. There were an estimated fifty-five thousand emigrants in 1850, and the stages of John Hockaday and William Liggett arrived in 1851. (The post also served briefly as a station on the famed Cheyenne-Deadwood stage route.) In 1851, too, and again in 1868 (*see* Fort Rice), important treaties were drawn up at Fort Laramie by which the Sioux, Cheyennes, and other tribes reluctantly gave up their claims to the region. The fort played a very prominent role in the Indian wars of the 1860's and 1870's, culminating in the Sioux campaigns of 1876.

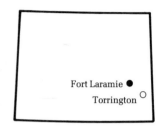

Fort Laramie •
Torrington ○

Fort Laramie, as painted by Alfred Jacob Miller in 1837, when he accompanied Sir William Drummond Stewart on an expedition to the Far West.

Courtesy Walters Art Gallery

The U.S. government purchased Fort Laramie (667 Oregon Trail miles west of Independence, Missouri) in 1849 for the sum of four thousand dollars and began construction of the military post almost immediately. Many of the fort's twenty-two structures have been restored in Fort Laramie National Historic Site and are open to visitors.

Courtesy Wyoming Travel Commission

South Pass Wyoming

"Here Hail Oregon" Joel Palmer wrote in 1845 as his wagon train reached the summit of South Pass, 947 miles from Independence and roughly the mid-point on the trail to Fort Vancouver. The journal entry was symbolically right. Here atop the Continental Divide, 7,550 feet above sea level, emigrants were on something of a psychological watershed. The trail ahead, if not easy, was at least downhill all the way.

This most celebrated of all pioneer passes was hardly a pass at all, actually, No well-defined gorge or striking notch in the mountains, it was rather a broad, treeless valley that could confuse no less a pathfinder than John C. Frémont. The ascent was so gradual "we were obliged to watch very closely to find the place at which we had reached the culminating point."

The discoverer of this remarkably easy pass is unknown. Lewis and Clark (1805) crossed the Divide in the Bitter Roots far to the northwest. The westbound Astorians under Wilson Price Hunt (1811) used near-by Union Pass. Both were above nine thousand feet and extremely rugged. Had no easier way been found across the mountains, historians speculate, the vast Oregon country might never have become American, and almost certainly its conquest by home-seeking emigrants would have been greatly delayed.

The ubiquitous fur trappers did stumble onto South Pass, however, probably in the early 1820's. Thomas Fitzpatrick and Jedediah Smith used the grassy gateway in 1824 and promptly reported its presence to William H. Ashley, who sent the first "wheels" through the pass in 1827—a four-pound cannon mounted on two wheels and drawn by four mules. Capt. B. L. E. Bonneville took the first wagon over South Pass on July 24, 1832.

By 1843 wagon trains began to wear deep ruts that are still visible today, and during the next two decades as many as 300,000 persons may have crossed the Rockies here. The stagecoach arrived in the late 1850's, the Pony Express in 1860, a telegraph line in 1861. Indian trouble caused freight and stage lines to be moved south in 1862 to what became known as the Overland Trail. The railroad (*see* Promontory) soon doomed both.

Gold was discovered in 1867, and South Pass City, twelve miles northeast of the pass, boomed briefly. Here the territorial legislature met on December 10, 1869, and became the first in the nation's history to grant equal rights to women. Four years later the town was deserted.

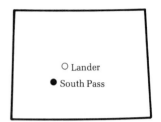

O Lander
● South Pass

South Pass, landmark on the Oregon Trail. Many travelers commented on how flat the pass was, how difficult it was to know when you'd crossed it.

Courtesy Wyoming Recreation Commission

South Pass City, situated near the pass and once Wyoming's largest community, is an outstanding example of a western ghost town.

Courtesy Wyoming Travel Commission

Mormon Ferry Wyoming

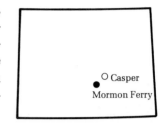

"In a large company of men, horses, wagons, and equipments, the crossing of rivers is quite an undertaking," Alfred Jacob Miller noted in 1837. He witnessed "trappers getting rid of their religion and their temper at the same time." Recalling that Laurence Sterne's Captain Shandy spoke of the army's swearing terribly in Flanders, he concluded' "In this . . . our devil-may-care Trappers have not degenerated."

Ten years later, when the Mormon pioneers reached the North Platte, swearing as a tool of transportation was denied the Saints, on religious grounds, and fording was eschewed for ferrying. On June 16, according to Preston Nibley, "President Young worked with all his strength, assisted by Doctor Richards and others, and made a first rate white pine and white cottonwood raft." This, together with a raft built a few days before by the advance party, put the Saints in the ferrying business. Young, always the shrewd businessman, promptly decided that "it would be wisdom to leave a few of the brethren at this ferry to assist . . . other emigrants and make enough in provisions to sustain themselves."

Appleton Harmon, one of nine men detailed to the operation, reports Young's instructions regarding rates: "For one waggon familey &c you will charge $1.50 cts payment in flour & provisions at State Prices or $3.00 in cash." Two Saints were sent back to Deer Creek to erect what must have been one of the first advertising signs on the Plains:

Notice
To the ferry 28 ms the ferry good &
safe maned
by experienced men black Smithing horse & ox
shoing done all so a wheel right
Thomas Grover

(Customers continued to arrive. On July 8, Harmon noted "thare was done $6.40cts worth of black Smithing & Some other jobs commenced Luke Johnson [an amateur doctor and dentist] got $3.00 for cleaning teeth & Doctoring which was put into the jineral pile.")

In 1859, Louis Guinard build an impressive 1,000-foot-long toll bridge—of cedar logs on stone-filled cribs—near the ferry site. To protect the emigrants, troops were stationed here only intermittently until 1863, when Platte Bridge Station was formally established. The biggest engagement in the vicinity occured July 26, 1865, when some three thousand Indians attacked a wagon train near Red Buttes. Among those killed was Lt. Caspar Collins, for whom the fort was subsequently named. (A clerical error in the official order resulted in the spelling *Casper*.) The bridge was abandoned on October 19, 1867, and later burned by the Indians.

Mormon Ferry on the North Platte River in 1849 (William Henry Tappan is believed to be the artist). Several sites in the general area of present-day Casper were used in the years before the first bridge was built.

Courtesy State Historical Society of Wisconsin

Reconstructed Fort Casper, on the North Platte River a mile west of Casper. It was named for Lt. Caspar Collins, killed near there July 26, 1865, while trying to defend a wagon train from Indians.

Courtesy Wyoming Travel Commission

284

Independence Rock Wyoming

Outstanding landmarks were sufficiently rare on the long Overland Trail that reaching one after days of weary travel seemed to call for a celebration. It was probably such an impromptu affair, falling fortuitously on July 4, which named Independence Rock (fifty-five miles southwest of Casper). No one knows for sure who first christened it, but John K. Townsend noted, in 1834, that the massive glacial relic was "called Rock Independence," and one commonly accepted story credits the actual naming to the Ashley-Henry expedition of 1822, comprising such mountain-man stalwarts as Jim Bridger, Jedediah Smith, Tom Fitzpatrick, Étienne Provost, and William Sublette. Better documented is the July 4, 1847 celebration, when as many as one thousand Oregon- and California-bound emigrants gathered here on the north bank of the Sweetwater and set off a charge of gunpowder in salute to the states they had so recently left.

Independence Rock also served, in Fr. Pierre Jean De Smet's words (1840), as "the great registry of the desert." He admits that "my name figures amongst so many others." Artist Alfred Jacob Miller noted three years earlier "the names of Sublette, Wyeth, Campbell, Bonneville, Pitcher &c., many carved deep into the stone," and he adds that "the temptation was too strong not to add our own;—to make amends for this assumption, and show our zeal for others, we found a man by the cognomer of Nelson had carved his name, and to insure *him* immortality we added to it, 'Of the Nile!' . . . what a pity it is he will never know his benefactors."

In 1842, John C. Frémont records: "I engraved on this rock of the far West a symbol of the Christian faith . . . a large cross." It has now disappeared (perhaps in the 1847 dynamite blast?), but it was used to inflame feeling against him in 1856 when he was an unsuccessful candidate for President. Happier was the experience of the Mormons. Recognizing that many travelers had neither the time nor the ability to mark their passage suitably, the Saints detailed experienced stonecutters to the site, charged from one to five dollars for each name engraved on the rock.

Thousands of names can still be read on Independence Rock, nor have wind and rain completely obliterated the dim wagon ruts at its base. Here, too, are memorial plaques to the Mormon emigrants; to Ezra Meeker; to Narcissa Whitman and Eliza Spalding, first white women to cross Wyoming; to Fr. De Smet, the state's first Jesuit missionary; and to Wyoming's first Masonic meeting, held atop Independence Rock on July 4, 1862.

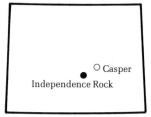

Independence Rock as seen in 1837 by Alfred Jacob Miller. From ten miles away "we were struck with its resemblance to a huge tortoise sprawling on the prairie." Capt. B. L. E. Bonneville, in 1832, saw it as "a half globe of imposing appearance rising out of a lonely landscape."

Courtesy Walters Art Gallery

A gray-brown granite monolith, Independence Rock is 1,552 yards in circumference, with a north-south height ranging from 193 feet to 167 feet. It has changed little since Alfred Jacob Miller first saw it.

Union Pacific photograph, courtesy Wyoming Travel Commission

Devil's Gate   Wyoming

All sites along the emigrant trails were marked with tragedy. This homely notation on a crude grave board recorded the death, in the early 1860's, of an eighteen-year-old girl who climbed to the ridge overlooking Devil's Gate, then slipped from the edge:

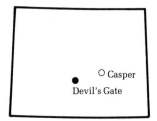

> Here lies the body of Caroline Todd
> Whose soul has lately gone to God;
> Ere redemption was too late,
> She was redeemed at Devil's Gate.

Far grimmer was the fate of the Mormon handcart company of inexperienced European converts marooned here the winter of 1856–57.

Delayed on the trail and eventually trapped by snow, the group built a crude fort in the gap, waited desperately for help. It came, finally, in the form of relief wagons dispatched from Salt Lake City by Brigham Young, but not before more than one hundred had died. When the meat of their oxen was gone, the converts were reduced to living off the hides (after scraping off the hair and boiling away the worst of the taste). "We asked the Lord," wrote Dan Jones, "to bless our stomachs and adapt them to this food." Evidently He did, for Jones records later, with wry humor: "We enjoyed this sumptuous fare for about six weeks and never had the gout."

Devil's Gate, six trail miles up the Sweetwater from Independence Rock (q.v.), is a spectacular granite-walled gorge some 350 feet deep and only 30 feet wide at the bottom. There is no evidence of erosion. Instead, the rock seems to have been cleft by some convulsion of nature.

Although from a distance the chasm appears to be an inviting notch in a low range of mountains, the emigrant trail wisely skirted it to the south. Still accurate is the description of newspaperman Matthew C. Field, with Sir William Drummond Stewart's 1843 hunting expedition to the Rockies: "It is a dark, frowning, narrow cleft . . . and the beautiful stream of the Sweetwater plunges through it in a sparkling torrent of milky foam, caused by the narrow rocky limit into which the current is compressed while escaping through."

Robert Stuart's Astorians, in 1812, were perhaps the first to note Devil's Gate. Alfred Jacob Miller sketched it in 1837, and John C. Frémont paused in 1842 to measure its length: three hundred yards. As for the Sweetwater River, it was named by William H. Ashley in 1823 after his trappers told him the water left a pleasant taste in their mouths. Tradition tells that a pack mule fell, while crossing the stream, and spilled its load of sugar into the water.

Devil's Gate in 1837. Alfred J. Miller thought it a "singular scene," but after attempting to describe it, he decided that "the sketch . . . will convey a better idea . . . than any written description can possibly accomplish."

Courtesy Walters Art Gallery

John C. Frémont visited Devil's Gate (shown here as it looks today) in 1842 and noted that "the stream in the gate is almost entirely choked up by masses which have fallen from above. In the wall on the right bank is a dike of trap rock, cutting through a fine grey granine."

Courtesy Wyoming Travel Commission

Fort Bridger Wyoming

Jim Bridger was shrewder than most. When the fur trade began to decline, threatening the mountain-man breed with extinction, he landed on his feet. In a letter written in December 1843 (undoubtedly dictated, since he was almost illiterate), Bridger outlined his scheme to St. Louis merchant Pierre Chouteau, Jr.:

I have established a small fort with a blacksmith shop and a supply of iron in the road of the emigrants on Black's Fork on Green River which promises fairly. They, in coming out, are generally well suplied with money, but by the time they get there are in want of all kinds of supplies. Horses, provisions, smith work, etc., bring ready cash from them, and should I receive the goods hereby ordered will do a considerable business in that way with them.

Contemporary accounts agree the post was "small." Joel Palmer, leader of one Oregon-bound emigrant train, camped near by in July 1845 and wrote: "It is built of poles and daubed with mud; it is a shabby concern. Here are about twenty-five lodges of Indians, or rather white trapper's lodges occupied by their Indian wives. They have a good supply of robes, dressed deer." The following year, one Mary Smith added, "This is not properly a fort, but several adobe buildings arranged for the purpose of defense."

But the establishment—said, half-facetiously, to be the first "tourist camp" west of the Mississippi—was both popular and profitable. It soon became the second greatest (after Fort Laramie) outfitting point for Oregon Trailers and attracted the attention of another shrewd businessman, Mormon leader Brigham Young, who first stopped there in 1847 on his way to Salt Lake City.

Whether through purchase (by Lewis Robinson, as the Church maintains) or by force (history is more indefinite than Bridger, who wrote in 1873, "I was robbed and threatened with death"), the Mormons took over the fort in 1853. In 1857, however, after investing sixty thousand dollars in it and near-by Fort Supply (q.v.), they abandoned and burned both before the advancing federal troops of Gen. Albert Sidney Johnston. (Curiously, the two hundred tons of supplies hauled west for Johnston's army by Alexander Majors and William H. Russell represent the first organized effort at large-scale freighting.)

The army promptly rebuilt Fort Bridger, and in the fall of 1857 it became a regular military base. It was not abandoned, permanently and officially, until November 6, 1890. Many of its old buildings remain today, carefully preserved, just off US 30, as a state park.

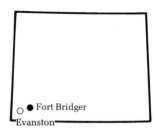

○ ● Fort Bridger
Evanston

Fort Bridger, on Black's Fork of the Green River in southwestern Wyoming, was one of the best-known "rest stops" on the Oregon, California, and Mormon trails. The view is an Ackerman lithograph from Howard Stansbury's Exploration and Survey of the Valley of the Great Salt Lake of Utah (1852).

Courtesy Library of Congress

Bridger State Park preserves the remaining buildings of the old trading post and military fort, one of which is now a museum. Here, too, is the first schoolhouse in Wyoming, and it was also here (probably in June 1863) that the state's first newspaper appeared— daily bulletins of Civil War news and other items issued by one H. Brundage, the fort's telegrapher.

Courtesy Union Pacific Railroad

Fort Supply Wyoming

If Fort Bridger (*q.v.*) was primarily a commercial venture, Fort Supply, twelve miles to the south was essentially an experiment in religious pragmatism. Brigham Young had two main objectives when, in the fall of 1853, he commissioned Orson Hyde to settle the Black's Fork Valley of southwestern Wyoming. Fort Supply, like Las Vegas and the Carson Valley in Nevada, San Bernardino in California, Moab in southeastern Utah, and Lemhi in Idaho, was part of the second phase of Mormon colonization, a long-range plan for the expansion of the Church beyond Utah's readily cultivatable valleys. The ultimate goal was to ring this central bastion with strategically located friendly colonies. (The area encompassed by this outer cordon— one thousand miles north-south, eight hundred east-west— amounted to almost one-sixth of the area of the United States, excluding Alaska and Hawaii.)

A more immediate (and humanitarian) objective was to provide a base for "relief trains" meeting the westward-moving Saints with food, fresh teams, and needed equipment. Young felt that extending this volunteer help to those unable to carry sufficient supplies for the entire eighty-day trek across the plains was the essence of Christianity, and in 1852 no less than two hundred wagon teams left Salt Lake City carrying fifty thousand pounds of flour and large quantities of vegetables.

Hyde selected the site for Fort Supply. Behind him came a second company of Saints with horses, mules, cattle, and wagons loaded with seed, farm implements, and other colonizing supplies. A winged, two-story log building was built at once to house the entire population. Fields were promptly planted and irrigated, representing two agricultural "firsts" for white men in present-day Wyoming.

But the future of Fort Supply (and Fort Bridger, which the Mormons acquired in 1853) was clouded by the so-called Utah War of 1857. Brigham Young called up the territorial militia, the Nauvoo Legion, and from it detached a 75-man Corps of Observation to scout Gen. Albert Sidney Johnston's approaching Utah Expedition. Eventually, other groups of raiders were sent out, one with instructions as follows:

On ascertaining the locality or route of the troops, proceed at once to annoy them in every possible way. Use every exertion to stampede their animals, and set fire to their trains. . . . Keep them from sleeping by night surprises. Blockade the road by felling trees, or destroying the fords when you can. . . . Take no life, but destroy their trains, and stampede or drive away their animals.

Curiously, one of the early actions of these raiders was to burn both Fort Bridger and Fort Supply. The latter was never rebuilt.

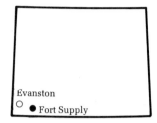

Fort Supply, established by the Mormons in the Black's Fork Valley of southwestern Wyoming in 1853, is shown here in a copy of an original drawing by Merritt D. Houghton.

Courtesy Wyoming State Historical Department

Historical marker on the site of Fort Supply. The post was burned by Mormon raiders to prevent its capture by Gen. Albert Sidney Johnston.

Courtesy David E. Miller

SITE OF
FORT
SUPPLY

ESTABLISHED IN NOVEMBER 1853,
BY CAPTAIN JOHN NEBEKER
AND CAPTAIN ISAAC BULLOCK
WHO LOCATED HERE WITH A
NUMBER OF LATTER DAY
SAINTS. THIS WAS THE FIRST
PLACE IN WYOMING WHERE
LAND WAS IRRIGATED

ABANDONED IN 1857

THIS SITE WAS GIVEN TO WYOMING BY
ANSON HANSEN
ERECTED BY
THE HISTORICAL LANDMARK COMMISSION
OF WYOMING
1937

Fort Phil Kearny Wyoming

Fort Phil Kearny was conceived in treachery. In 1865, the "Bloody Year on the Plains," a formal treaty with the Sioux guaranteed them exclusive use of a vast area now included in southeastern Montana, northeastern Wyoming, and the western Dakotas. In the meantime, however, gold was luring a steady stream of Argonauts to western Montana (*see* Bannack). Impatient of the circuitous route through Salt Lake City, they were soon streaming across Sioux lands from Fort Laramie to Bozeman. When the Indians retaliated savagely for this violation of their treaty, public indignation in the East soon brought the call for another peace commission and the decision to establish a line of forts along the new Bozeman Trail. The timing was unfortunate.

On June 13, 1866, while commissioners and Indians were still negotiating, a westbound wagon train of about seven hundred men under Col. Henry B. Carrington arrived at Fort Laramie. When it pulled out for Bozeman three days later—with twenty-one women and children plus household goods—the Indians realized what was up. As one hostile summed it up bitterly: "Great Father sends us presents and wants new road, but white chief goes with soldiers to steal road before Indian say yes or no!"

Carrington reached the Big Piney in mid-July and soon had construction under way. On the last day of October the post was finished sufficiently to warrant a "holiday," complete with formal parade, speech, and flag raising.

"The fort proper is six hundred feet by eight hundred," wrote Mrs. Carrington, "situated upon a natural plateau. . . . The Stockade is made of heavy pine trunks, eleven feet long, hewn to a touching surface of four inches so as to join closely, being pointed and loop-holed. . . . Blockhouses are at two diagonal corners."

Strong defenses were needed. Though brief, the fort's two-year existence was extremely bloody. Red Cloud and his Sioux had been unable to prevent its erection, but they kept it under continual siege. And then on December 21, 1866, they had their chance. Brevet Lt. Col. William J. Fetterman—a greenhorn who considered troopers superior to war-painted Indians per se, regardless of numbers—led out his Eighteenth Infantry to rescue a wood train under attack. Disobeying Carrington's explicit orders, he charged over a hill in pursuit of a band of Sioux decoys under Crazy Horse. The result: Fetterman and his entire command of seventy-nine soldiers and two civilians wiped out in a few bloody minutes.

The Wagon Box Fight, August 2, 1867, did not end so tragically, but life was never easy, nor was it without danger, at Fort Phil Kearny.

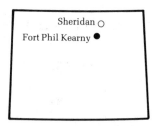

Fort Phil Kearny, as sketched in 1867 by Bugler Antonio Nicoli. Built in 1866 on big Piney Fork of Powder River about twenty-five miles south of present-day Sheridan, Wyoming, it was abandoned—and promptly burned, probably by the Sioux—in 1868."

Courtesy Archives and Western History Department, University of Wyoming Library

The site of Fort Phil Kearny is now a National Historic Landmark.

Wyoming Travel Commission

294

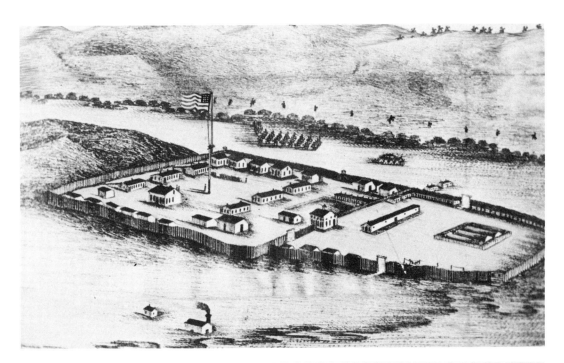

Index

Bold numbers indicate the pages on which an index entry is treated in full as individual site. All other page numbers are passing mentions of the entry.

Abercrombie, Lt. Col. John J.: 182
Abert, Lt. J. W.: 40
Adair, John G.: 248
Agriculture: California, 26, 28, 30; Colorado, 42; Idaho, 58; Montana, 114; Nebraska, 132; Washington, 274
Alamo, The: 238
Alarcón, Hernando de: 6
Albuquerque, New Mexico: **164–65**
Alcohol: 72, 86, 116, 130, 176, 178, 190
Alden, James: 274
Alder Gulch (Montana): *see* Virginia City, Montana
Allison, William: 118
Alvarado, Hernando de: 156, 158
American Fur Company: 40, 42, 64, 90, 102, 106, 108, 116, 130, 176, 178, 180, 224, 278, 280
Ames, Oaks: 260
Ames, Oliver: 260
Anaconda Copper Company: 118
Anza, Juan Bautista de: 4, 22
Apache Pass (Arizona): 10
Apache Springs (Arizona): 12
Applegate, Jesse: 140
Arbuckle, Col. Matthew: 190, 192
Arrow Rock Tavern (Missouri): 100
Ashley, William H.: 92, 114, 134, 250, 278, 282, 286, 288
Aspen, Colorado: 46
Astor, John Jacob: 208; *see also* Astorians
Astoria, Oregon: **208–209**
Astorians: 56, 134, 136, 208, 266, 268, 282, 288
Atkinson, Col. (later Gen.) Henry: 96, 132
Audubon, John James: 176, 178, 224
Auraria, Colorado: 46
Austin, Moses: 242
Austin, Stephen A.: 242
Ayala, Juan Manuel de: 22

Baird, James: 162
Baker, Jim: 44
Baker, Capt. Stephen: 128
Baker Bay (Washington): **264–65**
Ball, John: 272
Bannack, Montana: 116, **120–21**, 122, 124, 126
Baptists: 74, 130
Barrionuevo, Francisco de: 158
Bartlett, John Russell: 4
Battles
    Adobe Walls: 202
    Fetterman Massacre: 294
    Glorieta Pass: 164, 166
    Little Big Horn: **128–29**, 200, 226, 228, 234
    Wagon Box Fight: 294
    Washita: 200
    Wounded Knee: **234–35**
Baylor, Lt. Col. John R.: 170
Bayou Salado (Colorado): 42
Beale, Edward F.: 34, 160, 236
Beattie, H.S.: 146
"Beaver money": 212
Becknell, William: 100, 162
Beckwourth, James P.: 36, 158, 250
Bedbugs: 192
Belknap, Gen. William G.: 244
Bellevue, Nebraska: **130–31**, 140
Beltrán, Fr. Bernardino: 160
Bent, Charles: 40, 42, 158
Bent, George: 158
Bent, Robert: 158
Bent, William: 40, 42, 82, 102, 158
Benteen, Capt. Frederick W.: 128
Benton, Senator Thomas Hart: 116
Bent's Fort (Colorado): **40–41**
Bernalillo, New Mexico: 156, 164
Bidwell, John: 136, 280
Big Foot (Sioux): 234
Bigler, Henry W.: 32
Big Tree (Kiowa): 202
Bingham, George Caleb: 100
Bird Cage Theatre: 12
Bismarck, North Dakota: 184, 186
Black Hawk: 66, 96
Black Hawk Purchase: 66
Black Hawk War: 68
Black Hills: 228, 230, 232
Black Kettle: 200
Blanchette, Louis: 94
Bliss, Col. W.W.S.: 236
Bluff, Utah: 262
Bodega Bay (California): 28
Bodmer, Charles: 132, 174, 176, 178, 224
Boggy Depot (Oklahoma): **196–97**
Bonham, James: 238
Bonneville, Capt. B. L. E.: 56, 98, 136, 270, 278, 282, 286
Bonneville Dam: 218
Bonney, William H. "Billy the Kid": 168, 170
Boone, Daniel: 94

Boone Nathan: 190
Bouchard, Hypolite: 20
Bowie, James: 238
Brackenridge, Henry M.: 98
Bradbury, John: 98, 130
Bradford, Maj. William C.: 16
Bradley, Lt. James H.: 126, 128
Brady, Sheriff William: 168
Brannon, Samuel: 32
Bridger, Jim: 108, 134, 176, 278, 280, 286, 290
Bringhurst, William: 148
Browne, J. Ross: 2, 6, 10, 152
Buffalo: 84, 140, 204
Burr, Aaron: 38
Burt, Francis: 130
Burton, Richard F.: 136
Butte, Montana: **118–19**
Butterfield Stage: 16, 170, 244; *see also* Stagecoach
    service

Cabanné, J. P.: 92
Cabanné Post (Nebraska): 130
Cabeza de Vaca, Álvar Núñez: 12, 236
Cabrillo, Juan Rodríguez: 18, 20, 22
Caldwell, Kansas: 204
California Gulch (Colorado): 48
California Joe (scout): 188, 200
California Volunteers: 12
Cameahwait: 50
Camel Corps: 34, 160, 246
Campbell, Robert: 92, 280, 286
Campion, J.S.: 44
Camp Missouri (Nebraska): 132
"Camp of Israel": 70
Camp Robinson (Nebraska): *see* Robinson (Nebraska)
    under Forts
Camp Supply (Oklahoma): 84, **200–201**
"Carbonate Kings": 48
Cárdenas, García López de: 156
Caribou, Colorado: 46
Carleton, Brig. Gen. James H.: 12, 170
Carmelites: 18
Carrington, Col. Henry B.: 294
Carson, Kit: 40, 44, 100, 158
Carson Valley (Nevada): 292
Cascades of the Columbia: **218–19**
Casper, Wyoming: 284
Castañeda, Pedro de: 156
Catholic mission system: 6, 8, 26; *see also* Carme-
    lites, Franciscans, *and* Jesuits
Catlin, George: 72, 90, 110, 130, 174, 176, 182, 190,
    200, 224
Cattle industry: California, 26; New Mexico, 168;
    North Dakota, 188; Texas, 84, 248

Cavalry School: 80
Celilo Falls: 216
Central City, Colorado: 46
Cermeño, Sebastián Rodríguez: 22
Cerré, Michael Silvestre: 92
Chaboillez, Charles: 172
Champoeg, Oregon: **210–11**
Chamuscado, Capt. Francisco: 160, 170
Charbonneau, Touissant: 174, 222
Chardon, Francis A.: 178, 224
Charleston Mountains (Nevada): 148
Chateau de Mores (North Dakota): **188–89**
Cherokee Advocate: 194
Cheyenne Transporter: 204
Chimney Rock (Nebraska): **136–37**
Chinese: 62, 260
Chisum, John: 168
Chittenden, Hiram M.: 52, 130
Cholera: 102, 106
Chouteau, Auguste: 92, 94, 176
Chouteau, Pierre, Jr.: 92, 102, 108, 224, 290
Christian Advocate and Journal: 58
Cíbola: 18, 156, 160
Civil War: 4, 12, 74, 78, 80, 96, 152, 154, 164, 166,
    170, 190, 192, 194, 196, 198, 244, 246
Clark, William: 64, 92, 94, 98, 108, 110, 112, 174,
    206; *see also* Lewis and Clark expedition
Clark, W. P.: 144
Clarke, John: 266
Clemens, Samuel L.: 152
Clowes, John C.: 258
Clyman, James: 134
Cochise: 12
Cody, William F. "Buffalo Bill": 154
Collins, Lt. Caspar: 284
Coloma, California: **32–33**
Colter, John: 108, 112
Colyer, Vincent: 190
Comcomly (Chinook): 208
Comstock Lode (Nevada): 146, 150, **152–53**
Concho, Oklahoma: 204
Cooke, Lt. Col. Philip St. George: 10, 136
Cooke, W.W.: 128
Copper mining: 118
Corinne, Utah: 260
Coronado, Francisco Vásquez de: 76, 156, 160, 164,
    248
Council Bluffs (Nebraska): 132
Council Bluffs, Iowa: **64–65**, 70, 140
Council Grove, Kansas: **76–77**
Cove Fort (Utah): **258–59**
"Cow Column": 140, 280
Cox, Ross: 208, 268
Craig, William: 56

Crazy Horse: 128, 144, 294
Credit Island (Iowa): 68
Crespi, Fr. Juan: 24
Crittenden, Gen. G.B.: 96
Crocker, Charles: 260
Crockett, David: 238
Croghan, Inspector General George: 72, 190
Crook, Gen. George: 12, 144
Crooks, Ramsay: 130
Cruz, Fr. Juan de la: 156
Cuervo y Valdés, Don Francisco: 164
Curly (scout): 128
Custer, Elizabeth B.: 86, 186
Custer, Gen. George A.: 80, 84, 86, 112, 128, 144, 186, 200, 226, 230
Custer, South Dakota: 230
Custer Battlefield (Montana): **128–29**, 200, 226, 228, 234

Daly, Marcus: 118
Daly, Pete: 124
Dana, Charles A.: 102, 104
Dana, Richard Henry: 22
Daniel, Wyoming: 278
Darling, Lucia: 120
Darlington, Brinton: 204
Darlington Agency (Oklahoma): **204–205**
Davenport, Col. George: 68
Davidson, Lt. Col. John W.: 202
Davis, Jefferson: 34, 96, 122, 200, 246
Davis, W.W.H.: 164
Deadwood, South Dakota: **232–33**
Decker, Elizabeth Morris: 262
Denver, Colorado: **46–47**
De Smet, Fr. Pierre Jean: 60, 64, 106, 108, 114, 134, 136, 176, 184, 226, 280, 286
Devil's Canyon (Oklahoma): 200
Devil's Gate (Wyoming): **288–89**
DeVoto, Bernard: 40, 178
Dimsdale, Thomas J.: 124
Dodge, Grenville M.: 64, 84, 260
Dodge, Col. Henry I.: 84
Dodge City, Kansas: 84
Domínguez, Fr. Francisco Antanasio: 254
Don Fernando de Taos, New Mexico: *see* Taos, New Mexico
Donner party: 150
Dougherty, John: 130
Douglas, David: 272
Drake, Sir Francis: 18, 22
Drake's Bay (California): **18–19**, 22
Dred Scott: *see* Scott, Dred
Driggs, Howard R.: 140

Drips, Andrew: 130, 224
Drouillard, George: 108
Dubuque, Julien: 66
Duhaut-Cilly, Auguste Bernard: 28
Dull Knife: 204
Dunbar, John: 130
Durant, Thomas C.: 260

Eads, William: 120
Earp, Wyatt: 14
Eastman, Seth: 90, 238, 240
Edgar, Henry: 122
Edgerton, Sidney: 120
Eells, Myron F.: 276
El Morro (New Mexico): **160–61**
El Paso, Texas: 170, 198, **236–37**
El Pueblo (California): *see* Los Angeles, California
El Pueblo (Colorado): **36–37**
Epitaph (Tombstone, Arizona): 14
Escalante, Fr. Francisco Silvestre Vílez de: 254
Escalante, Utah: 262
Escalona, Fr. Luis de: 156
Espejo, Capt. Antonio de: 160, 236, 246
Espinosa Gang: 44

Fairweather, Bill: 122
Fall, Albert B.: 170
Faribault, Jean Baptiste: 90
Farlin, William L.: 118
Feliz, Corp. José Vicente: 24
Fergusson, Erna: 160
Ferris, Warren A.: 136
Fetterman, Brevet Lt. Col. William J.: 294
Field, Matthew C.: 288
First U. S. Dragoons: 72, 78, 96, 190, 200, 280
Fitzpatrick, Thomas: 36, 114, 134, 280, 282, 286
Flagg, Edmund: 92, 94
Florence, Nebraska: 138
Font, Fr. Pedro: 22
Forsyth, Lt. Col. James W.: 112
Fort Madison, Iowa: 66
Fort Pierre, South Dakota: 220, 224
Fort Randall Dam: 226
Forts
    Abercrombie (North Dakota): **182–83**
    Abraham Lincoln (North Dakota): **186–87**
    Armstrong (Iowa): 68
    Atkinson (Nebraska): 130, **132–33**
    Atkinson (North Dakota): 180
    Baker (Nevada): 148
    Belknap (Texas): **244–45**
    Bellefontaine (Missouri): 96
    Bennett (South Dakota): 228

Forts (*continued*)
Benton (Montana): **116–17**, 180, 182
Berthold (North Dakota): **180–81**
Bliss (Texas): 236
Boise (Idaho): 54, **56–57**
Bonneville (Wyoming): 278
Bowie (Arizona): **12–13**
Bridger (Wyoming): 54, **290–91**, 292
Buenaventura (Utah): 250
Buford (North Dakota): 176, 182
Canby (Washington): 264
Casper (Wyoming): 284
Chadbourne (Texas): 244
Churchill (Nevada): **154–55**
Clark (North Dakota): **178–79**
Clatsop (Oregon): **206–207**, 264
Columbia (Washington): 264
Colville (Washington): 60, 266
Croghan (Texas): 244
Daer (North Dakota): 172
Dalles (Oregon): 216
Davis (Texas): **246–47**
Dodge (Kansas): **84–85**, 200
Elliot (Texas): 204
Fillmore (New Mexico): 170
Fletcher (Kansas): 86
Floyd (North Dakota-Montana): 176
Garland (Colorado): **44–45**
Garry (Manitoba): 182
Gates (Texas): 244
George (Oregon): 208, 270
Gibson (Oklahoma): 16, 78, **190–91**, 192
Graham (Texas): 244
Guijarros (California): 18
Hall (Idaho): **54–55**, 56, 114, 250, 272
Hays (Kansas): 84, **86–87**
Jackson (Colorado): 42
Jesup (Louisiana): 78
John (Wyoming): 280
Kearny (Nebraska): **140–41**
Lancaster (Colorado): *see* Lupton *below*
Laramie (Wyoming): 42, **280–81**, 294
La Reine (Manitoba): 220
Larned (Kansas): **82–83**
Leavenworth (Kansas): **72–73**, 78, 80, 176
Lee (Oregon): 216
Lemhi (Idaho): **50–51**, 292
Lewis (Montana): 116
Lisa (Nebraska): 222
Lupton (Colorado): 42
McKavett (Texas): 244
McKeen (North Dakota): 186
McKenzie (Montana): 116

Madison (Iowa): **66–67**
Mandan (North Dakota): 112, **174–75**, 186
Manuel (Montana): 222
Manuel (South Dakota): **222–23**
Mason (Texas): 244
Massachusetts (Colorado): 44
Nez Percés (Washington): **270–71**
Nisqually (Washington): **274–75**
Nonsense (Wyoming): 278
Okanogan (Washington): **268–69**
Osage (Missouri): **98–99**
Owen (Montana): 114
Pembina (North Dakota): **172–73**
Phil Kearny (Wyoming): **294–95**
Piegan (Montana): 116
Pierre (South Dakota): 178, **224–25**
Randall (South Dakota): 224, **226–27**
Reno (Oklahoma): 204
Rice (North Dakota): **184–85**
Riley (Kansas): **80–81**
Robinson (Nebraska): **144–45**
Ross (California): **28–29**
St. Anthony (Minnesota): 88
St. Vrain (Colorado): 42
Scott (Kansas): **78–79**
Sill (Oklahoma): **202–203**, 204
Smith (Arkansas): **14–15**, 192, 196
Snelling (Minnesota): 68, 78, **88–89**, 90, 182
Stanton (New Mexico): 168
Stevenson (North Dakota): 180, 182
Sully (South Dakota): **228–29**
Supply (Oklahoma): 200
Supply (Wyoming): 290, **292–93**
Tecumseh (South Dakota): 224
Tejón (California): **34–35**
Totten (North Dakota): 182
Towson (Oklahoma): **192–93**
Union (New Mexico): **166–67**
Union (North Dakota–Montana): **176–77**, 178, 224
Utah (Utah): **254–55**
Vancouver (Washington): 114, 208, 212, 214, **272–73**, 274, 276, 282
Vásquez (Colorado): 42
Walla Walla (Washington): 56
Washakie (Wyoming): 222
Washita (Oklahoma): 196, **198–99**
William (Colorado): *see* Bent's Fort (Colorado)
William (Wyoming): *see* Laramie *above*
Worth (Texas): 244
Yuma (California): 4, 170
Fort Smith, Arkansas: 16
Fountain, Col. A. J.: 170
Fourth of July Canyon (Idaho): 60

Fowler, Maj. Jacob: 36, 98
Fraeb, Henry: 42
Franciscans: 8, 10, 158, 164, 238, 240
Franklin, Missouri: **100–101**, 104
Freeman, Daniel: 142
Frémont, John C.: 22, 30, 40, 42, 90, 96, 102, 134, 148, 272, 282, 286, 288
"French Bottoms": 102
Fry, Johnny: 106, 154
Fuller, C. W.: 150
Fur trade: 28, 42, 62, 90, 92, 108, 158, 176, 178, 224, 266, 278; *see also* Alcohol

Gadsden Purchase: 170
Gall (Sioux): 184
Galtier, Fr. Lucian: 90
Galvanized Yankees: 86
Gálvez, José de: 18
Garcés, Fr. Francisco Tomás: 6, 10
Garrard, Lewis H.: 158
Garrett, Pat: 170
Genoa, Nevada: 146, 154
Georgetown, Colorado: 46
Geronimo: 12, 202
"Ghost Dance": 228, 234
Gibbon, Gen. John: 112
Gibbs, George: 210
Glen Canyon (Utah): 262
Glisan, Assistant Surgeon Rodney: 198
Glorieta Pass (New Mexico): 164, 166
Gold discoveries: California, 6, 12, 16, 22, 30, 32, 106; Colorado, 46, 48; Idaho, 62; Montana, 116, 120, 122, 126; South Dakota, 184, 188, 228, 230, 232; Wyoming, 282
Golden Gate: 22
Goode, Rev. W. M.: 192
Goodnight, Charles: 248
Goodnight Ranch (Texas): **248–49**
Goodyear, Miles: 250
Gordon, John: 230
Gordon Stockade (South Dakota): **230–31**
Gore, Sir George: 176
Grant, Capt. Richard: 54
Grant, U. S.: 204
Gray, Capt. Robert: 264
Gray, William H.: 250
"Great Migration": 56
Great Salt Lake (Utah): 250, 252, 254, 260
Great Salt Plains (Oklahoma): 190
Greeley, Horace: 46
Green River Rendezvous (Wyoming): 54, 56, **278–79**
Gregg, Josiah: 76, 162
Gregory Gulch (Colorado): 46
Grierson, Gen. Benjamin H.: 202

Grinnell, George Bird: 40, 204
Guinard, Louis: 284
Guittar, Francis: 64

Hamilton, Lt. Thomas: 66
Hancock, Gen. W. S.: 86
Handy's Point (South Dakota): 226
Harmon, Appleton: 140, 284
Harney, Gen. William S.: 224, 226
Harris, Benjamin Butler: 4
Harris, Cyrus: 196
Harris, Edward, 224
Hart's Bluff (Iowa): 64
Hash-Knife Ranch: 188
Haslam, Robert H. "Pony Bob": 154
Hatcher, John: 158
Hawikúh Pueblo (New Mexico): 160
Hays, A. A.: 48
Hays, Seth M.: 76
Heap, Gwinn Harris: 148
Heger, Joseph: 166
Helena, Montana: *see* Last Chance Gulch (Montana)
Hennepin, Fr. Louis: 88
Henry, Alexander, Jr.: 172, 174, 210
Hewes, David: 218
Hickey, Michael: 118
Hickok, James Butler "Wild Bill": 86, 232
Higbee, John S.: 254
Hildreth, James: 190
Hockaday, John: 280
Hole-in-the-Rock (Utah): **262–63**
Homestake Mine (South Dakota): 232
Homestead Act (1862): 142
Homestead National Monument (Nebraska): **142–43**
Hopkins, Mark: 260
Houghton, Merritt D.: 293
Houston, Sam: 190
Howe, Henry: 74
Hudson's Bay Company: 28, 34, 52, 54, 56, 172, 208, 210, 212, 214, 250, 266, 268, 270, 272, 274, 276, 278
Huffaker, Thomas Sears: 76
Hughes, James T.: 248
Huizar, Pedro: 240
Humphrey, G. O.: 118
Hunt, Jefferson: 148
Hunt, Wilson Price: 98, 208, 282
Huntington, Collis P.: 260
Huntsman, Orson: 256
Hyde, Orson: 64, 146, 150, 292

Independence, Missouri: 54, 56, 102, **104–105**, 106, 140, 282

Independence Rock (Wyoming): **286–87**
Indians
 Apaches: 4, 6, 8, 10, 12, 44, 166, 202, 246
 Arapahos: 40, 134, 200, 204
 Arikaras: 132, 180
 Bannocks: 120, 154
 Blackfeet: 108
 Cayuses: 276
 Cherokees: 16, 190, 192, 194
 Cheyennes: 40, 134, 200, 204
 Chickasaws: 196, 198
 Chinooks: 206, 208, 264
 Choctaws: 190, 192, 196, 198
 Coeur d'Alenes: 60
 Comanches: 158, 166, 198, 202, 244, 246, 248
 Creeks: 190, 192
 Crows: 128
 Flatheads: 58, 60, 114, 214
 Foxes: *see* Sauks and Foxes *below*
 Gros Ventres: 180
 Hopis: 160
 Kalispels: 52
 Kashia Pomos: 28
 Kaws: 76
 Kiowas: 166, 202, 244, 248
 Mandans: 108, 174, 178, 180, 222
 Minnetarees: 174
 Missouris: 130
 Navahos: 166
 Nez Percés: 50, 58, 60, 114, 214, 276
 Omahas: 130
 Osages: 16, 76, 98, 194
 Otos: 64, 130
 Paiutes: 154, 234
 Papagos: 10
 Pawnees: 130
 Pecos: 156
 Pend d'Oreilles: 52
 Pimas: 8, 10
 Potawatomis: 64
 Quivirans: 76
 Sauks and Foxes: 66
 Seminoles: 190
 Shawnees: 74
 Shoshones: 50
 Sioux: 88, 128, 134, 144, 180, 182, 184, 200, 222,
  224, 226, 228, 230, 232, 234, 280, 294
 Taos: 158
 Tiguas: 156, 236
 Tiguex: *see* Tiguas *above*
 Utes: 36, 44, 166, 254
 Wascos: 216
 Wichitas: 202
 Winnebagos: 64
 Yangnas: 24
 Zuñis: 156
Ingalls, Eleaser: 106
Irish: 260
Irvine, Caleb E.: 118
Irving, John Treat, Jr.: 72
Irving, Washington: 72, 92, 190, 218

Jackson, William Henry: 258, 282
Jackson-Jeffries fight (1910): 150
Jaeger, L.J.F.: 6
James, Thomas: 16
Jefferson, Thomas: 98, 108, 208
Jefferson Barracks (Missouri): **96–97**
"Jene Baptiest": 112, 174
Jenney, W. P.: 188
Jesuits: 4, 8, 114, 286; *see also* De Smet, Fr. Pierre
 Jean
Johnson, Rev. Thomas: 74
Johnston, Gen. Albert Sidney: 290, 292
Jones, Dan: 288
Jones, Com. Thomas Ap Catesby: 20

Kanesville, Iowa: 64, 138
Kansas City, Kansas: 74
Kansas City, Missouri: 102, 104; *see also* Westport
 Landing (Missouri)
Kearny, Col. (later Gen.) Stephen Watts: 40, 134, 158,
 160, 162, 164, 280
Kelley, Cornelius F.: 118
Keokuk, Chief: 68
Kettle Falls (Washington): 268
Kimball, Heber C.: 50
Kingsbury, Rev. Cyrus: 192, 196
Kino, Fr. Eusebio Francisco: 4, 6, 8
Kipp, James: 178
Kodiak, Alaska: 28
Koppel, Charles: 16, 24
Kuaua Pueblo (New Mexico): 156
Kullyspell House (Idaho): **52–53**
Kurz, Rudolph: 106
Kuskov, Ivan Aleksandrovich: 28

Labadie, Sylvester: 92
Laclède, Pierre: 92
Laidlaw, William: 224
Lake, M. C.: 150
Lake's Crossing (Nevada): **150–51**
La Lande, Jean Baptiste: 158
La Ramée, Jacques: 280
Larned, Kansas: 82
Larocque, François Antoine: 174

Last Chance Gulch (Montana): **126–27**
Las Vegas Fort (Nevada): **148–49**, 292
Las Vegas Optic (New Mexico): 166
Latrobe, Charles J.: 88, 104, 190
Lead mining: 66
Leadville, Colorado: 46, **48–49**
Leavenworth, Col. Henry H.: 72, 88, 132, 190, 192, 200
Lebecque, Peter: 34
Le Claire, Antoine: 68
Lee, Abe: 48
Lee, Daniel: 214, 216
Lee, Jason: 54, 134, 212, 214
Lee, Oliver: 170
Le Flore, Chief Basil: 196
Lemhi Pass (Idaho): 50, 62
Leslie, David: 274
Le Sueur, Pierre Charles: 88
Letterman, Assistant Surgeon John: 166
Lewis, Meriwether: 50, 66, 108, 110; *see also* Lewis and Clark expedition
Lewis and Clark expedition: 50, 58, 64, 92, 108, 110, 112, 174, 186, 206, 216, 264, 270, 282; *see also* Clark, William, *and* Lewis, Meriwether
Liggett, William: 280
Like-a-Fishhook Village (North Dakota): 180
Lincoln, Dr. Able B.: 6
Lincoln, Abraham: 64, 68, 142
Lincoln, New Mexico: **168–69**
Lincoln County War (New Mexico): 168
Lisa, Manuel: 92, 98, 112, 130, 222
Lisa's Fort (North Dakota): 222
Little, Jesse C.: 254
Little Wolf: 204
Llano Estacado: *see* Staked Plains
Long, Maj. Stephen H.: 16, 42, 98, 130, 132, 172
Los Angeles, California: **24–25**
Louisiana Purchase: 38, 88, 92, 96, 98
"Louis Veneri": 206
Lowe, Percival G.: 80
Lucin Cutoff (Utah): 260
Lucky Cuss mine: 14
Lupton, Lt. Lancaster P.: 42
Luttig, John C.: 222
Luxán, Pérez de: 160
Lyman, Platte D.: 262

McClellan, Lt. (later Capt.) George B.: 198, 244
McCoy, John C.: 102
McDonald, Angus: 52
McDonald, Archibald: 274
McDonald, Duncan: 52
McDonald, Finan: 266

McDougal, Duncan: 208
"Macedonian Call": 58, 60, 214
McGillivray, Joseph: 268
McKay, James: 174
McKay, Tom: 56
McKay, William T.: 230
McKenzie, Donald: 56, 270
McKenzie, Kenneth: 176
Mackenzie, Ranald S.: 144
McKnight, Robert: 162
McLaughlin, James: 234
McLellan, Robert: 130
McLoughlin, Dr. John: 210, 212, 214, 272, 274
McNeal, Hugh: 50
McSween, Alexander: 168
Magoffinsville, Texas: 236
Mail service: 104, 106, 148, 182, 204
Majors, Alexander: 290
Mangas Coloradas (Apache): 12
Marcy, Mary: 192, 198
Marcy, Capt. Randolph B.: 192, 198, 202, 244
Marsh, Dr. Elias J.: 226
Marsh, Capt. Grant: 112, 186
Marshall, James Wilson: 32, 106
Martínez, Gov. Don Féliz: 160
Mattes, Merrill J.: 140, 226
Mattison, Ray H.: 178
Maxey, Gen. S. B.: 192
Maximilian, Prince of Wied: 94, 106, 132, 176, 178, 224
Maxwell, Lucien: 158
Maynadier, Lt. Henry E.: 112
Meares, Capt. John: 264
Medora, North Dakota: 188
Meek, Joe: 56
Meeker, Ezra: 140, 286
Meline, Col. J. F.: 162
Menard, Pierre: 108
Mendota, Minnesota: **90–91**, 172
Mengarini, Fr. Gregory: 114
Mennonites: 204
Meriwether, David: 162, 170
Merrill, Rev. Moses: 130
Mesilla, New Mexico: **170–71**
"Messiah Craze": *see* "Ghost Dance"
Methodists: 58, 74, 76, 192, 214, 216, 274
Métis: 172
Mexican War: 20, 24, 40, 138, 170, 192, 236, 244
Miles, John D.: 204
Miles, Gen. Nelson A.: 12, 84, 144
Miles Goodyear Farm (Utah): **250–51**
Miller, Alfred Jacob: 102, 134, 136, 278, 280, 284, 286, 288

Miller, David E.: 262
Miller's Hollow (Iowa): 64
Minneapolis, Minnesota: 88, 90
Missions
    Cataldo (Idaho): *see* Sacred Heart (Idaho) *below*
    Cedar City (Utah): 256
    Concepción (Texas): 238
    Dolores (California): 22
    Dwight (Oklahoma): 194
    Espada (Texas): 238
    Fort Berthold (North Dakota): 180
    Kaw (Kansas): 76
    Lapwai (Idaho): **58–59**
    Merrill (Nebraska): 130
    Methodist (Salem, Oregon): **214–15**
    Park Hill (Oklahoma): 194
    Parowan (Utah): 256
    Sacred Heart (Idaho): **60–61**
    St. Mary's (Montana): 60, **114–15**
    San Antonio de Padua (Texas): 238, 240
    San Antonio de Valero (Texas): 238
    San Carlos de Borromeo (California): 20
    San Diego de Alcalá (California): 18
    San Gabriel (California): 24
    San Gerónimo de Taos (New Mexico): 158
    San José del Tucson (Arizona): 10
    San José de Tumacacori (Arizona): 4
    San José y San Miguel de Aguayo (Texas): **240–41**
    San Juan (Texas): 238
    San Juan River (Utah): 262
    Santa Barbara (California): **26–27**
    San Xavier del Bac (Arizona): **8–9**
    Shawnee (Kansas): **74–75**, 80
    Spalding (Idaho): *see* Lapwai (Idaho) *above*
    Union (Oklahoma): 194
    Waiilatpu (Washington): **276–77**
    Whitman (Washington): *see* Waiilatpu (Washington) *above*
    Ysleta (Texas): 236
Missouri Fur Company: 92, 108, 130, 222
Mizner, Maj. John K.: 204
Molybdenum: 48
Montana City, Colorado: 46
Monterey, California: **20–21**, 22
Monterey Bay (California): 20
Montgomery, Capt. John B.: 22
Moreno, Fr. Manuel: 164
Mores, Marquis de: 188
Morfi, Fr. Juan Antonio, 240
Mormon Battalion: 10, 138
Mormon Ferry (Wyoming): **284–85**
Mormons: 32, 50, 64, 70, 104, 134, 138, 140, 146,
    148, 150, 196, 250, 252, 254, 256, 258, 262, 284,
    286, 288, 290, 292

Mormon Station (Nevada): **146–47**
Morrow, Stanley J.: 228
Mosca Pass (Colorado): 38
Mount Hood (Oregon): 218
Mount Pisgah (Iowa): **70–71**
Mullan, Capt. John: 60, 116
Mundt, Senator Karl: 234
Murphy, L. G.: 168
Murrell House (Oklahoma): 194
Myer, Dr. Albert J.: 246
Myers, L. B.: 254

Nachez (Apache): 12
Nauvoo, Illinois: 70, 138
Newell, Robert "Doc": 56
New Helvetia (California): 28, **30–31**, 32
Nibley, Preston: 284
Nicoli, Antonio: 294
Nicollet, Joseph: 90
Nieto, Gov. Francisco Manuel de Silva: 160
Niza, Fr. Marcos de: 18
North West Company: 52, 56, 172, 174, 206, 208,
    210, 266, 268, 270
Nuttall, Thomas: 16, 98

Oahe Dam (South Dakota): 223, 225, 228
Ogden, Peter Skene: 250, 276
Ogden, Utah: 250, 260
O. K. Corral: 14
Olivares, Fr. Antonio de San Buenaventura: 238
Olvera, Judge Augustín: 24
Omaha, Nebraska: 130, 132, 138, 222, 260
Oñate, Juan de: 158, 160, 170, 236
Oregon City, Oregon: 210, **212–13**
Oregon Institute: 214
Oregon Pony (locomotive): 218
Oregon Temperance Society: 212
Oregon Volunteers: 54
Oro City, Colorado: 48
Ortega, Capt. José Francisco: 26
Overland Mail Company: *see* Butterfield Stage *and*
    Stagecoach service
Owen, Maj. John: 114
Owyhee Mountains: 62

Pacific Fur Company: *see* Astorians
Padilla, Fr. Juan: 76, 156
Page, Capt. John H.: 200
Paha Sapa: *see* Black Hills
Paiute War: 154
Palace of the Governors (New Mexico): 162
Palmer, Joel: 282, 290
Palo Duro Canyon (Texas): 248
Palou, Fr. Francisco: 16

Parker, Judge Isaac C.: 16
Parker, Dr. Samuel: 134, 136, 278, 280
Parker, Quanah: 202
Park Hill (Oklahoma): **194–95**
Parkman, Francis: 36, 42, 102, 134, 280
Parks Mill (Iowa): 64
Pawnee, Kansas: 80
Pawnee Rock (Kansas): 82
Payette, Francis: 56
Pearson, John B.: 232
Pembina, North Dakota: 90, **172–73**, 182
Peosta (Fox): 66
Peralta, Don Pedro de: 162
Perkins, H.K.W.: 216
Pierre, South Dakota: 220, 228
Pig's Eye, Minnesota: 90
Pike, Albert: 248
Pike, Zebulon M.: 36, 38, 42, 88, 162, 236
Pikes Peak: 36, 42, 46
Pike's Stockade (Colorado): **38–39**
Pilcher, Joshua: 130, 136
Pine Ridge Agency (South Dakota): 234
Platte Bridge Station (Wyoming): 284
Plummer, Henry: 120, 124
Point, Fr. Nicholas: 60, 114
Point Loma (California): 18
Pompeys Pillar (Montana): **112–13**
Pony Express: 30, 106, 136, 154, 282
Portolá, Don Gaspar de: 18, 20, 22
Poston, Charles D.: 4
Potts, John: 108
Powell, M.: 140
Pratt, H. C.: 236
Pratt, Orson: 70, 252
Presbyterians: 130, 134, 192
Preuss, Charles: 136
Price, Gen. Sterling: 40, 158
Promontory, Utah: 150, 218, **260–61**
Provost, Étienne: 254, 286
Pueblo, Colorado: *see* El Pueblo (Colorado)
Pueblo Revolt (1680): 160, 162, 164, 236
Puget Sound Agricultural Company: 274
Pulpit Rock (Oregon): 216
Purcell, James: 42

Quakers: 74, 204
Quivira: 156

Rae, Frances M.: 200
Railroads
  Central Pacific: 150, 260
  Hannibal & St. Joseph: 106
  Kansas Pacific: 86
  Missouri-Kansas-Texas: 196
  Northern Pacific: 188, 228
  Oregon Tramway: 218
  Rock Island: 64, 68
  Santa Fe: 24, 84, 164
  Southern Pacific: 6
  Union Pacific: 64, 140, 260
Ramsdell, Joseph: 118
Ramsey, Alexander: 172
Rats: 178
Ravalli, Fr. Anthony: 60, 114
Red Cloud Agency (Nebraska): 144, 294
Red River carts: 172
Reed, John: 56
Reeder, Gov. Andrew H.: 75, 80
Reese, Col. John: 146
Reno, Gen. Jesse Lee: 150
Reno, Maj. Marcus A.: 128, 186
Reno, Nevada: *see* Lake's Crossing (Nevada)
Revere, J. W.: 30
Rezanov, Nikolai: 22
Rhodes, Eugene Manlove: 170
Richardson, Albert D.: 102
Richmond, Dr. John P.: 274
Riley, Bennet: 80
Rindisbacher, Peter: 172
Rivers
  American: 30, 32
  Arkansas: 16, 36, 38, 40, 78, 82, 84, 102, 190
  Bad: 224
  Beaverhead: 120
  Big Horn: 128
  Boggy: 196
  Boise: 56
  Brazos: 242, 244
  Carson: 146, 152, 154
  Clark Fork: 52
  Clearwater: 58
  Coeur d'Alene: 60
  Colorado: 6, 262
  Columbia: 50, 54, 56, 206, 208, 212, 216, 218, 264,
    266, 268, 270, 272, 276
  Conejos: 38
  Gallatin: 108
  Grand: 190
  Green: 54, 56, 278, 290
  Heart: 186
  Illinois: 194
  Jefferson: 108
  Kansas (Kaw): 72, 74, 80, 102
  Knife: 174
  Laramie: 280
  Lewis and Clark: 206

Rivers (*continued*)
    Little Big Horn: 112, 128, 184, 186
    Little Missouri: 188
    Little Spokane: 266
    Madison: 108, 122
    Marmaton: 78
    Minnesota: 88, 90
    Mississippi: 38, 66, 68, 70, 78, 88, 90, 92, 172, 182
    Missouri: 50, 56, 64, 70, 72, 78, 92, 94, 96, 98,
      102, 104, 106, 108, 110, 116, 128, 130, 132, 140,
      162, 174, 176, 178, 180, 184, 186, 220, 222, 224,
      226, 228
    Neosho: 76
    North Canadian: 200, 204
    North Platte: 134, 136, 140, 184, 280, 284
    Ogden: 250
    Okanogan: 268
    Pembina: 172
    Platte: 64, 132, 140
    Porciúncula (Los Angeles): 24
    Portneuf: 54
    Poteau: 14
    Powder: 184, 294
    Provo: 254
    Red: 38, 78, 192, 198, 244
    Red (of the North): 90, 172, 182
    Republican: 80
    Río Grande: 38, 156, 164, 168, 170, 236
    Rosebud: 222
    Russian: 28
    St. Joe: 60
    Salmon: 62
    San Antonio: 238
    San Juan: 262
    Santa Clara: 256
    Santa Cruz: 10
    Smoky Hill: 80
    Snake: 54, 56, 266
    South Platte: 42, 46
    Spokane: 266
    Sweetwater: 140, 288
    Truckee: 150
    Verdigris: 190
    Virgin: 256
    Walla Walla: 270, 276
    Washita: 198
    Weber: 250
    Willamette: 210, 212, 214
    Wind: 56
    Yellowstone: 112, 128, 132, 176, 184, 186
Roads: *see* Trails
Robbers' Roost (Montana): **124–25**
Robidoux, Joseph: 106

Robinson, Dr. John H.: 38
Robinson, Lewis: 290
Rock Island: 68
Rocky Mountain Fur Company: 54, 108
Rocky Mountain News: 46
Rodríguez, Fr. Agustín: 160, 170, 236
Roosevelt, Theodore: 188
Ross, Alexander: 266, 268, 270
Ross, Horatio N.: 230
Rotchev, Aleksandr: 28
Roy, Peter: 102
Russell, T. H.: 230
Russell, William Green: 46
Russell, William H.: 290
Russia: 22, 28
Russian-America Company: 28
Ruxton, George Frederick: 36, 158, 162

Sacagawea: 50, 108, 112, 174, 222
Sacramento, California: 30
Sage, Rufus B.: 136
St. Anthony's Falls (Minnesota): 88, 90
St. Charles, Colorado: 46
St. Charles, Missouri: **94–95**, 98
St. George, Utah: **256–57**
St. Joseph, Missouri: **106–107**, 140
St. Louis, Missouri: 14, 38, 84, **92–93**, 96, 106, 108,
    114
St. Louis Missouri Fur Company: 222
St. Paul, Minnesota: 88, 90, 172
St. Vrain, Céran: 40, 42, 102, 158
Salem, Oregon: 214
Salish House (Montana): 52
Salmon fishing: 216
Salt Lake City, Utah: 50, 70, 104, 146, 148, **252–53**,
    254, 288, 292, 294
San Antonio, Texas: **238–39**, 240
Sandels, G. M.: 30
San Diego, California: **18–19**, 20
San Diego Bay: 18
San Francisco, California: 4, 16, 18, **22–23**, 26, 28,
    32
San Francisco Bay: 18, 20, 22
Sangre de Cristo Mountains: 38
San Luis Valley (Colorado): 38, 44
Santa Anna, Gen. Antonio López de: 238
Santa Fe, New Mexico: 38, 102, 104, **162–63**, 164,
    170
Sarpy, Peter A.: 42, 130
Satank: 202
Satanta: 202
Schieffelin, Ed: 14
Scott, Dred: 90

Scott, Gen. Winfield: 72, 88
Scotts Bluff (Nebraska): **134–35**
Seawell, Lt. Col. Washington: 246
Second Cavalry: 96
Seger, John H.: 204
Selkirk, Earl of: 172
Serra, Fr. Junípero: 16, 20, 26
Seventh Cavalry: 80, 86, 186, 200, 234
Seventh Infantry: 190
Sheridan, Gen. Philip H.: 84, 86, 200, 202, 226
Sherman, Gen. William Tecumseh: 96, 226
Shiel, Dr. Edward: 210
Ships and steamboats
  Anson Northrup: 182
  Beaver: 208, 274
  California: 22
  Chippewa: 116
  Chirikov: 28
  Columbia Rediviva: 264
  Effie Alton: 68
  Far West: 128, 186
  Fenix: 210
  Fort Des Moines: 68
  Independence: 100
  Josephine: 112
  Llama: 274
  Miner: 166
  Nimrod: 130
  Omaha: 138
  Omega: 130, 226
  Otter: 20
  Porpoise: 274
  Portsmouth: 22
  St. Peter's: 176, 178
  San Salvador: 18
  Tonquin: 208
  Victoria: 18
  Vincennes: 274
  Virginia: 90, 172
  Western Engineer: 98, 132
  Yellowstone: 176, 224
  Zebulon M. Pike: 92
Sibley, George C.: 98
Sibley, Gen. Henry H.: 90, 166
Sibley, Dr. John: 196
Silver Bow Town, Montana: 118
Silver City, Idaho: **62–63**
Silver discoveries: Arizona, 4, 14; Colorado, 46, 48;
  Nevada, 146, 150, 152
Simons, George: 64
Simpson, George: 268
Simpson, Lt. James H.: 160
Sioux War (1862): 182

Sitler, H. L.: 84
Sitting Bull (Oglala): 184, 226, 234
Slabtown, Colorado: 48
Sloat, Com. John D.: 20
Smallpox: 176, 178, 180, 208, 224
Smith, Hyrum: 70
Smith, Jedediah: 134, 158, 282, 286
Smith, Joseph: 70
Smith, Jackson and Sublette Company: 56
Snelling, Col. Josiah: 88
Somerville, John: 126
South Pass (Wyoming): 98, 140, **282–83**
South Pass City, Wyoming: 282
South Platte Posts, The: **42–43**
Sowiette (Ute): 254
Spalding, Eliza: 58, 134, 278, 286
Spalding, Rev. Henry: 58, 134, 276
Spokane House (Washington): 52, **266–67**, 270
Spotted Tail: 226
Stagecoach service: 16, 104, 170, 244, 280; *see also*
  Butterfield Stage
Staked Plains: 248
Stand Watie: 192
Stanford, Gov. Leland: 260
Stanley, Henry M.: 82
Stanley, John Mix: 50, 60, 176, 268
Stansbury, Howard: 254, 290
Steamboats: *see* Ships and steamboats
Stevens, Isaac I.: 60, 176
Stewart, Capt. Joseph: 154
Stewart, Sir William Drummond: 102, 278, 280, 288
Stockton, Com. Robert F.: 26
Stuart, David: 208, 268
Stuart, James: 112
Stuart, Robert: 216, 218, 280, 288
Sublette, Andrew: 42
Sublette, Milton: 158, 280
Sublette, William: 92, 280, 286
Sully, Gen. Alfred H.: 176, 184, 226, 228
Sumner, Col. E. V.: 166
Sutro Tunnel: 152
Sutter, John A.: 28, 30, 32
Sutter's Fort: *see* New Helvetia (California)

Tabor, Augusta: 48
Tabor, H.A.W.: 48
Tacoma, Washington: 274
Tahlequah, Oklahoma: 194
Taliaferro, Maj. Lawrence: 90
Tallent, Mrs. Annie D.: 230
Taos, New Mexico: 42, 46, **158–59**
Taos Lightning: 46, 158
Taos Pueblo: 158

Tappan, Col. Samuel F.: 44
Tappan, William Henry: 284
Taylor, Bayard: 20
Taylor, Gen. Zachary: 14, 68, 198
Tehachapi Mountains: 34
Tejon Ranch (California): 34
Territorial Enterprise: 146, 152
Terry, Gen. Alfred H.: 128, 226
Thoen Stone: 232
Thomas, Lewis F.: 94
Thompson, David: 52, 174
Three Forks (Montana): **108–109**, 174
Three Forks (Oklahoma): 190
Tiguex (New Mexico): **156–57**
Tixier, Victor: 104
Tobin, Tom: 44
Tolmie, Dr. William Frazier: 274
Tombstone, Arizona: 14–15
Toole, K. Ross: 128
Townsend, John K.: 286
Trail of Tears: 194
Trails
  Barlow Toll Road; 216, 218
  Boon's Lick: 98
  Bozeman: 294
  Caribou: 268
  Cheyenne-Deadwood: 280
  Chisholm: 204
  Cimarron Cutoff: 84, 166
  El Camino del Diablo: 6
  El Camino Real: 170
  Fort Smith-Boggy Depot: 196
  Fort Totten: 182
  Goodnight: 248
  Humboldt: 146
  Mormon: 70, 134, 280, 290
  Mullan: 60, 116, 270
  Oregon: 54, 134, 136, 140, 216, 272, 276, 280, 282, 286, 290
  Overland: 54, 106, 280, 282, 286, 290
  Red River: 172, 182
  Santa Fe: 40, 72, 76, 82, 84, 100, 102, 162, 166
  Smoky Hill: 86
  Texas: 190, 196
  Western: 84, 200
  Whoop-up: 116
Travis, Col. William B.: 238
Treaties
  Black Hawk (1832): 68
  Cahuenga (1847): 24
  Council Grove (1825): 76
  Ghent (1814): 88
  Guadalupe Hidalgo (1848): 236

  Indian Removal Act (1830): 78
  Oregon (1846): 56, 268
  Sioux (1868): 128, 184, 230, 280
Trobriand, Gen. Philippe Régis de: 180, 184, 228
Tubac, Arizona: **4–5**, 8
Tucson, Arizona: 8, **10–11**, 12
Tunstall, John H.: 168
Twain, Mark: *see* Clemens, Samuel L.

Union Pass (Wyoming): 282

Vaca, Álvar Núñez Cabeza de: *see* Cabeza de Vaca, Álvar Núñez
Vancouver, Capt. George: 22
Vancouver Barracks (Washington): 272
Vanderburgh, Henry: 108
Van Dorn, Maj. Earl: 244
Varennes, Pierre Gaultier de: *see* Vérendrye, Sieur de La
Vargas, Don Diego de: 160, 162
Vashon, George: 76
Vásquez, Louis: 42, 46
Vérendrye, François: 220
Vérendrye, Louis: 220
Vérendrye, Sieur de La: 174, 220
Verendrye Hill (South Dakota): **220–21**
Victorio (Apache): 246
Vigilantes of Montana: 120, 122, 124, 126
Villagrá, Don Gaspar Pérez de: 236
Virginia City, Montana: 118, 120, **122–23**, 124, 126
Virginia City, Nevada: 150, 152
Vizcaíno, Sebastián: 18, 20, 22
Vose, Lt. Col. J. H.: 192

Walker (Ute): 254
Walker, C. M.: 56
Walker, Joel P.: 54
Walker, Joseph Reddeford: 10
Wallace, Lew: 162
Walla Walla, Washington: 116, 276
Wallula, Washington: 270
War of 1812: 98, 100, 208, 222, 268
Warre, Henry James: 212, 272
Warren, J. Newton: 230
Washoe City, Nevada: 150, 152
Washoe Valley (Nevada): 152, 154
Weston, Samuel: 104
Westport, Missouri: 74, 102, 106, 140
Westport Landing (Missouri): **102–103**, 114
Wheels across the West: 54, 56, 98, 282
Whipple, Lt. A. W.: 4, 14
White, John: 120
Whitman, Alice Clarissa: 276

Whitman, Dr. Marcus: 54, 56, 58, 134, 216, 250, 276, 278, 280
Whitman, Narcissa: 134, 272, 276, 278, 286
Whitney, R. R.: 230
Wild, J. C.: 94, 96
Wilkes, Capt. Charles: 274
Wilkins, Caleb: 56
Wilkinson, Lt. (later Gen.) James B.: 38, 190
Williams, James: 154
Williams, Joseph: 280
Williams, Old Bill: 40, 158
Williamson, R. S.: 34
Willson, Dr. William Holden: 274
Wimmer, Peter L.: 32
Winnemucca, Chief: 150
Winnipeg, Manitoba: 172, 182, 220
Wint, Capt. T.: 204
Winter Quarters (Nebraska): **138–39**
Wislizenus, Dr. Frederick A.: 162, 280
Wolf, Capt. Lambert: 82
"Wolf Meetings": 210, 214

Woodbury, Lt. Daniel P.: 140
Woodson, Samuel H.: 104
Wootton, Richens Lacy "Uncle Dick": 40, 46, 158
Worcester, Rev. Samuel Austin: 194
Workman, David: 100
Wounded Knee Battlefield (South Dakota): **234–35**
Wovoka (Paiute): 234
Wright, Chief Allen: 196
Wyeth, Nathaniel J.: 54, 56, 136, 176, 216, 270, 272, 286

X Y Company: 172

Yellowstone Expedition: 96, 98, 132
Yerba Buena, California: 22
Young, Brigham: 70, 134, 138, 140, 148, 250, 252, 254, 256, 258, 284, 288, 290, 292
Young, Ewing: 158, 214
Yugeuingge, New Mexico: 170
Yuma, Arizona: **6–7**
Yuma, Territorial Prison: 6